IMAGES
of America

PARMA AND HILTON

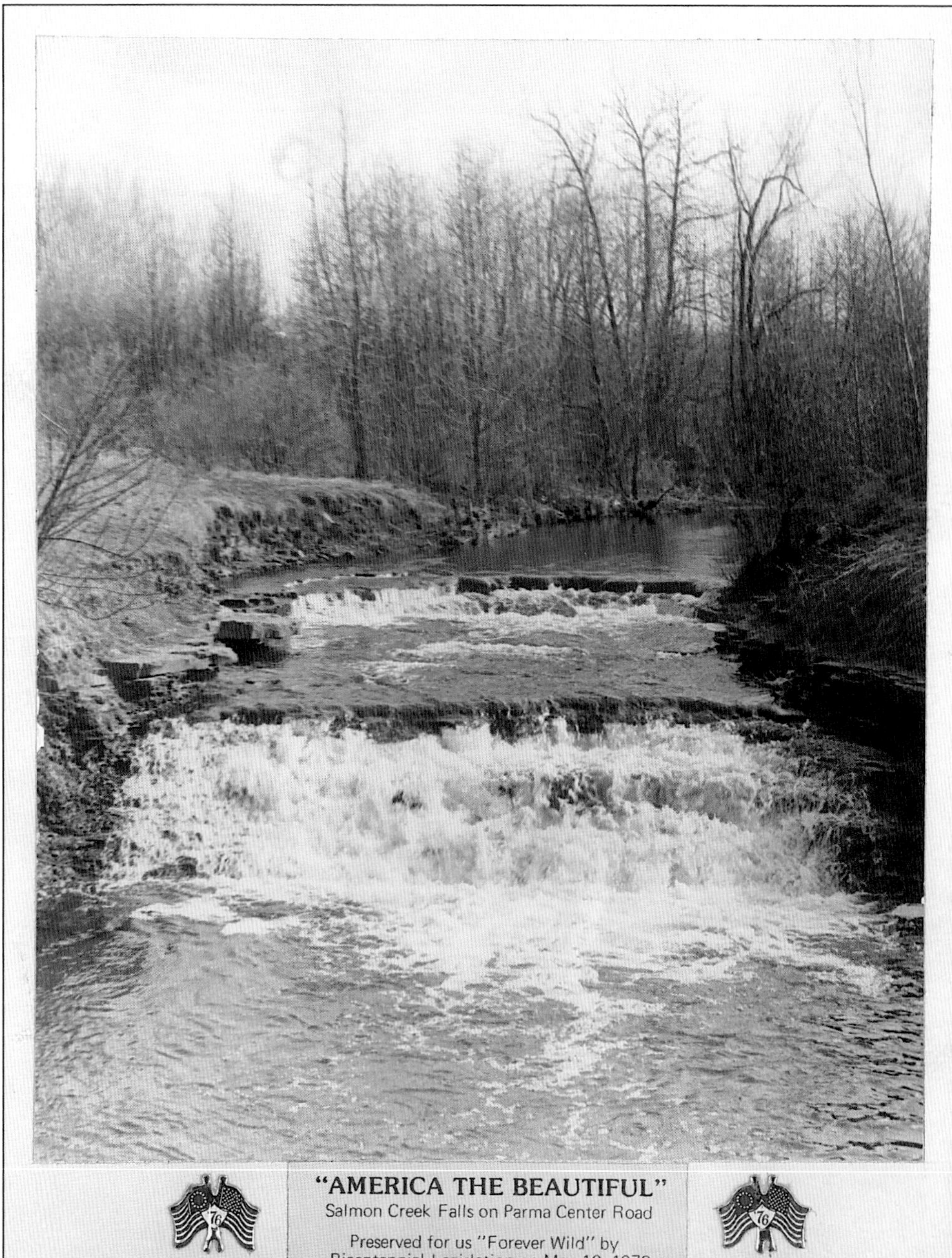

SALMON CREEK FALLS. Parma's most beautiful landmark, the waterfall at Salmon Creek, dates from only the 20th century. Local resident Brayton Miles remembers well how blasting work was done to straighten out the creek beside an early industrial site off Parma Center Road, the mill of Bezaleel Atchinson, one of Parma's first pioneers. The creeks changed over time, too; their flow increased or decreased as the Erie Canal was constructed through Spencerport. This view reveals the site's beauty when the falls, owned by the county of Monroe, were designated a scenic landmark.

IMAGES
of America

PARMA AND HILTON

Shirley Cox Husted

ARCADIA
PUBLISHING

ISBN 978-0-7385-0340-0

Published by Arcadia Publishing
Charleston, South Carolina

Printed in the United States of America

Library of Congress Catalog Card Number: 2009921965

For all general information contact Arcadia Publishing at:
Telephone 843-853-2070
Fax 843-853-0044
E-mail sales@arcadiapublishing.com
For customer service and orders:
Toll-Free 1-888-313-2665

Visit us on the Internet at www.arcadiapublishing.com

On the Cover: The 1912 Peck & Pratt Inc. Canning Factory. The largest industry in Hilton village was the canning factory on Canning Street, purchased by Smithfield's Pure Food Company in 1926. In the 1930s, many of its workers posed for this remarkable photograph beside huge apple piles. In 1916, more apples were canned there than at any other factory of its size in the U.S. While serving abroad, a local soldier delightedly discovered Smithfield canned goods with labels printed at the Hilton Record's print shop, "a little taste of home" from the home front to the war front. (Reproduced courtesy of the Hilton Village Historian.)

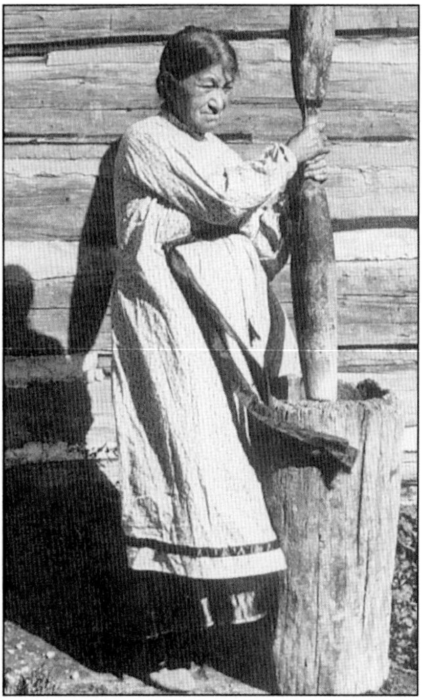

Native-American Woman. Parma lies within the mill seat tract, a gift of 84,000 acres paralleling the Genesee River. All Native-American claims to this tract were given up in 1788 in exchange for a promise that a gristmill would be built to grind grain for them, thus ending the laborious work of pounding corn into flour in a wooden stump mortar. Parma's western boundary follows the line demarking this territory, roughly 12 miles west of the river, extending 24 miles from Lake Ontario to a point in the town of Wheatland. White landowners in Massachusetts expected 3¢ an acre, but much of that money was never paid. The Native Americans received $5,000 for 6.25 million acres; but for the mill seat acreage, they were given nothing. Ebenezer "Indian" Allen did build a log mill, using about an acre of this swindled land; but because it soon fell into disrepair from lack of use, the Native-American women were forced to keep on pounding grain.

CONTENTS

DEDICATION

Parma and Hilton is dedicated to all of the following: the people of Parma, who have created the town's history; Dr. Charles G. Lenhart, who brought me into this world; Dr. Charles Keller Sr. and Jr. and Dr. Dominic DiVincenzo, who have kept me healthy; Dr. Patrick C. Lee, who has many times saved my life; my dentists, especially Dr. Robert Morriss, "the singing dentist"; the Rev. Dr. Frank Weston, who inspired my Christian ideals; all the worthy teachers and principals who helped shape my ideals, especially Agnes Chattin Low, Mary E. Taber, Imogene Smith, Mary Bess Jennejahn, Leonard Wright, Howard and Cora Updyke, Dr. Paul Adams, and Harry Anderson; Lee Davenport, who encouraged me to write books; George Scheible and John Cooper, Charles Cooper, and C. Harlan Cooper, whose guidance helped to launch my journalistic career; Supvr. Edwin A. Foster and his successor, John F. Jennejahn Jr.; Thomas Younker and Rick Lemcke, whose support made my historian work possible; George Lusk, Gordon Howe, and Lucien Morin, who sponsored my work as Monroe county historian; Eugene Mazzola, who invited me to become Irondequoit's historian, a task I highly treasured; Elizabeth VanDorn Keller, Leith Wright, and Mary Townsend, Hilton's officially appointed historians, who often aided my work; Brian Glenn Husted, who continually aids me now; and most of all my beloved father, Ward William Cox, whose stories of how life used to be inspired my interest in history, despite my mother's constant admonitions to "forget all that 'useta' stuff." I'll never stop loving the tales of yesteryear . . . all that useta stuff!

ACKNOWLEDGMENTS

Since my appointment as Parma town historian in September 1967, I have amassed a pictorial collection of several hundred photographs. Some were taken by myself or by Donald, Rosemary, and Brian Husted. Others were contributed by friends of history, including the following: William V. Newcomb, Harry McCarty (by Anne Pfarrer Hall), Fred Hill (by Esther Hill), Denny W. Wright, Leith Cox Wright, Florence Lee, Earl Hilfiker, Vernon Tyner, Ann Kolb, Alvin McMann, Alan Hovey, Priscilla Tyner Beeman, Dixie Miller Dunn, Audrey Derosia Wheeler, Ruth Rosenberg Naparsteck, Jean Wadsworth, Lucille Pfarrer, David Fox, Elsie Webster, Mary E. Smith, Kathleen Coakley Hershey, Grace Witty, Virginia Tomkiewicz, Magdalene VanDorn, Robert Sickelco, David Abbott, Jeffrey Tipton, Jolyon Kramer, Mary Townsend, Elmer LaDue, Rick Hooper, Marion Schepler, Betty Vary, Arlo "Buss" Bacon's family, the Mitchells, the Dimocks, the Nicholses, the Pasterkamps, the Chattins, Nellie Hunt Martin, Kay Bingalli, Joseph Choka, Rev. I.V. Lloyd, Thomas Burger, David Crumb, Margaret Huffer Bennett, Earl Hilfiker, Robert Gustafson, Madelyn Schalk, Charles Lenhart, C. Harlan Cooper, Larry Gursslin, Harriet Wyant, Adolph Watkins, Walter Sassaman, Edwin Spellman, Gordon Howe, Merritt Elwell, Marlene Leeming, Laura Quinn, Florence Lee, Arthur Perry, Ruth Perry Eaton, Violet Green, Luella Dean, Mike Boyle, Verna Chassman, Mary Gavigan, Donald Pisher, Edgar McWilliams, Joseph Heinrich, Grace Cox, Thomas Younker, Mrs. Alvah Miller, David Maynard, Lois McCracken, Harold Silloway, Alvin McMann, James Scott, William Watters, the Parma Baptist Church, the Eastman Kodak Company, Rowe Photos, the Village Photographer at Hilton, Corgan & Balestiere, and a few unidentified camera artists. To all, especially those no longer on this earth, we are grateful for their willingness to preserve these cherished pictures of the past. Their photographic gifts have made this book possible.

For research assistance, I am grateful to Greg Schmitz, reference librarian at the Oshkosh (MI) Public Library; Charleen Tiebell, Winnefax Wisconsin Communities; Ken Huisjen, Multi-Mag Inc.; William R. Gordon; Ted N. Husted; and my editors, Rosalind Hopkins, Pamela O'Neil, and Michael Guillory of Arcadia Publishing.

—Shirley Elizabeth Cox Husted
shusted1@rochester.rr.com
Parma Center, New York

INTRODUCTION

Native Americans and early explorers followed an ancient trail running between Lake Ontario and the Native-American village of Canawaugas (meaning "stinking waters," so named because of its location by sulfur springs near Avon). The Canawaugas trail crossed Ridge Road at what became known first as Parma and later as Parma Corners. The foot-wide trail proceeded near Atchinsons' Corners, later called Parma Centre, to the village now dubbed Hilton. There, a branch, today's East Avenue, led toward Braddock Bay, roughly paralleling Salmon Creek. Another branch, now Lake Avenue and North Avenue, continued northward and skirted a cranberry bog to reach Lake Ontario, called Skenadario ("beautiful lake").

Now somewhat straightened and designated as Route 259, the road acquired various names over the years, historically relevant at the time and always subject to change. The names have also depended upon the direction of travel: the Hilton-Parma Center Road or the Parma Center-Hilton Road, the Parma Corners-Hilton Road or the Hilton-Parma Corners Road, and the Hilton-Spencerport Road or the Spencerport-Hilton Road. In the late 1960s, the name was abridged to the Hilton-Parma Road, with the portion stretching from Ridge Road to Spencerport retaining its earlier name of Union Street. Local punsters call it the Hilton-South Hilton Road, while those in Spencerport village call it the Spencerport-North Spencerport Road.

In 1796, pioneers blazed notches into trees to mark the first man-made road, which two years later became the west side's first surveyed road. It led from the Atchinson family's settlement on Hill Road to the Genesee River crossing at McCrackenville, now part of the city of Rochester near Driving Park bridge. A branch led to King's Landing, later called Hanford's Landing, near Kodak Park. Stephen Peabody's first distillery was there, making the nascent road one that led from a mill to a still—not unusual because grain could be sold for making liquor or corn whiskey. Even more important to the pioneers was the opportunity for farmers to ship produce to Canada from those river landings or to receive needed goods. Now potash ashes—manufactured by burning trees, salt, barrel staves, fruit, grain, and vegetables—could become cash crops.

Because the headwaters of Braddock Bay lay within Parma, Braddock Bay Township was the first name given to the northern portion of the town, encompassing all of the area north of Hilton's West Avenue. The southern section was called Fairfield, with a strip south of Peck Road called the Gore. The area was renamed by the state surveyor general's office in 1808, supposedly after Parma, Italy. The Italian city, named for the Parma River and well known for its excellent Parmesan cheeses and prosciutto hams, rose in 183 B.C. on the ruins of a prehistoric village founded *c.* 525 B.C. by Etruscans. The name seems to be associated with the Arabic word *barma*, meaning "circle." In 1817, the southern portion of the town of Parma split away, changing its name from Fairfield, the locality in Connecticut from which local pioneers came, to Ogden, in recognition of William Ogden and early proprietors of the Ogden Land

Company, a New York City land agency not always known for its honesty.

The main village was called the Crossroads, Tylers Corners, Salmon Creek, Unionville, and North Parma until it was renamed Hilton in 1896 to honor the Rev. Charles A. Hilton, a Civil War veteran and beloved Baptist minister. Hinkleyville, up the creek in the southern part of town, also commemorated an early Baptist parson, the Rev. Jonathan Hinckley. In his spare time Reverend Hinckley ran a mill and sometimes turned out good grain whiskey, to the horror of sedate Presbyterians in the nearby community of Adams Basin. To the west in Hamlin, East Hamlin was renamed Walker to honor their Baptist minister. Monroe County's only communities named in honor of early Christian leaders, these place names are evidence of the local belief that this land was indeed God's Country.

The acres that became Parma offered pioneers something more than the stony land of New England. The loamy alluvial soil, once the bottom of an old glacial lake, was rich silt deposited by an ancient glacier and left behind in the bed of Lake Iroquois, prehistoric waters that once stretched northward from Big Ridge Road, old Route 104. Lake Ontario is the shrunken remnant of that snowy glacier's melted waters.

From Lake Ontario's azure waters, the land that became Parma extended southward. Shallow marshes fed by sparkling streams, majestic virgin forests, wild berries, wild rose marshes, cranberry bogs, and wildflowers all flourished in the lake-warmed climate. Fruit also grew best near the shore, where temperatures were milder. The largest 20-ounce apple orchards in the world were planted near the lake on the Collamer Farms in Parma and Hamlin. Rare plant varieties were found around the bay in the 19th century by Dr. Samuel Beach Bradley and were filmed in the 20th century by naturalist filmmaker Earl Hilfiker for use in public and school presentations. The Bradley and Hilfiker collections are now in university libraries.

Here, vast forests of tall, magnificent trees offered valuable lumber with which to build homes, schools, and churches, business places, sailing ships, wagons, carriages, fences, barns, and outbuildings. Streams teemed with plump fish and waterfowl; marshes attracted wild game, frogs, beaver, deer, and birds. An abundance of food and shelter opportunities awaited; and for those who chose a plot of land, ten years of credit were available before the mortgage came due—ten years to decide whether to stay on that spot or move on to greener pastures. Here and there was the unexpected bonus of a spring or a salt lick. Good land sold for $2 an acre, about 1/1,000th of the current price.

The region had even more blessings: here there was freedom, an independent lifestyle without control by old foreign governments, and few taxes imposed on local development. There was so little governmental business that the town fathers met only once a year, every March. In 1809, the first town meeting's only business matters were to elect officers and to vote to build a pound at Parma Corners to confine stray animals.

Settlers found all this and something else: the attractive romance of life on the frontier. Here was an unexplored sanctuary for men and women—a place to hew a homesite from the wilderness, to clear fields, to build a home and outbuildings, and to leave an imprint on the land. Today, many streets bear the names of early farmers and civic leaders. Churches and schools stand proudly where pioneers once struggled to clear the forest and drain the swampland. Parma's legacy comes from those dedicated pioneers, whose hard work and steady perseverance brought progress. Emblazoned on Parma's town emblem is the motto "Pioneers, Perseverance, Progress." Designed by Eleanor Witty in 1970, the emblem is shaped like an old record book, opened to tell Parma's story.

The Native Americans who discovered Parma while food gathering were trekking to the cranberry bogs and fishing grounds near the lake. It must have been disheartening after the white pioneers first came, when wolves ate their sheep, dogs chewed cowhides, weather destroyed crops, livestock strayed away, snakes crept into their beds, chills and fevers raged, and fire decimated buildings. .

Women were lonely and men were fatigued by the hardships of the pre-Industrial Age, but they didn't complain about it. They kept on keeping on and because they did, Parma emerged from the tree-covered wilderness to become a grain center, then a fruit capital, and finally an educational leader, valuing and encouraging its authors, progressive teachers, musicians, and athletes in much the same way as did the Parma of northern Italy, a province of 400,000. People here still applaud when the bands go by, vote Republican more often than not, and happily brag about their community. May the town never lose that sense of pride that has given it the reputation of a being a community that cares about causes and children, older residents and human rights, just as it did in the middle of the 19th century when slaves escaping bondage passed through here on the Underground Railroad.

Some former residents resettled in Jackson County, Michigan, where they named their village after their home here. Others unsuccessfully sought personal wealth during the 1840s gold rush in the West. Others traveled to Oil Creek, Pennsylvania, in 1865 to check out an oil speculation bubble. When that bubble burst, two disillusioned Hilton men said, "Let us go back to God's Country." Whereupon they returned to Hilton and never left home again.

Built by the "muscle power" of the pioneers, Hilton benefited from the "sweat power" of those who built the Lake Ontario Shore Railroad in 1876, enabling rapid industrial growth. Then came "brain power," with electricity, rayon, plastics, wonder drugs, telephones, telegraphs, television, Teflon, Velcro, and scores of astonishing technological and mechanical inventions, literary and educational achievements of our modern era. Still, by whatever the name it was designated, the community was always considered God's Country . . . swept time and again by the agonies of war . . . saddened by the influence of drugs that may have led to, among other things, the burning of the Hilton Methodist Church . . . horrified from time to time by scandals involving preachers, teachers, principals, bus drivers, a bank official, doctors, lawyers, druggists, sports figures, politicians, murderers, musicians, students, and even children.

Yet it was still God's Country, with residents proud of the "Star-Spangled Banner," ever honoring God and country, 99.44% pure despite occasional peccadilloes that, if not forgotten, were usually forgiven. Parma Center once was boastfully called the Hub of the Universe, and as the 20th century ended and computers became commonplace, even Parma Center was easily brought into instant contact with the entire world, via electronic mail.

First, last, and always a community that cares, the village's proud slogans—"Unionville Against the World," "The Apple Capital of the World," and "The Little Town with a Big Heart," as village historian Betty Van Dorn Keller liked to call it—were, perhaps, a questionable bit of proud parochial puffery. But they remain evidence that here is a place important to most of us simply because it is home, the center of our personal universe. For many of us, just the privilege of living here is the greatest adventure of all. May we consider it to be God's County for all the years to come, for now the future belongs to all those who believe in the beauty of their dreams and strive to make them become reality.

Author's note: How old is the world? Over 300 million years old, some scientists say. If so, then Parma began in the foggy mists of time at a date unknown. But if Jesus was born c. 5 B.C., as theologians believe, then our third millennium since Christ's birth already began c. 1995. Julius Caesar tried to correct the calendar in 63 B.C., and so did Pope Gregory XIII in 1582. However, if a monk tinkering with the Gregorian calendar made a mathematical error and began the present calendar with the year one instead of zero, by that "new" calendar the third millennium would actually begin January 1, 2001, not January 1, 2000, of the Christian calendar when most people will celebrate. But, as Einstein might say, all time is relative. There's the Jewish calendar version, 5761; the Muslim one, 1421; the Buddhist one in Thailand, 2543; Taiwan's year, 89 counting from the fall of the last imperial dynasty; and the Chinese year, 4698, on the 12-year lunar calendar, with years honoring animals coming up again every 12 years, by our definition of a year. And not all new years start on January 1. So, celebrate whenever you choose. For *Parma and Hilton*, we will use the Gregorian dates and hope that the dreaded man-made Y2K bug stays away from the door in the new Chinese year of the dragon.

One

A Look Around

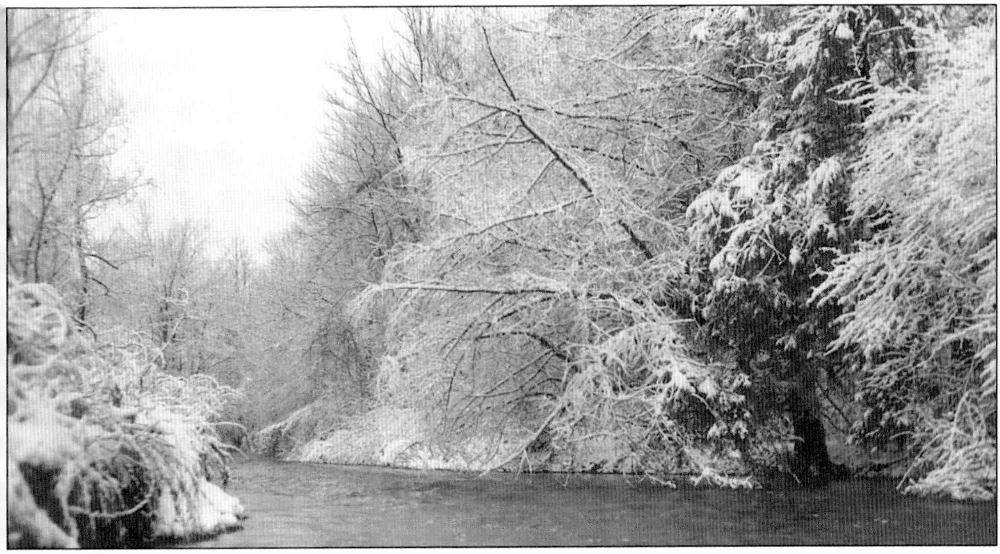

Salmon Creek in Winter. Salmon Creek bears the name of its delicious fish, once so plentiful that children could wade into the waters and catch salmon in their hands. It perpetuated life for those who ate the eels, salmon, trout, and other fish taken from it. Long before white pioneers arrived, nearby Braddock Bay attracted Native Americans, who came here in warm weather to fish in the lake, the bay, and fast-flowing streams that drain into the bay. Salmon Creek was the name chosen for the first village post office (1845) located at the country crossroads that became Hilton. The creek supported almost all of the early industry: gristmills and sawmills, which converted grain and logs into the flour and lumber that fed and sheltered the pioneers and their farm animals. But the creek's rushing waters provided something else. The muddy creek, which Native Americans called the Place of Minnows, was a source of flooding and infectious germs that made living in the area hazardous. A young girl drowned in the creek, trapped under winter ice. Vermonter Jonathan Underwood, Hilton's first pioneer, operated a potashery on the hill overlooking the flats. Underwood first came here in 1806. The flats by the creek, where a Native-American campsite was found and an early militia unit trained, have become the site of a shopping plaza, apartments, and despite long opposition, a now popular McDonald's restaurant. This view, which captures the beauty of the creek in winter, was taken by photographer Harry McCarty.

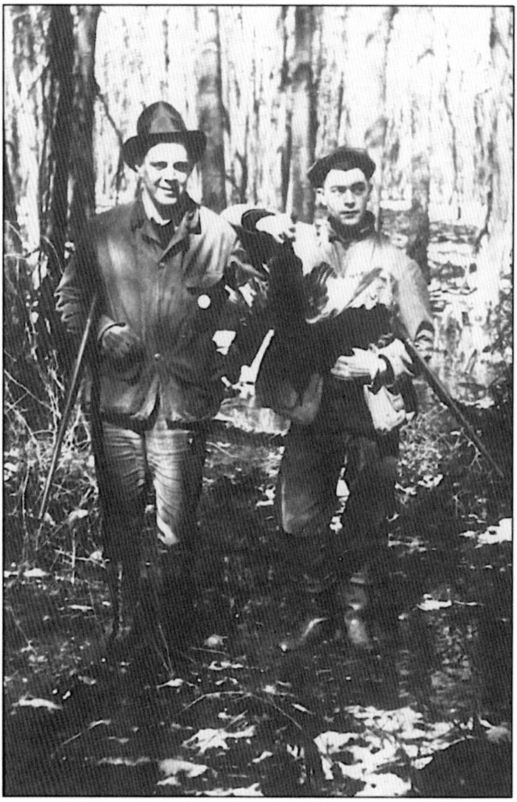

Hunting Grounds. In pioneer times, passenger pigeons, ducks, geese, wild boars, bears, deer, and fish were plentiful throughout the area. Hunting continued into the 20th century. At the left, Millard "Pete" Rowley and Fenton "Fent" Coakley pause for a moment during their hunting trip. Coakley later became under sheriff of Monroe County, right-hand man to Sheriff Albert Skinner. Below, deer hunters display their plunder in a 1940s photograph taken by Harry McCarty. Deer, fox, peacocks, wild turkeys, muskrats, and other wildlife still thrive on public lands near the lake.

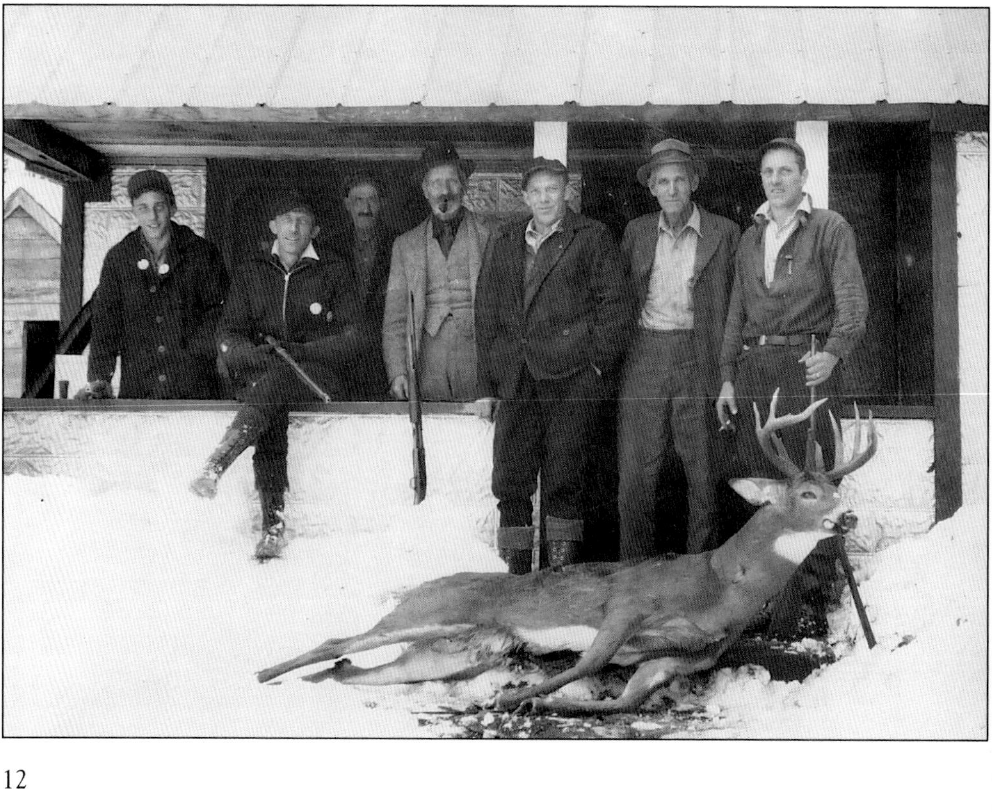

Hovey Square. The Victorian village clock given by John Klock to honor his grandfather, John Cooper, is an attractive centerpiece in Hovey Square at the center of Hilton village. Walt Horylev (a village trustee), the local historian, and Mayor Larry Gursslin proudly dedicated the square as a family memorial, in recognition that Jesse Hovey's gift of land for a train station and public street crossing had attracted a railroad, ensuring the growth of the village. Justus VanAllan Hovey became the village's first undertaker in 1883 and also ran a hotel. Jesse Justus Hovey, his father, was the local constable, and was responsible for escorting imprudent drinkers to the village lockup. At the edge of the square, the popular Hilton Family Restaurant features unique Tommy Burgers, named after its proprietor, Tommy Platt.

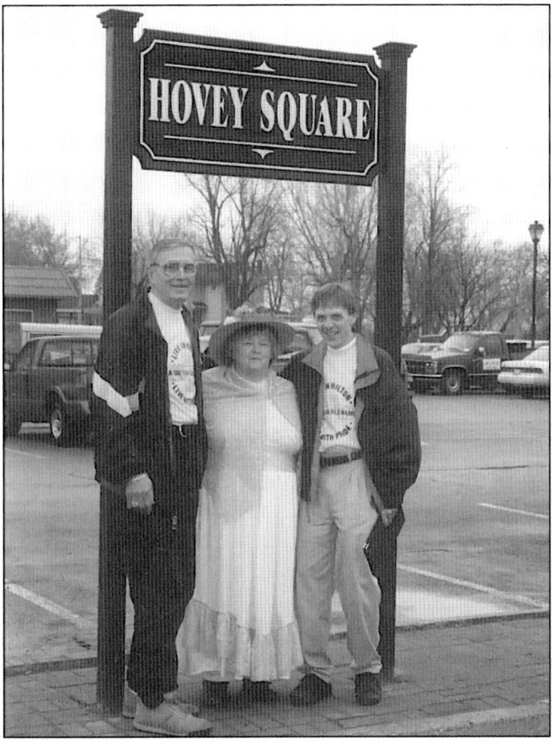

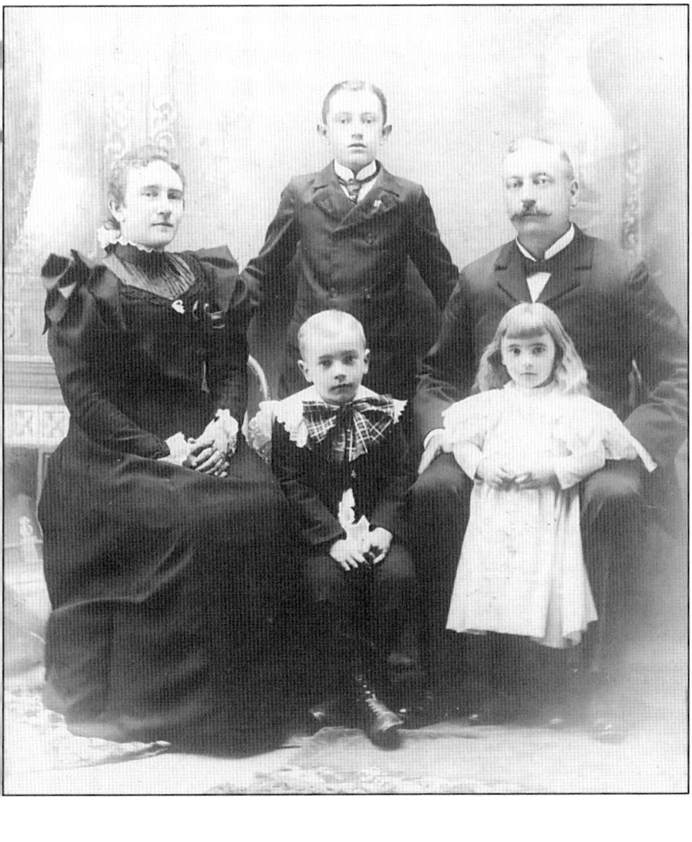

Hovey Family. Sophronia Hovey (left), secretary of the local Women's Christian Temperance Union, often sent memorandums about the evils of intemperance to be read from the Baptist church pulpit, while her undertaker husband, Justus VanAllan Hovey (right), was running the hotel bar nearby. Note young Allan Hovey (front center) in his fashionable lace collar and ribbon tie. He was born in 1891. With the houses and most of Hovey Street gone, the family is now best remembered by Hovey Square, a shopping center dedicated to the Hoveys in 1996.

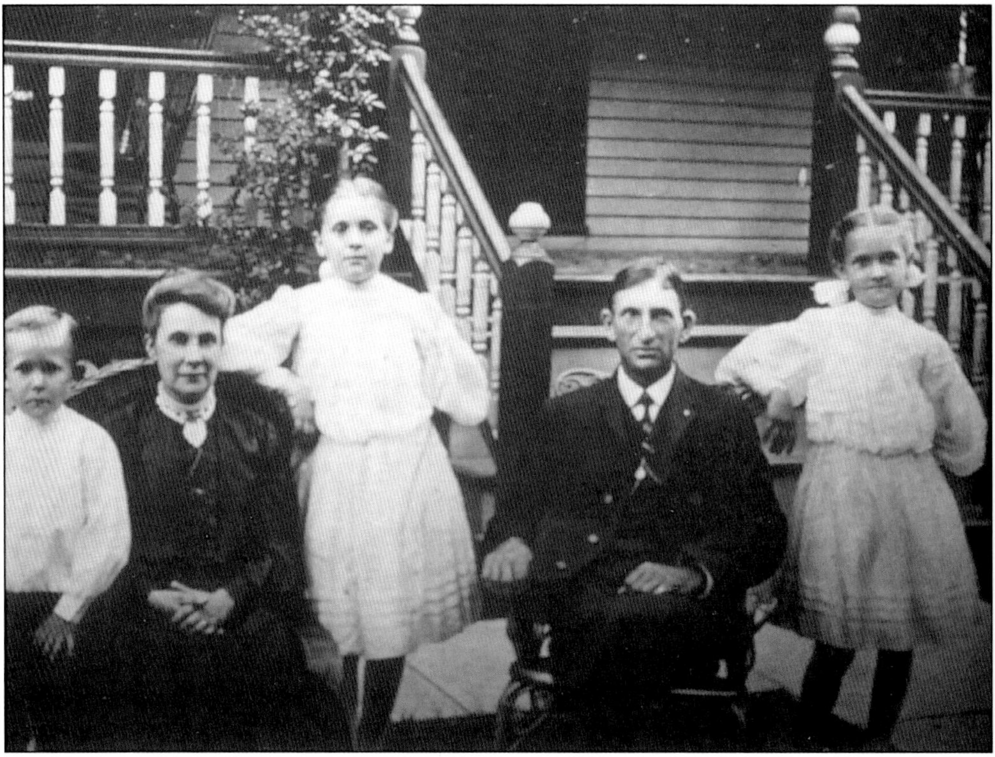

W.I. Smith Family. Members of the Smith family pose outside their house on the southwest corner of Collamer and Dunbar Roads. The Collamer 20-ounce apple originated as a sport, or freak, on a tree growing on the farm of Collamer brother-in-law W.I. Smith. The Collamers bought part of the Smith farm to acquire the tree. The house pictured here burned in a fire, was rebuilt, and still stands at the same location today.

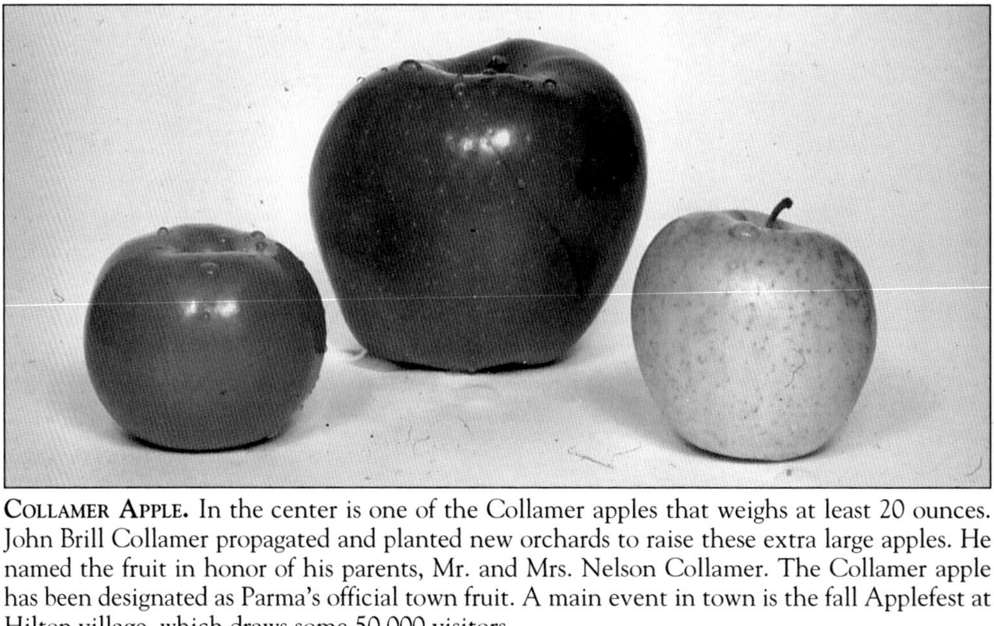

Collamer Apple. In the center is one of the Collamer apples that weighs at least 20 ounces. John Brill Collamer propagated and planted new orchards to raise these extra large apples. He named the fruit in honor of his parents, Mr. and Mrs. Nelson Collamer. The Collamer apple has been designated as Parma's official town fruit. A main event in town is the fall Applefest at Hilton village, which draws some 50,000 visitors.

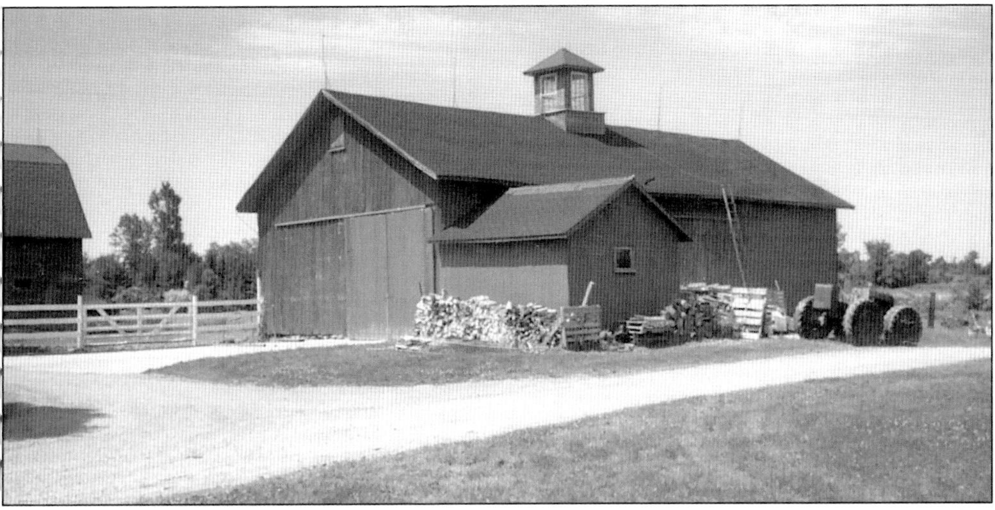

Frame Barn. Revolutionary War veteran Matthias Lane was the first owner of the farm that later became the Chase family's farm. Lane helped guard Congress as it escaped from Philadelphia during the American Revolution. The picturesque Chase-Flack-Wyant house at 1191 Manitou Road sheltered runaway slaves while owned by Parma Supvr. Isaac Chase. Today, its barn is part of the farm market operation established by Harold and Harriet Flack Wyant in 1969.

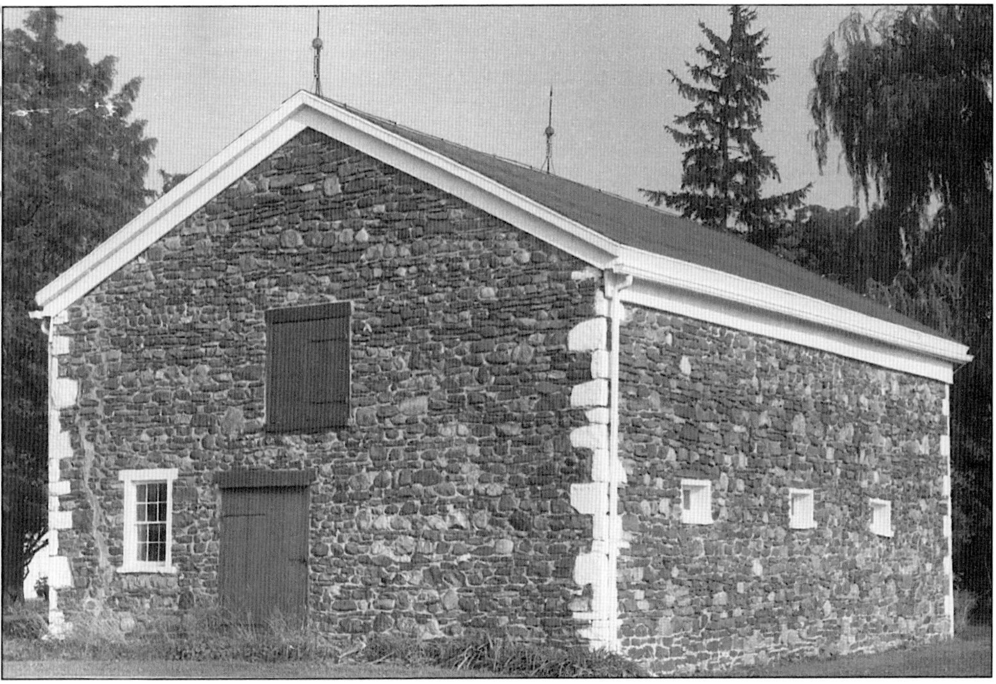

Stone Barn. Aaron Blakeman's apple barn on the Blakeman-Lenz-Coyle farm, Parma Center Road, is a fine example of Parma's cobblestone buildings. Robert Krzaczek purchased 5 acres and the Coyle farmhouse and barn in July 1999. It was later used as a garage. The barn, the foundation walls of Blakeman's earlier home at Parma Center, and the farmhouse of Blakeman's father-in-law, Isaac Chase Jr., were painstakingly built from stones washed smooth by Lake Ontario's waters. The Chase cobblestone farmhouse was the first Parma structure listed in the National Register of Historic Places.

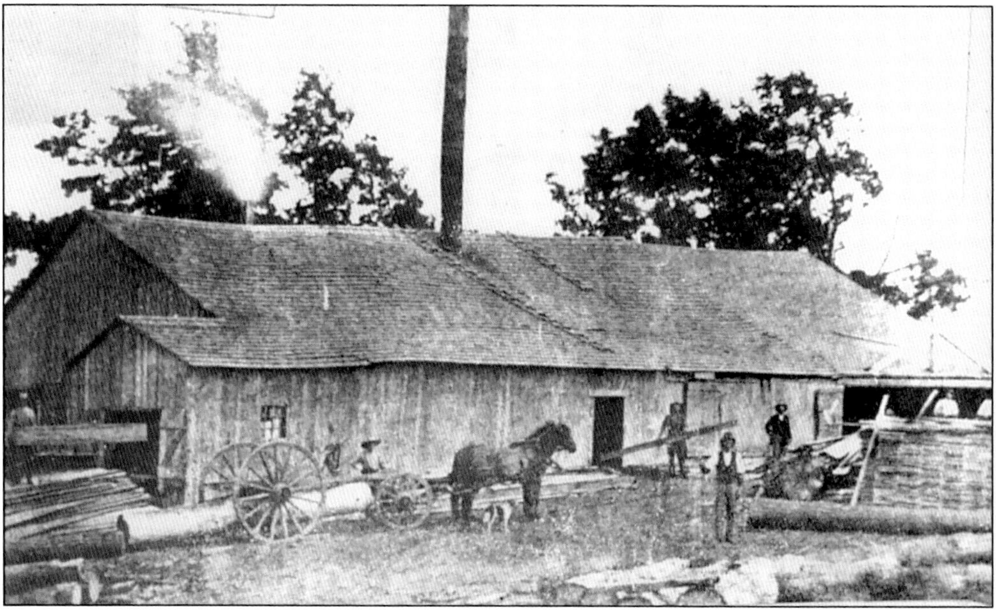

HISCOCK MILLS. Just north of today's Braddock Bay Hotel, blacksmith James Hiscock's employees cut lumber at a sawmill originally built by Clark & Atwell. Oliver Bagley's shop produced barrels and the firm shipped logs imported from Canada on to Hilton to be sawn into boards. The locality is now known as "The Bridges" because three bridges carry Manitou Road over the bay where a log causeway had once crossed. Hiscock-Fishbaugh Post, American Legion, was named after Lester Hiscock and Glenn Fishbaugh, World War I casualties. One hundred local men served in the war; nine were killed.

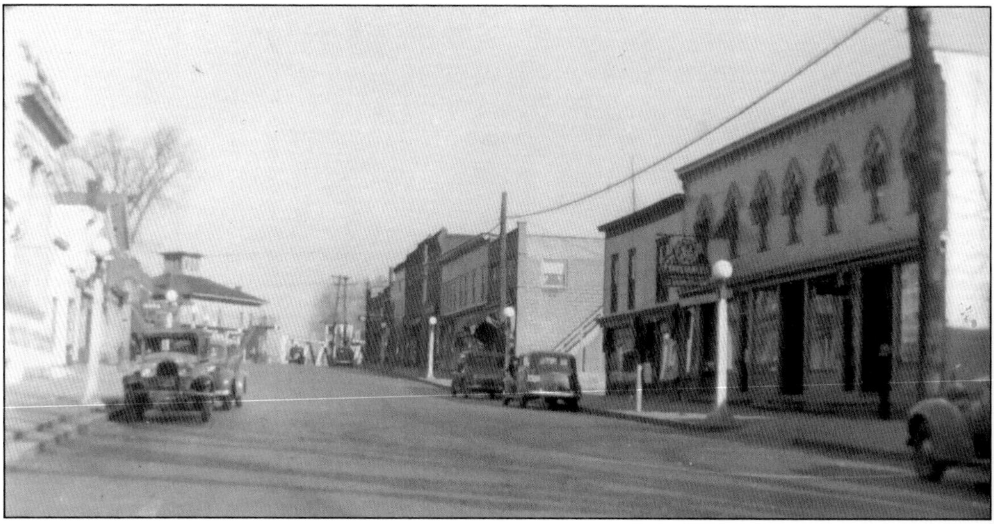

"SOUTH HILTON" IN THE 1930S. Vernon Tyner took this photograph of Spencerport's Main Street, which was originally part of Parma. Daniel Spencer's canal basin helped attract business life to the area after the Erie Canal came through. The Mattheos Ice Cream company, which began in a building at left on Main Street, became an important manufacturer of velvety ice cream and heavenly "Ooh-La-Las," cone-shaped vanilla delights on a stick with a sweet dark chocolate coating festively topped with nuts. They were available for only 10¢ at several Parma stores.

Two

Pioneer Places

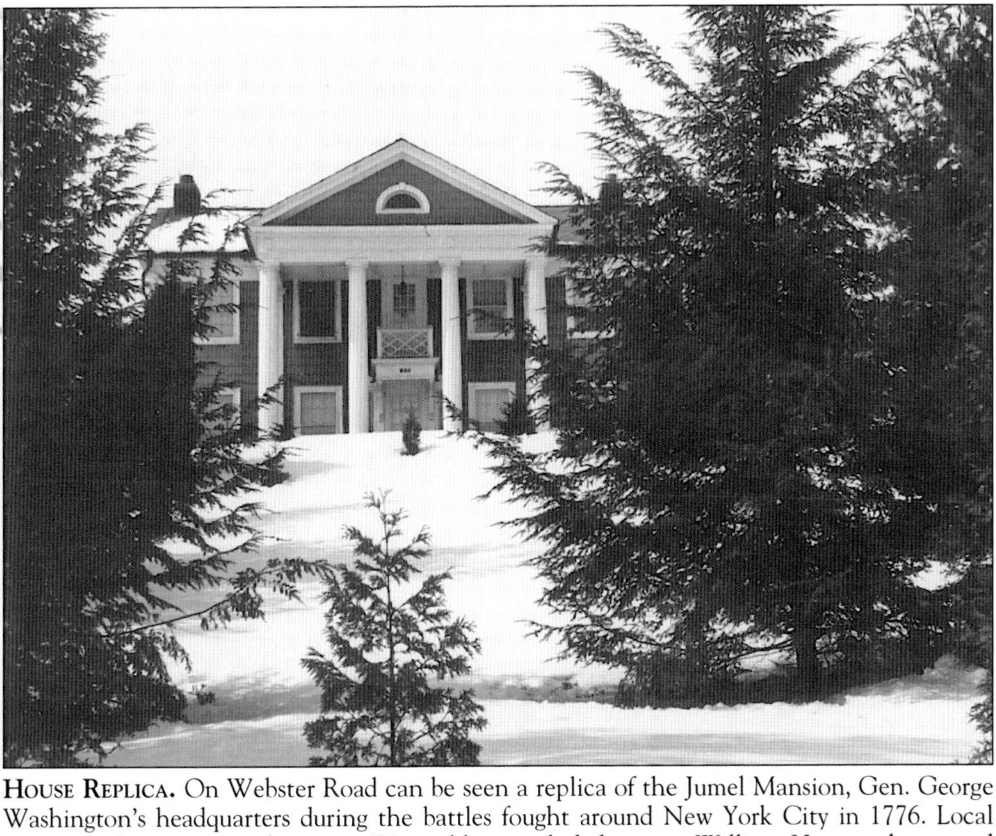

House Replica. On Webster Road can be seen a replica of the Jumel Mansion, Gen. George Washington's headquarters during the battles fought around New York City in 1776. Local pioneers who were Revolutionary War soldiers included patriot William Henry, who owned much of the land on the west side of Hilton Hill extending down to the creek. Henry is buried in North Avenue's Smith Family Cemetery. His granddaughter, Elizabeth Henry, married John Gorton. The family names are perpetuated today by Henry Street and Gorton Avenue.

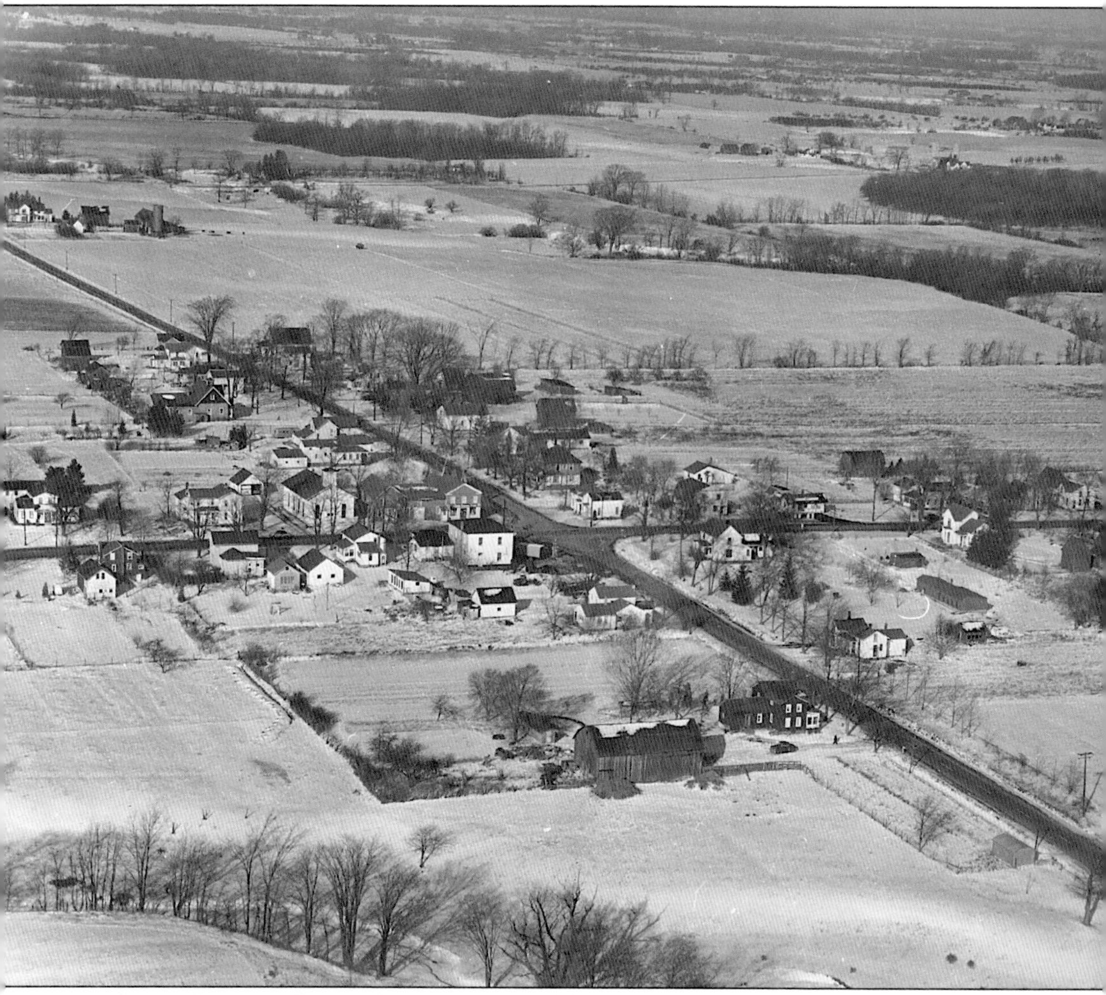

Aerial View of Parma Center. Fire and demolition changed the Parma Center seen in this 1940s photograph. The K&K Food Mart has replaced the Methodist church and the home of Gettysburg veteran Alvah Wyncoop. The Free Methodist Church is a tire garage and its parsonage has been moved away for a private home. Fire destroyed the general store on the southwest corner; the old harness shop adjoining it is being rebuilt. Only the 1831 home of state senator John Patterson on the northwest corner remains virtually unchanged. In the small law office and post office behind the Patterson house, Lewis Patterson, the senator's blind nephew, made brooms. He cut the lawn's grass by hand, using clippers and a board marker. In the distance can be seen the lands of the Atchinson Settlement. Austin and Roswell Atchinson, sons of Bezaleel Atchinson Jr., began developing the community after Austin built the first house in 1809. The community was first called Atchinsons' Corners since Austin owned lands north of Parma Center Road and Roswell owned lands to the south. Roswell Atchinson's house still stands near Parma Town Hall.

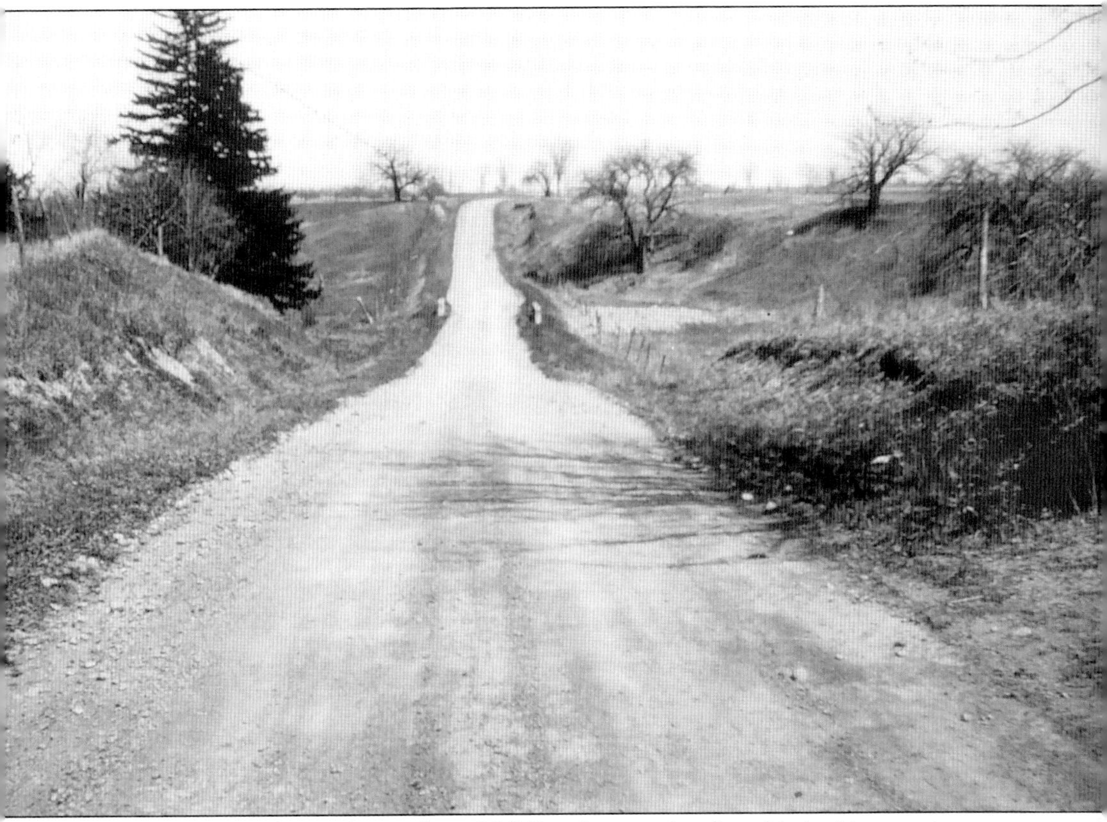

HILL ROAD. Settlement began here where Hill Road passes by the old Atchinson pioneer cemetery and curves past the homesite of Bezaleel Atchinson Jr. Atchinson's father, a soldier in the American Revolution, came here later and lived on Hill Road. Though the first Atchinsons came in 1796, veteran Michael Beach had staked a claim here in 1795, just south of Peck Road. The first church services, led by Methodist circuit rider Rev. Loring Grant, were held in Beach's log home. Other settlers soon began farming along Burritt and Peck Roads.

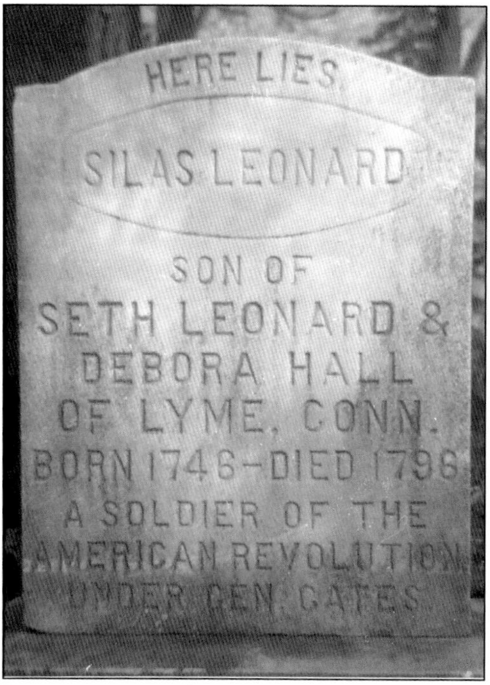

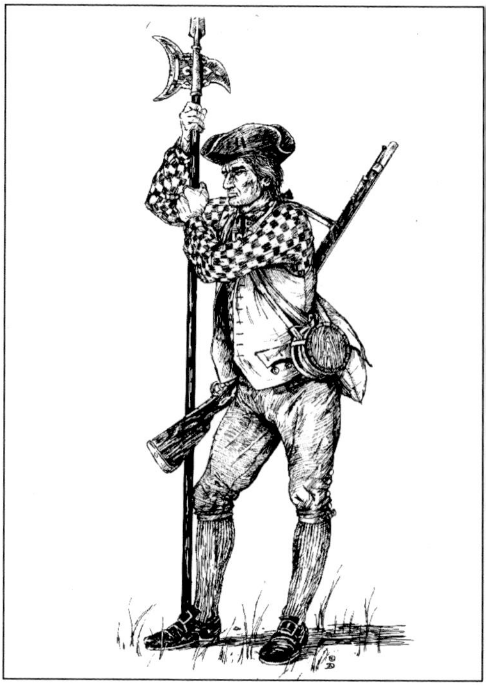

REVOLUTIONARY SOLDIERS. In the Atchinson Cemetery on a portion of Hill Road laid out in 1801 as the Braddock Bay Road can be found the tombstone of Silas Leonard, a Revolutionary War veteran. The death date given on the stone precedes the date of the family's arrival here. Family legend states that he died en route. It was sometimes customary for a family to erect a stone in memory of a previous member buried elsewhere. In 1803, Route 259 became a newer branch of the Braddock Bay trail. David Abbott's sketch shows another Revolutionary soldier, Sgt. William Henry, in the checkered shirt worn by his Hartford, Connecticut militia outfit. Henry was nearly 60 when he settled here.

REFRIGERATOR ADVERTISEMENT. Silas Leonard's great-grandson, Charles Heman Leonard, gave America several wonderful inventions including the Leonard's Cleanable Refrigerator, introduced in Grand Rapids, Michigan, in 1883. His later invention, a 1914 porcelain-coated wooden icebox cooled by a motor, is now in the Smithsonian Institution at Washington, D.C. His inventions made him a millionaire.

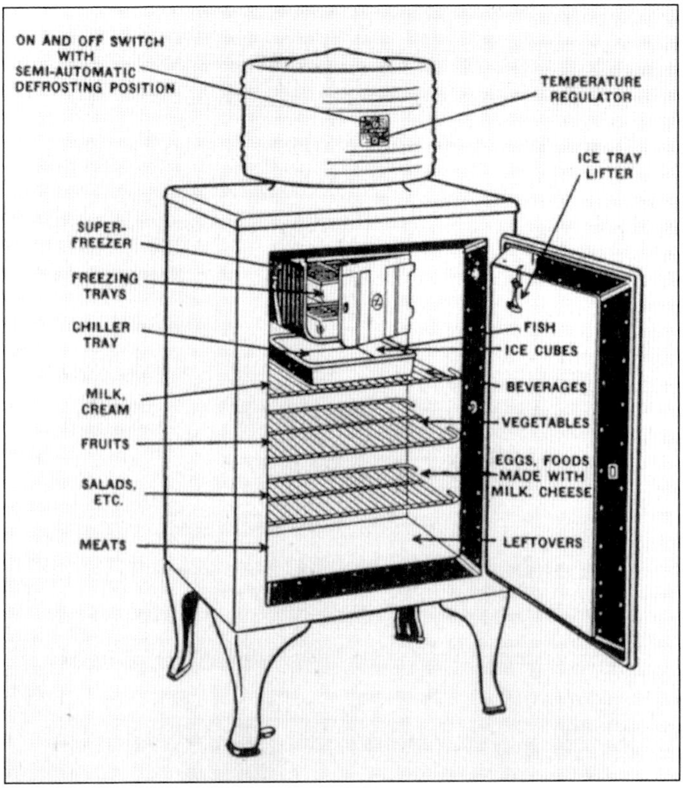

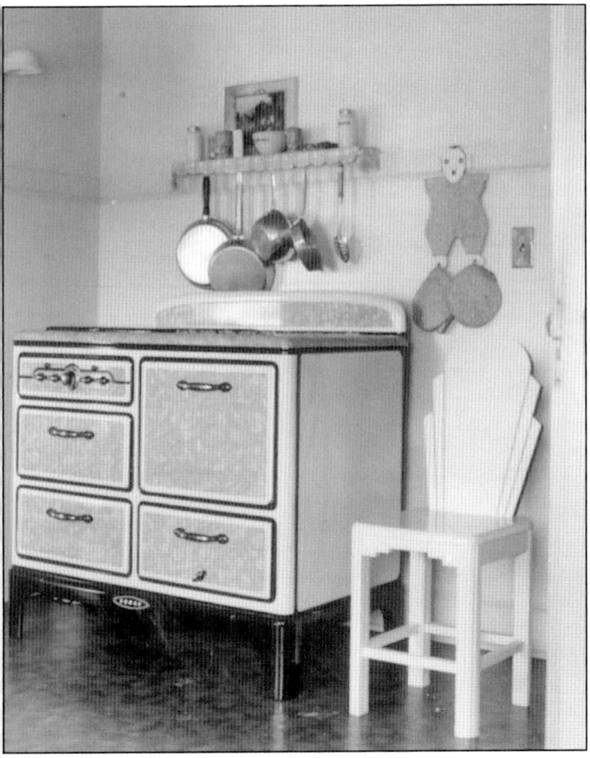

MITCHELL KITCHEN. Ruth and Lynn Mitchell were happy to have this remodeled kitchen in their Burritt Road home in the 1930s. The kitchen featured a new stove and an art deco style. There was, of course, a refrigerator, thanks to the legacy of their nearby neighbors' descendant Charles Leonard. The last iceman to deliver blocks of ice to local homes for cooling purposes was Glenn Wright, who was still supplying ice to lakeside cottagers in the 1950s.

THE WELLS PATENT BARN TRUSS.

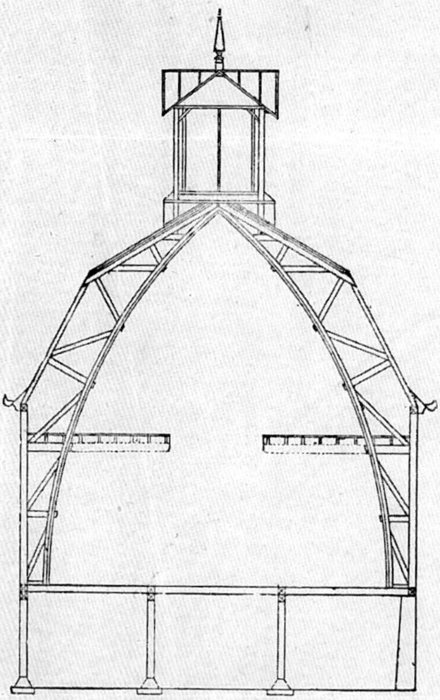

THIS CUT REPRESENTS THE

WELLS PATENT TRUSS

FOR

GRAIN AND HAY BARNS,

and shows a section over the drive floor, with a Scaffold supported by iron rods from above, which will leave the interior of the Barn free from Posts.

The lower story in the cut represents the basement.

The features we wish to call particular attention to is the absence of all Cross Beams, this allows the load to be run into the Mow as soon as it clears the wagon, the advantages arising from this combination are valuable, it does away with the necessity of hoisting the load clear of the track, thus saving time and travel of the horses, the load does not have to drop from the peak of the barn to the mow, thereby packing so hard as to cause mow burning; the sling full of Wheat, Oats or Hay hangs near the mow, and the operator can swing it to any part of the mow.

This Barn Frame can be sawed out on the farm with a Portable Saw Mill, if there is timber suitable, such as Spruce, Ash, Red Elm, Soft Maple, Hemlock or any wood that is tough.

This style of barn can be put up without a Mortice, Tenon or Gain, cut in the Sill or the Plate, thereby saving in the cost of labor, there is no large Timber above the Sills, the End Bents are built after an improved plan, which does away with any large posts or beams.

Correspondence solicited.

Working plans, terms and right of use can be obtained by addressing

J. T. WELLS & SONS,

Scottsville,

Monroe Co., N. Y.

WELLS BARN. Because Braddock Bay fever, a form of deadly malaria spread by mosquitoes from the marshes, sometimes wiped out entire families or left orphaned children to be raised by neighbors, settlement farther south along Ridge Road became more desirable. Myra Goodhue, Parma's firstborn white child, married Moses Wells and became the grandmother of John Wells. In 1889, John Wells patented the famous Wells Barn, an enormous trussed structure with a window in the front gable end.

A Hoosick Family. Pictured here are the Abraham Babcock family and house. Farther west on Ridge Road was the Pease family cooper shop, and down Dean Road was the Dean's blacksmith shop, so the sound of workmen's hammers ringing against steel was often heard in the neighborhood. When Manitou Road was straightened, the Babcock house was demolished and part of Hoosick Cemetery was destroyed. Caskets and human remains were loaded into trucks and hauled to the dump.

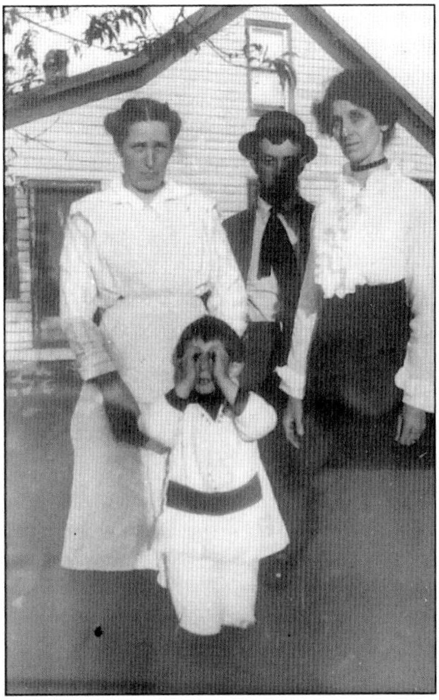

Village Blacksmith. Abe Babcock was Hoosick's village blacksmith. His rambling, weathered smithy on the top of Hoosick Hill was pushed down the hill in the late 1960s and eventually was covered by the RG&E fly ash landfill. Although most of Hoosick's old houses are gone now, the Greek Revival farm home of Supvr. A.P. Beebe, still stands. Beebe headed the committee responsible for building Monroe County's Italian Renaissance courthouse, now the county office building.

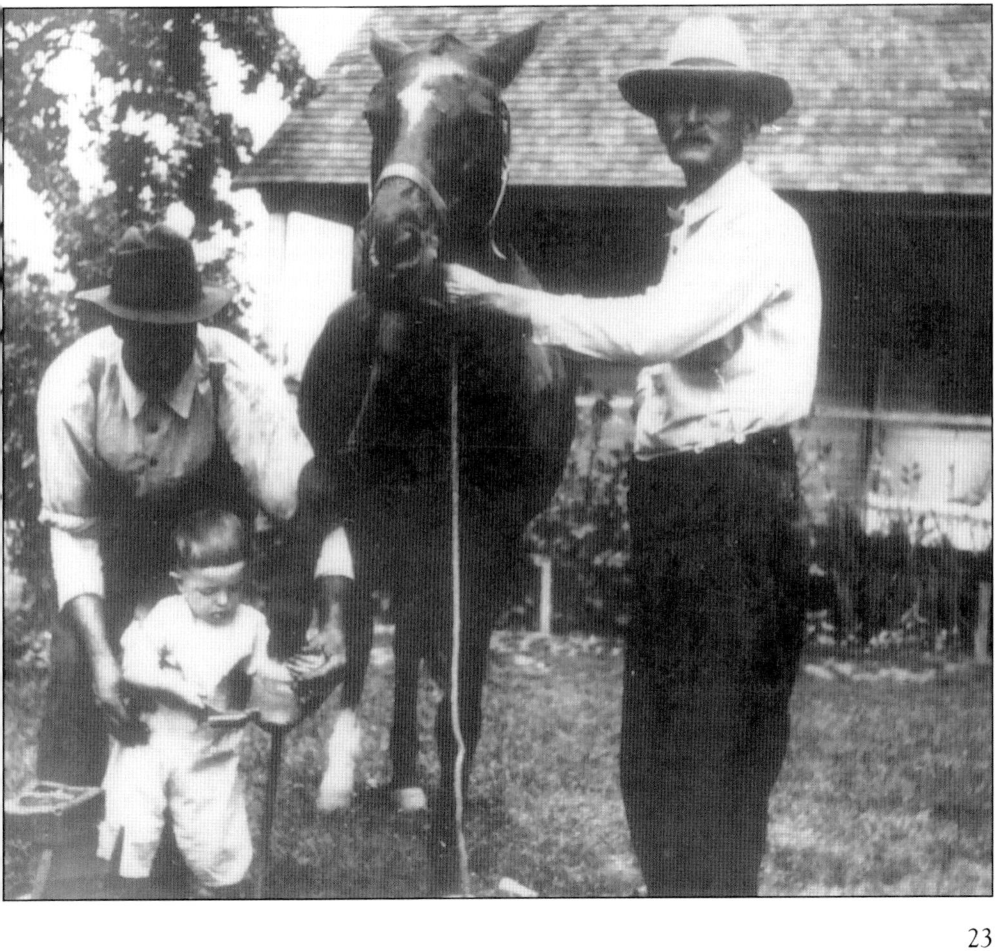

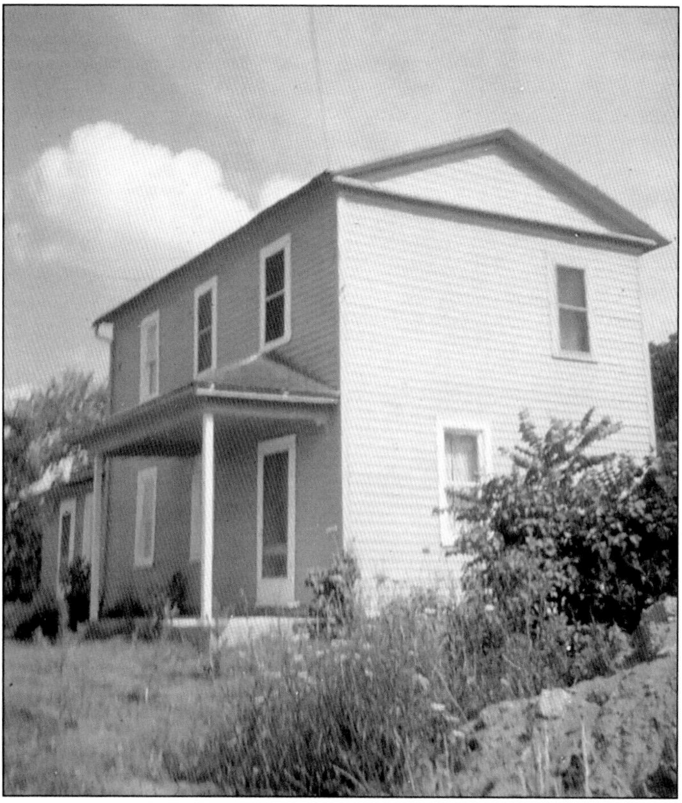

Sheldon House. Fire destroyed Jonathan Sheldon's 1814 Federal-style house on Ridge Road, supposedly the second frame house built in the town. The wood shop where Sheldon built everything from cradles to coffins, serving customers "from the cradle to the grave," still stands. Sheldon supervised the building of the Congregational church at Hoosick, part of whose cemetery still remains. Sheldon's land was first owned by Josiah Fish, first supervisor of old Northampton, all area lands west of the Genesee River.

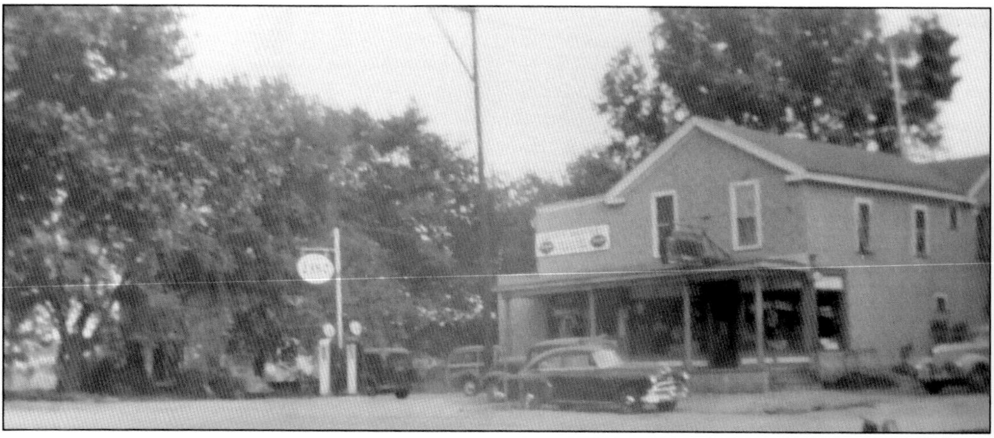

Parma Corners Tavern. Arlo "Buss" Bacon's Parma Corners tavern was rumored to have been one of the secret stops made by captors of William Morgan, the Mason, after he was abducted at Canandaigua in 1826. John Whitney, head of a Rochester lodge, told editor Thurlow Weed that he helped drown Morgan in the Niagara River. A Houston descendant insisted that she saw Morgan's body being buried in the cellar of their Clarkson tavern. Fire destroyed the Parma tavern in 1968. (McCarty photograph.)

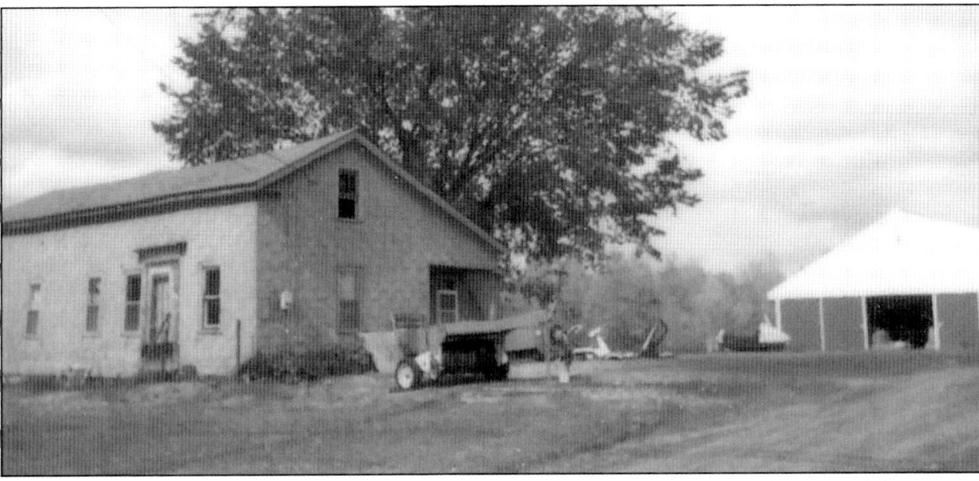

Cox House. William Cox, an 1823 pioneer, built this saltbox home on the site of the present Buttonwood Farm Nursery, established in 1989 by Frank and Ellen Palumbo at 1094 Hilton Parma Road. Constable Cox sold land at Hilton Beach to Walter Vond, a black fisherman. Vond concealed escaping slaves inside his lakeside boathouse and then rowed them to St. Catherine's, Canada, where Harriet Tubman's church provided shelter, food, and friendship.

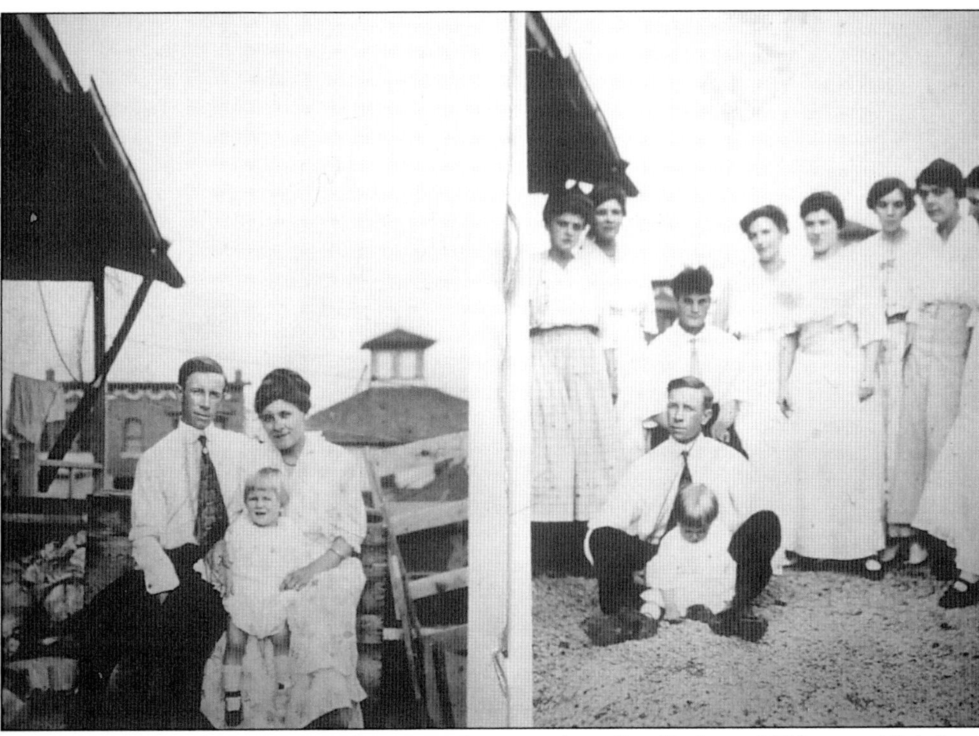

Burritt Family. The pioneering Burritts, who came from Sand Lake in 1832 to establish farms on Burritt Road, left many descendants in the local area. The Burritts became esteemed citizens and enthusiastic supporters of the fire department and local baseball teams. One of the most beloved was Loyd L. "Hy" Burritt (1889–1978) and his son Lloyd "Hy" (1918–1993), pictured here in his father's lap, across from Albert J. Stothard's hardware store, Hilton's oldest business block, built *c.* 1878.

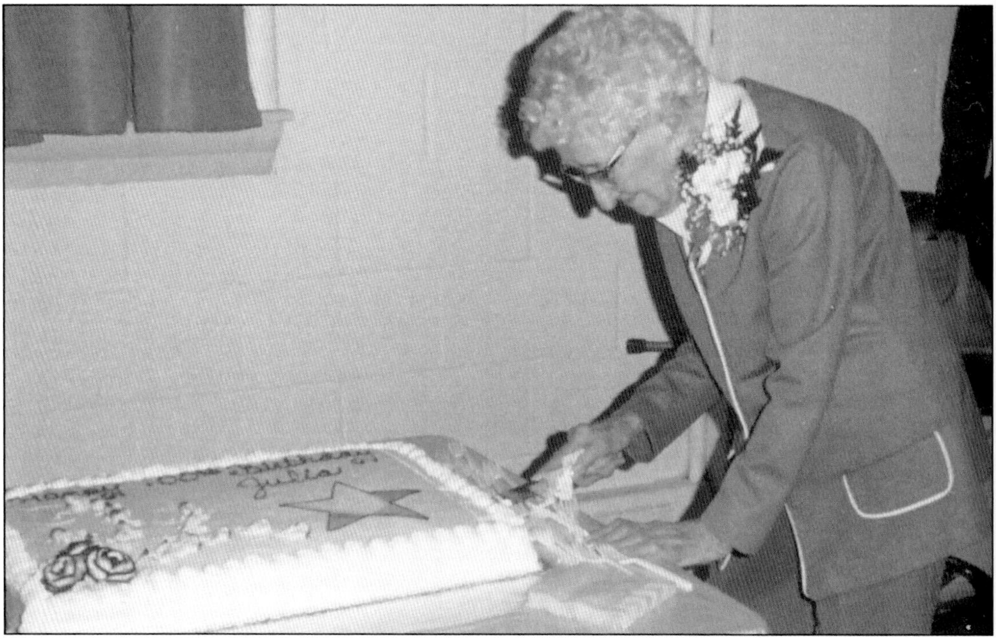

Cross Family Descendant. Julia Cross Kentner, a descendant of the 1811 pioneer Luman Cross, proudly became a centenarian from North Parma, or Bartlett's Corners. The hamlet, which was often called Bartlett's Shop because Thomas Bartlett's blacksmith shop occupied the southeast corner, also had a Methodist church and a district schoolhouse. Elam A. Cross was the first president of Hilton. Among later occupants of the Cross house was Mrs. Willette "Betty" Vary, Hilton's first woman principal.

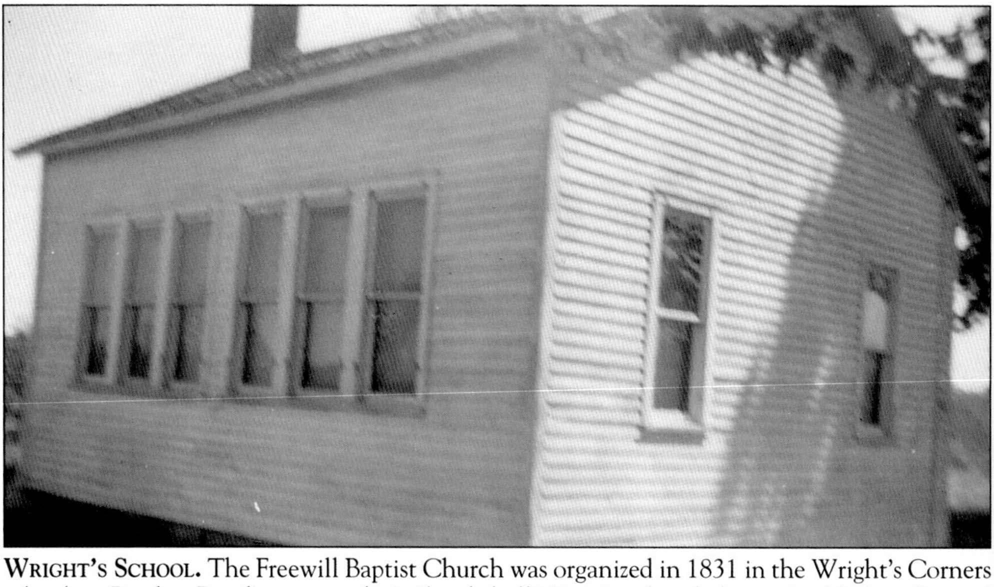

Wright's School. The Freewill Baptist Church was organized in 1831 in the Wright's Corners school at Dunbar Road's west end. A "hard-shell" Baptist church began in 1809 at Samuel Hicks's home at the Hicks's settlement on Peck Road. Both congregations moved to Hilton village, built new sanctuaries, carried on despite fires, and then united in 1920 to form the Hilton Baptist Church. The 1878 First Baptist sanctuary, 49 West Avenue, was used for school gym classes before it became an apartment house.

Three

ON THE WATERFRONT

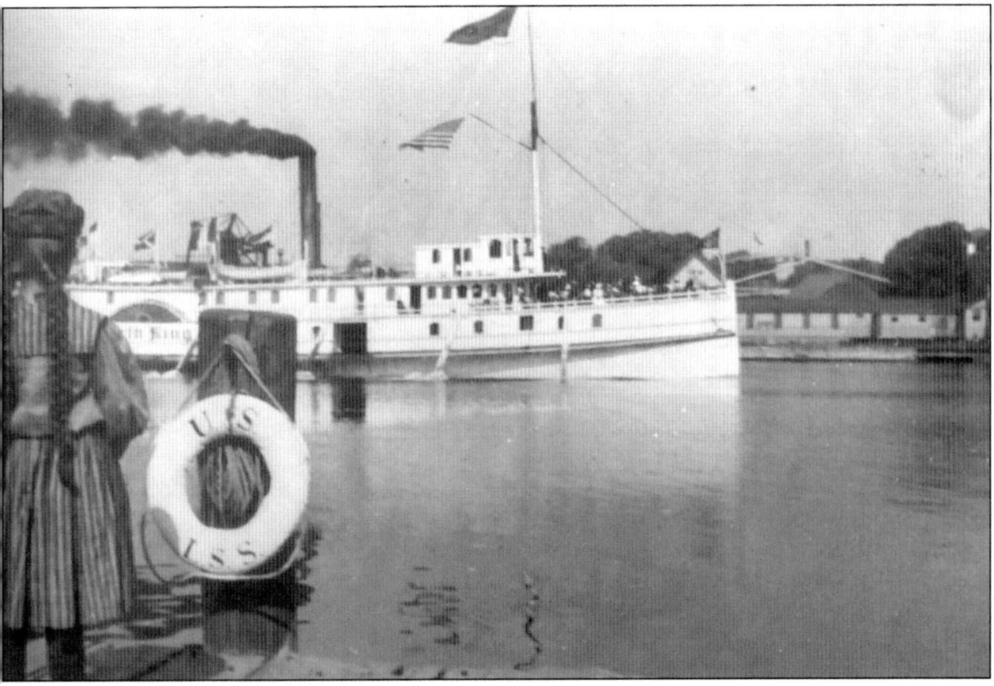

HARBOR SCENE. The port of Rochester at Charlotte became the main lake port for the Genesee region in 1805. One could visit a popular amusement park and public bathing beach there, take a trolley ride to Manitou Beach, or board a ferry to Cobourg, Canada. Lucky youngsters got to slurp down a delicious, dripping Abott's frozen custard cone at Charlotte or a strange, cone-shaped dip of vanilla at Cobourg. From 1907 until 1950, the two 300-foot open-stern boats *Ontario 1* and *Ontario 2* hauled some 500 passengers and some 2,000 tons of coal across the lake each day, an unforgettable sight when they passed by at night, their lights sparkling bright against an ebony sky. The boat runs were so regular that you could set your clocks by them. After the coal business declined, the two boats were sold for scrap metal.

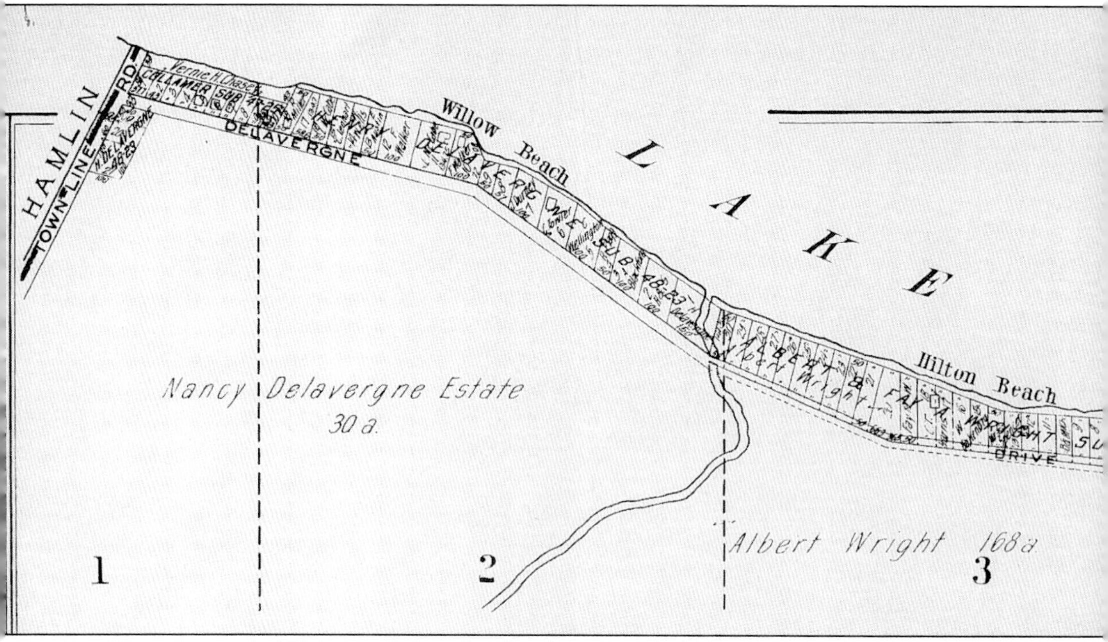

FIRST LOTS. A 1924 map shows the first lot owners along Parma's lakeshore. About 100 feet of the original shore is now underwater. Flooding occurred about every 20 years, and the controversial Gut Dam, built in Canada to control flooding, has not been entirely successful. Dr. Sherwood Sawyer sold lots at West Wautoma, giving it a Midwestern Indian name meaning "a good place." Wisconsin's Chief Tomah was a tall Menominee Indian known as a peacemaker and friend of the white men. Chief Oshkosh succeeded Tomah, who died while seeking supplies and food for his tribe and was buried on Michilimackinac Island in 1818. Bert Smith, Arthur Morgan, and Ward Cox built the first cottages at West Wautoma. The oldest structure on the beach is the Holcomb farmhouse .

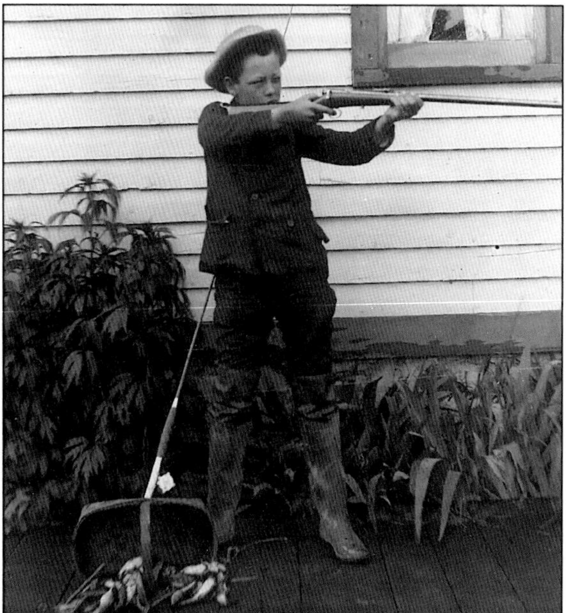

J. ALLAN HOVEY WITH A GOOD DAY'S CATCH.

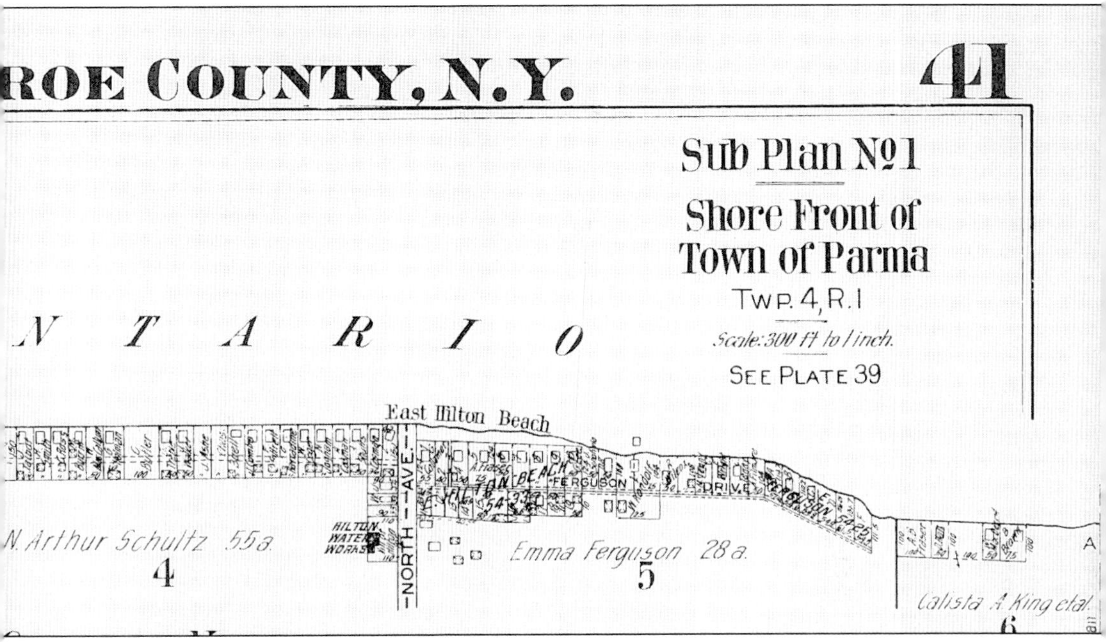

First Cottages. A rippling sandy bottom and seaweed beds off East Wautoma, first called Willow Beach, provided such good fishing that Milton and Henry DeLavergne, who farmed the land, rented boats to fishermen. Henry sold off lots on the beach. The Walkers and McCabes, Spencerportonians, built the first cottages. The Colony Club, a businessmen's club from Pittsburgh, camped out at least once at Wautoma and many summers at Manitou Beach. "They never drew a sober breath!" a Manitou Beach barkeeper, George Wiedman, remembered. When the Holcombs sheltered the crew of the ill-fated *James H. Shrigley*, a coal barge that went aground off East Wautoma in 1920, crewmen spent the night in the barn and the female cook was given a room in the farmhouse. After the owners decided not to salvage it, the barge remained aground off East Wautoma for several years, occasionally boarded by inquisitive citizens, some of whom illegally appropriated items found aboard. Eventually it sank.

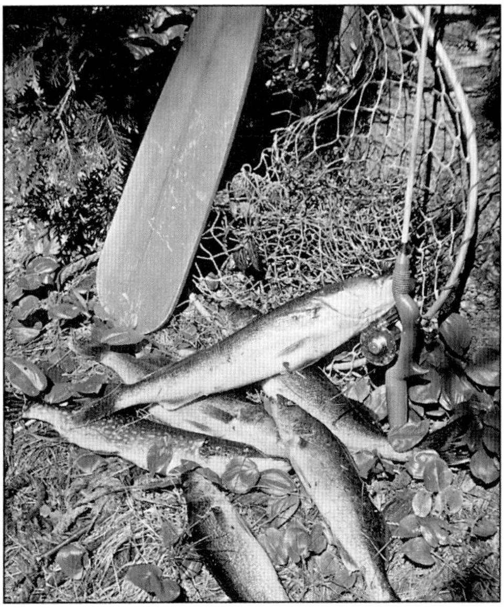

Harry McCarty Photograph of Dinner and the Means by which It Was Obtained.

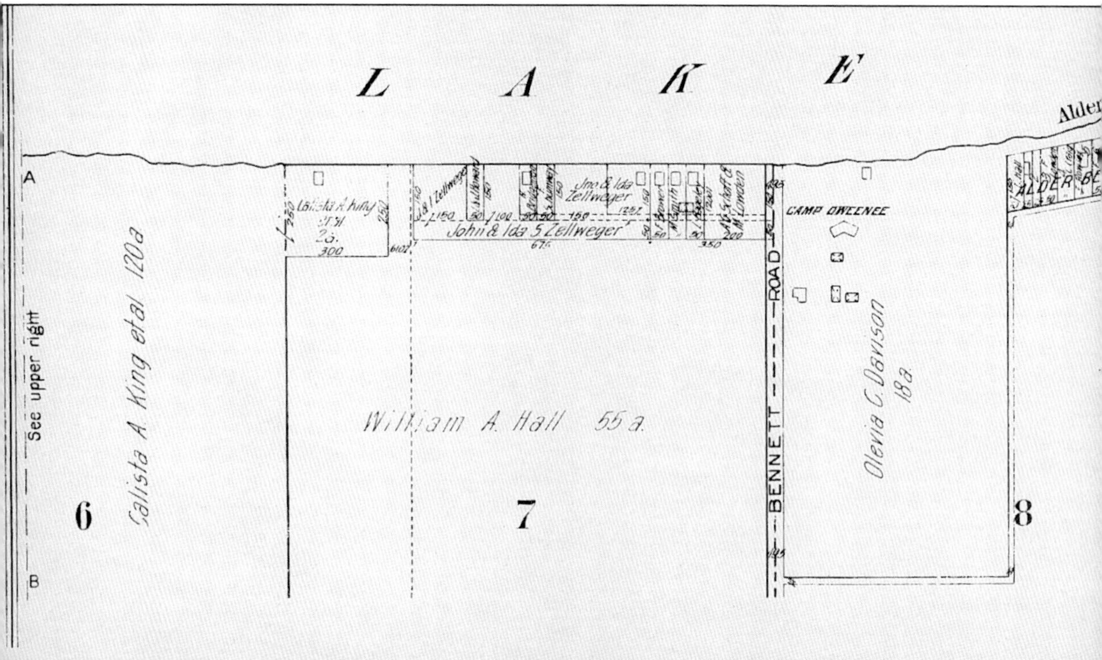

BEACH NAMES. Zellweger Beach and Davison Beach bear the names of their early owners, John and Ida Zellweger and Ed Davison. Zellweger Beach was once known as Dickson's Beach, but the Zellwegers sold off lots, developed it, and claimed the naming rights, as did the Davisons. Alder Beach was named for the trees growing prolifically along the shore. Ampor Beach perpetuated the name of its private club. Lighthouse Beach memorialized its lighthouse.

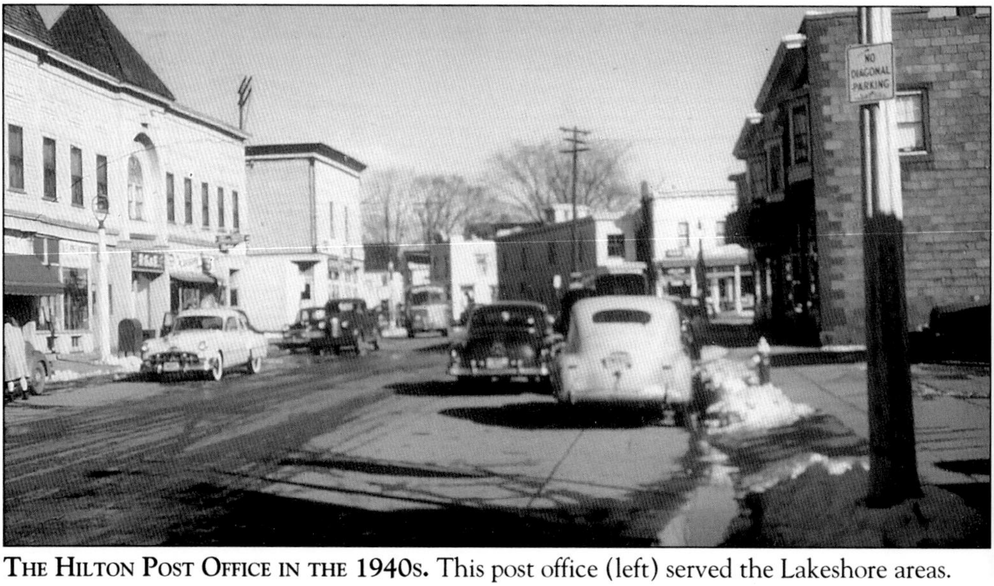

THE HILTON POST OFFICE IN THE 1940S. This post office (left) served the Lakeshore areas.

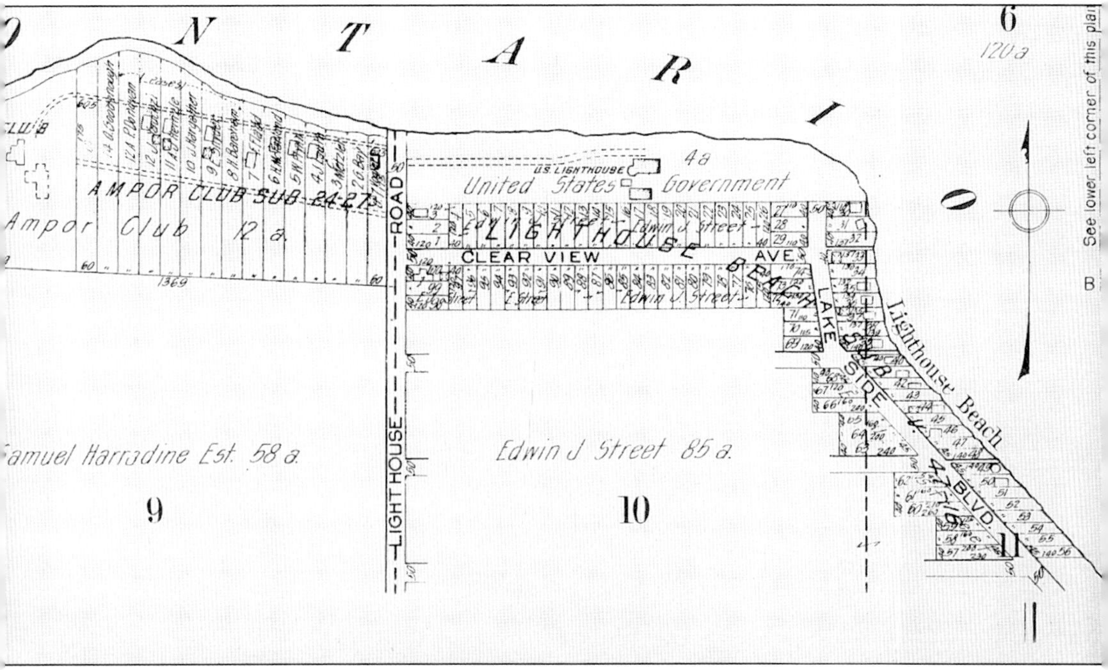

Deep Waters. Sometimes the deep waters were mystifying: the lake level rose 3 feet in 10 minutes on August 7, 1979, when a tornado passed over. Sometimes the waters harbored tragedies. Two girls died when their sailboat overturned near Hilton Beach in 1936. Later, a young father, Leon Doud, died in the same area while trying to save the life of an African-American youth visiting from New York City; the New York boy was drowning and clutched Doud's throat while panic stricken, accidentally strangling him. One springtime, a young Canadian boy's body washed ashore by Ward Cox's Wautoma cottage. A still unidentified serial killer left ravaged bodies near the quiet lake.

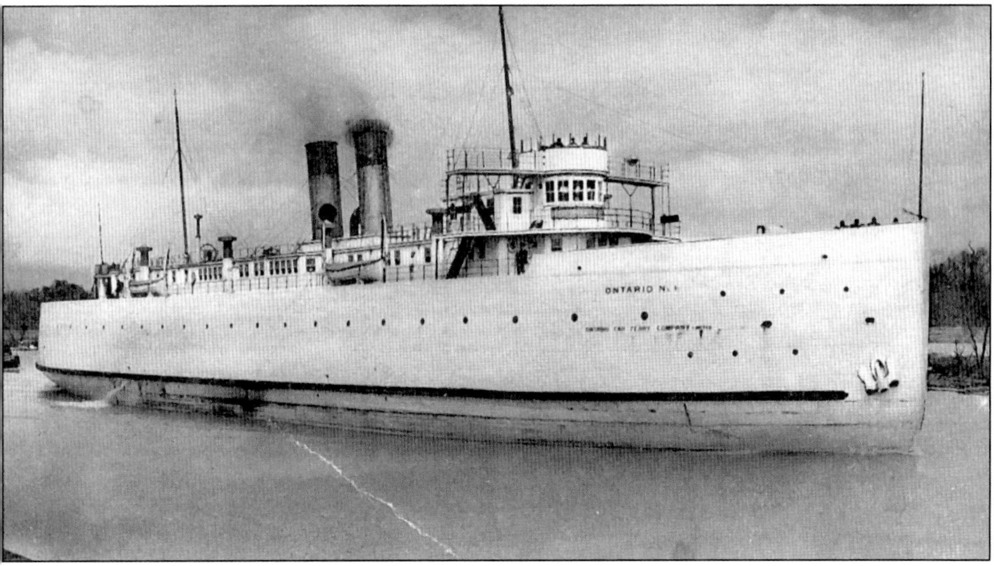

Postcard View of the Ontario Car Ferry.

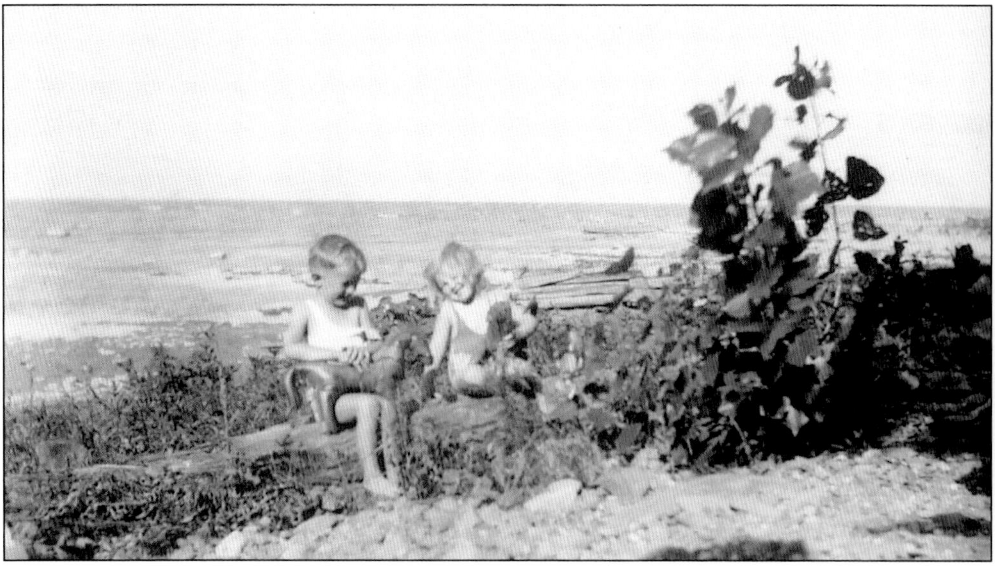

Children on the Beach. Playing at Wautoma Beach are Norman Wright and Shirley Cox, who knew well the joy of swimming in Ontario's azure waters. What fun it was to see shiners, small white alewives, wash in after they battled and lost their fight with the strong storm waves. Kids thought nothing of wading through the odoriferous mush of dead fish and seaweed left upon the beach after a storm. Rotting muck may have made an excellent mulch, but Ontario's storm-tossed waters left an icky green coating on your skin.

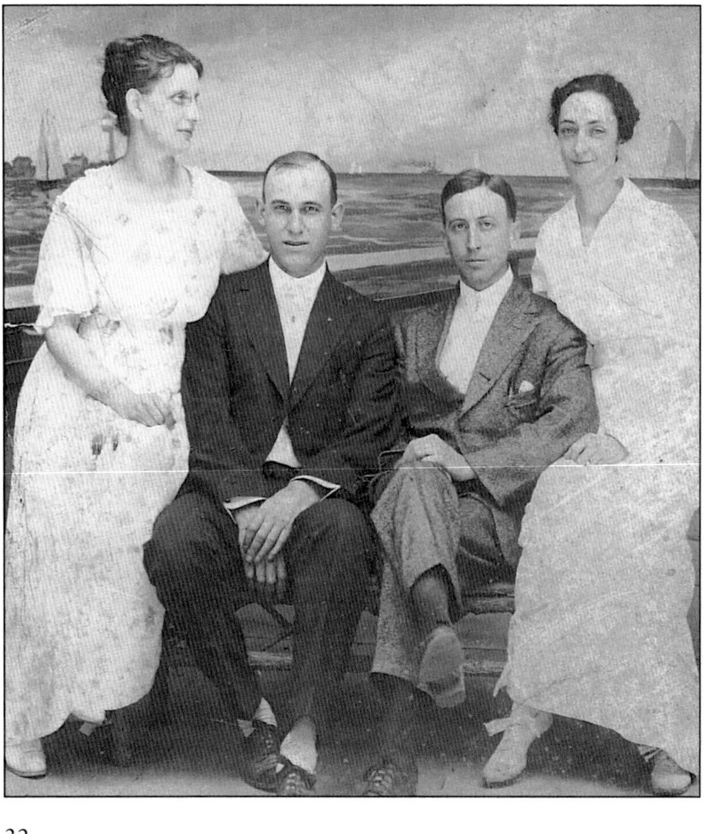

Leisure Hour. Dr. Charles G. Lenhart brought Norm Wright, Shirley Cox, and hundreds of other children into the world. Posing here on a boardwalk are Lenhart's first wife, Florella "Billie" Williamson, Lenhart, Dr. W.D. Wells, and Mrs. Wells. The Lenharts enjoyed leisure time at his cottage on DeLavergne Drive. A family legend relates that he was given a stretch of shoreline by a patient, decided to distribute lots to his Spencerport friends, pitched a tent on the beach, charged $25 a chair, and played cards to choose sites. The winners got to pick first.

LIGHTHOUSE. Bogus Point, home of the majestic 1895 Braddock Point lighthouse, was so called because counterfeiters reputedly hid fake (bogus) money in a nearby cave and then smuggled it away. Another kind of smuggling was a frequent night activity along the shore during Prohibition times, when flashlights beamed signals and nets filled with bottles were dropped overboard near the shore to be hauled up and resold by daring bootleggers.

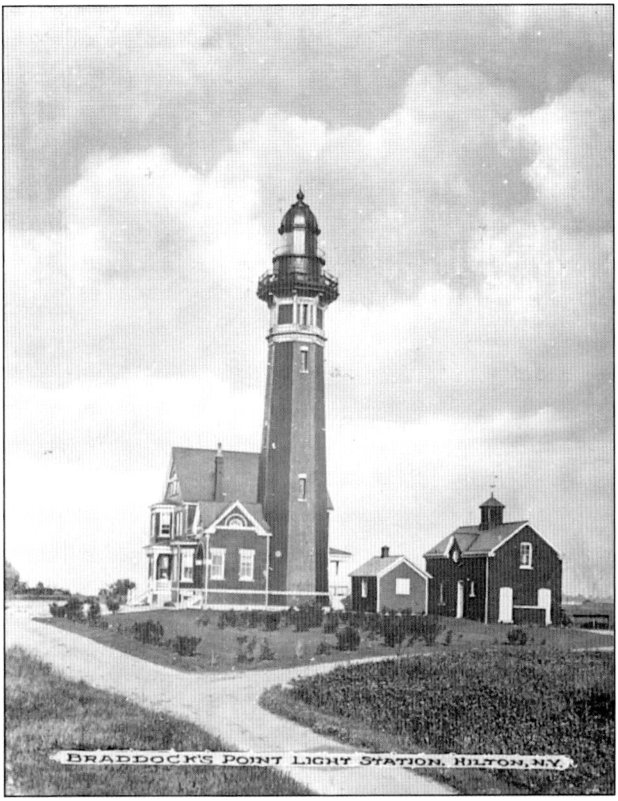

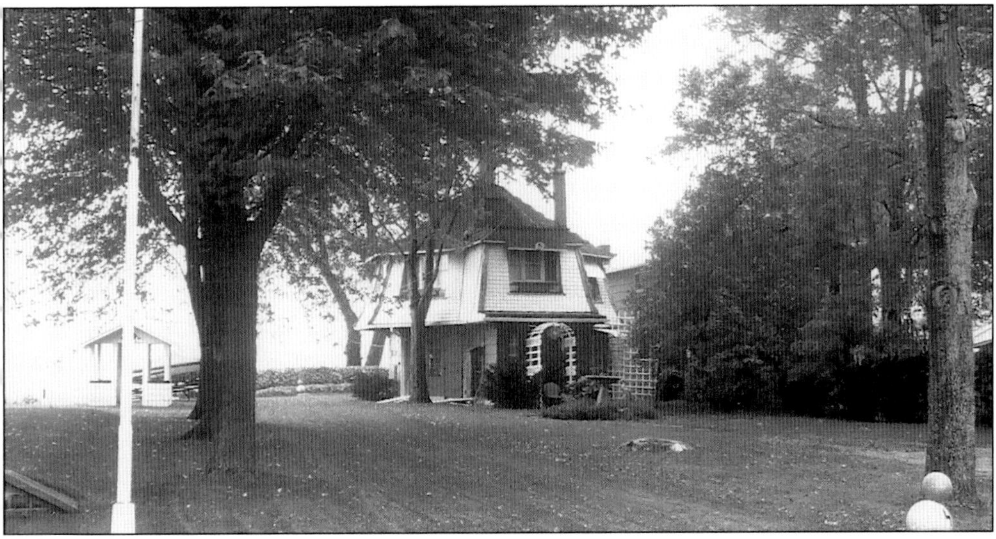

OCTAGON COTTAGE. Near the lighthouse, artist B. Aylesworth Haines designed and built the Forget-me-not, an eight-sided cottage. It was the only octagon resort home on the south side of Lake Ontario. Working on it from 1919 to 1937, Haines embellished inside walls with delicate landscape paintings, including many forget-me-not flowers, a reminder of an 18th-century military button with a forget-me-not decoration that washed ashore. Note the riprap barriers on the far left that were placed along the shoreline by the U.S. Army Corps of Engineers to check erosion.

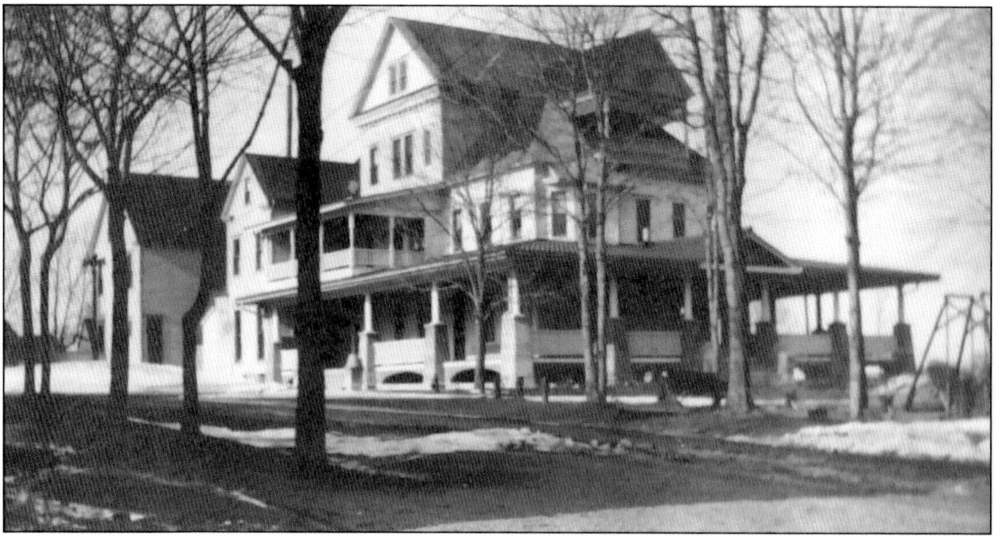

MANITOU BEACH HOTEL. At the end of Manitou Beach Road lay Hick's Point, renamed Manitou Beach by its developers, James Matthews and Silas Servis, in 1888, after a famous resort at Manitou Springs, Colorado. The 1889 Hotel Manitou, pictured here, was the most impressive building on the beach. William Reis's hand-carved carousel horses so delighted young riders that Reis built another carousel and moved his first one to Wautoma, where masses of goldenrod attracted bright orange Monarch butterflies, lake sunsets were unforgettable, and Joe Mergey's huge power boat and yacht club vessels attracted attention.

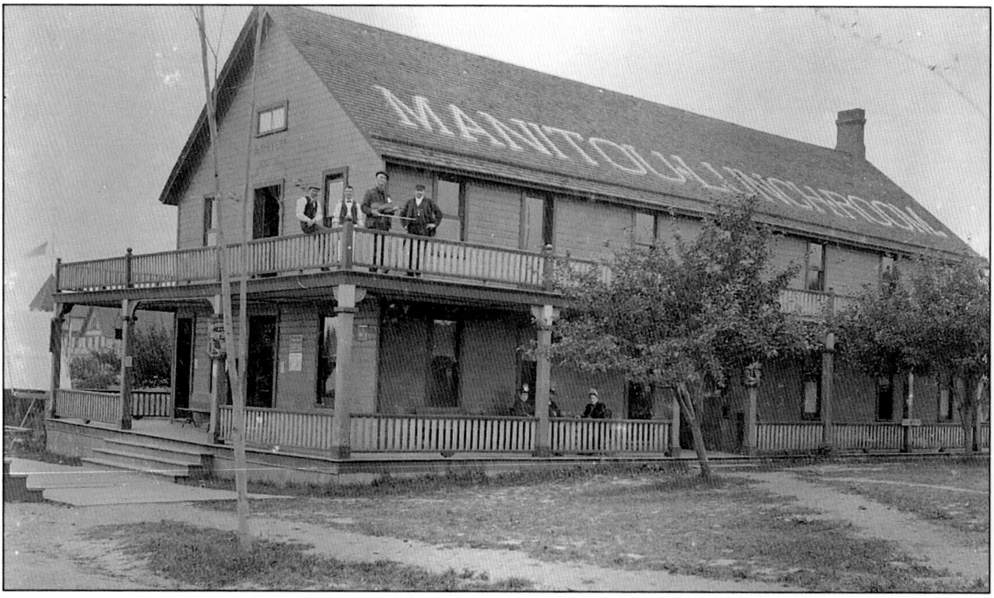

MANITOU LUNCHROOM. Faulding Skinner's hotel beside Braddock Bay was a fishermen's mecca at Manitou Beach, succeeded by the 1890 Elmheart Hotel and a bar and lunchroom, shown here, with an upstairs dance hall. Crowds came to Manitou by carriage, trolley, boat, bicycle, horseback, and on foot. They came to enjoy 75¢ fish and chicken dinners at Hotel Manitou, to ride the merry-go-round, to swim, to brave the water slide, to rent boats, to fish, to watch baseball games, to hear bands, to dance, to eat, to picnic, to drink, or just to enjoy watching people. Business declined after the Manitou Beach trolley line closed in 1924.

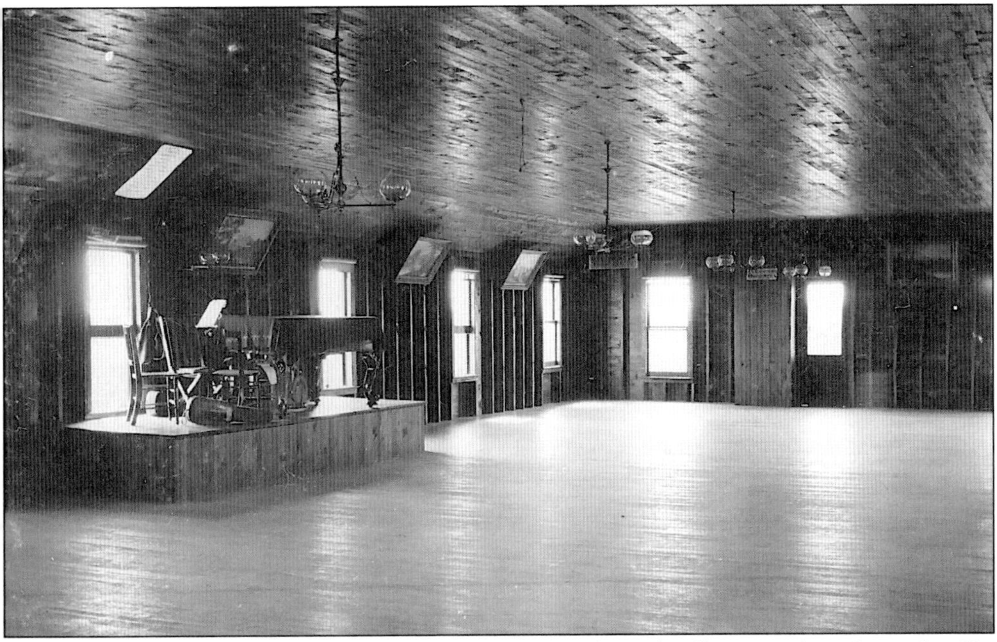

DANCE HALL. When a hot roast beef sandwich and a glass of milk cost only a dime, the 50¢ admission to the dance hall, pictured here, was more than many young people could afford. Some never saw the interior's second floor, where couples whirled to the music of Vincent Lopez and other name bands. They stood outside listening or danced under the open-air canopy, erected every August by the Colony Club for the enjoyment of its 200 or more members and the public.

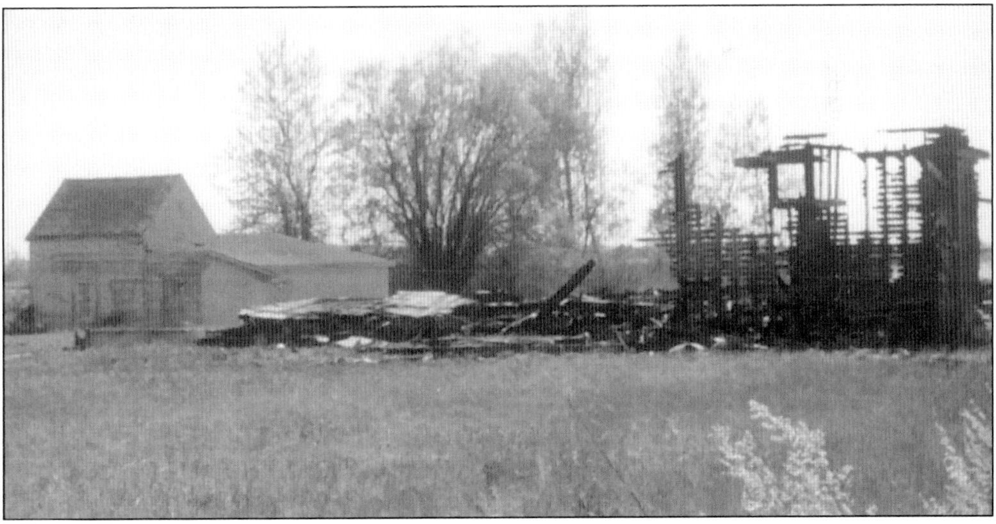

REMNANTS AFTER THE FIRE. Rooms at the Elmheart Hotel were no longer rented out after 1931, and the refreshment stand on the beach finally closed. Peppery old George Wiedman kept his bar and card tables open, charging a small fee for admission to the picnic area and telling customers, "I've seen the rise and fall of Manitou Beach!" The hotels burned and then the dance hall, too, its music stopped forever. Beside the charred ruins of the dance hall, only little outbuildings remained to evoke fond memories of the happy throngs that had once enjoyed the annual Farmers' Pioneer Picnics.

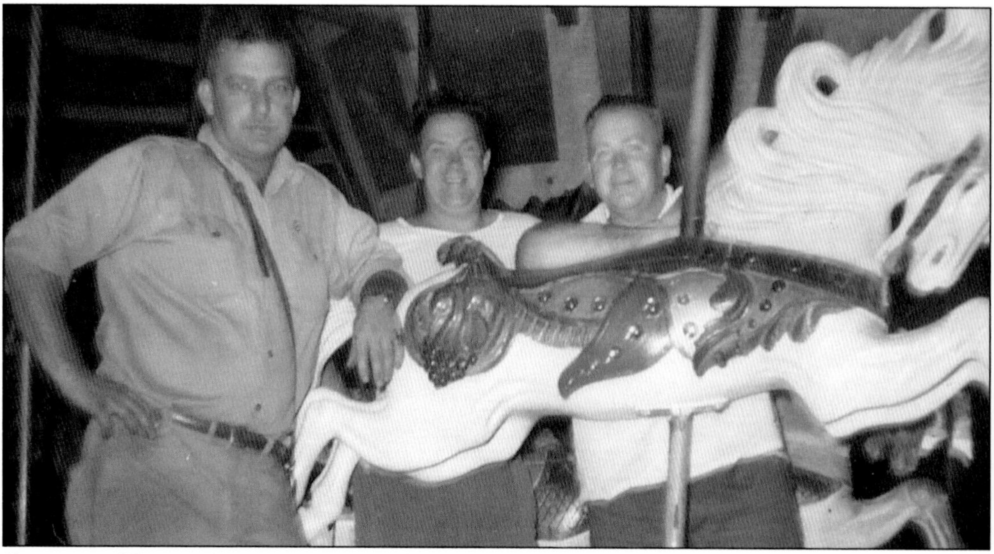

CAROUSEL HORSE. As Wautoma Beach flourished, Willam Reis added a picnic area and the Lago Vista dance hall, and the Gardner family opened a shooting gallery next to the merry-go-round, shown here. Prestigious professionals, such as radio broadcaster Al Sigl, enjoyed summer siestas at Wautoma cottages. Laura Reis ran a small grocery store on the beach and eventually married Alvah Miller (left), seen here with one of the carousel horses. Miller later took down the carousel and sold it off piecemeal to antique dealers. Its Wurlitzer military band organ went to Pennsylvania.

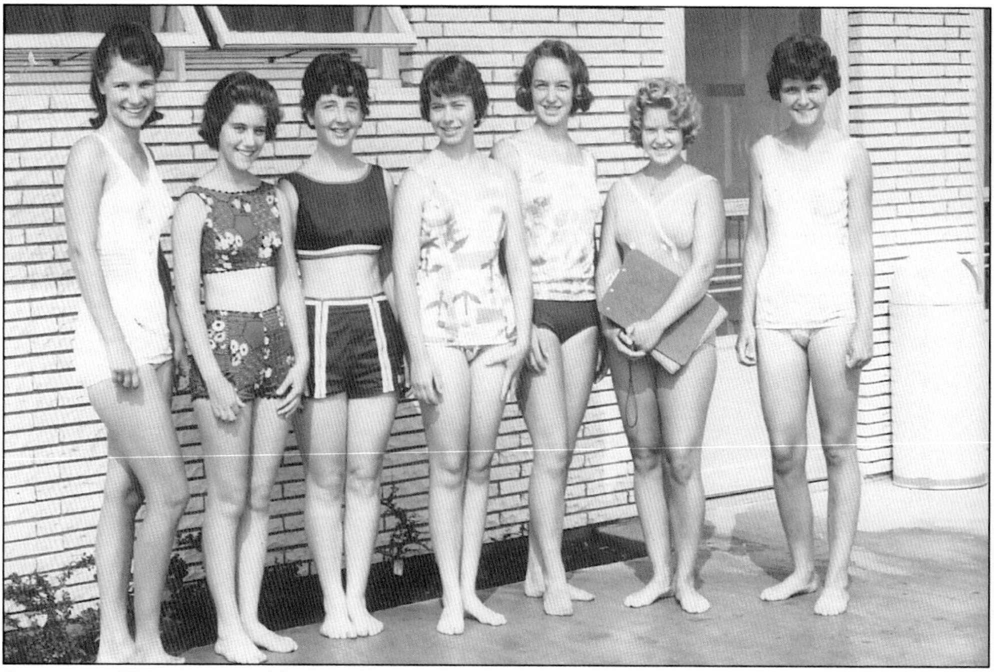

SWIMMING TEACHERS. Public swimming instructors and aides posing for this photograph are, from left to right, Judy Collamer, Nancy Greenfield, Joanne Vary, Ellen Holden, Marion Dieckman, Linda Metherell, and Pamela Ferron. Red Cross instructors still offer swimming courses through the Hilton-Parma Recreation program.

Four

GOVERNMENT SERVICES

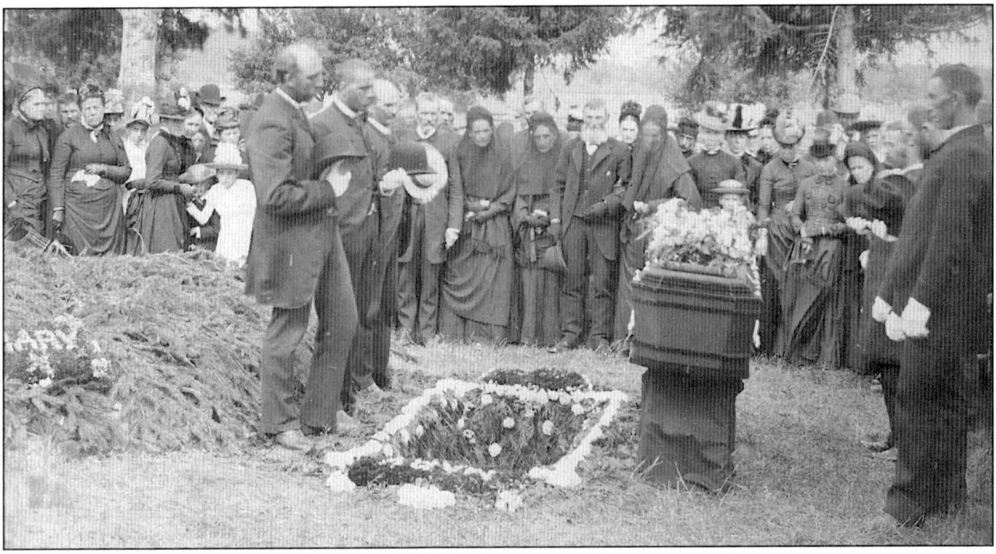

MARY'S FUNERAL. Who was the small girl named Mary being buried at Parma Union in this compelling picture? Near Bennett Road a "lost" farm cemetery, seen only by hunters, contains the graves of pioneer Levi VanWormer and family. A tree has grown around Levi's stone. Pvt. John VanWormer was killed in the Civil War. A Moul Road cemetery contains no visible stones; only one stone remains in Hilton's East Avenue cemetery. Health records reported two children were buried behind the house at 1222 Hilton-Parma Road; there is now no sign of burials. Supvr. Edson Taber chaired the Parma Union Cemetery Association (1918–1930), and other supervisors have served on its governing board. Parma Union, a cemetery created in 1853, became the largest public cemetery after small family cemeteries were outlawed by health laws and maintenance of small cemetery plots became a governmental responsibility. Originally $50 each, individual burial lots at Parma Union now sell for $350.

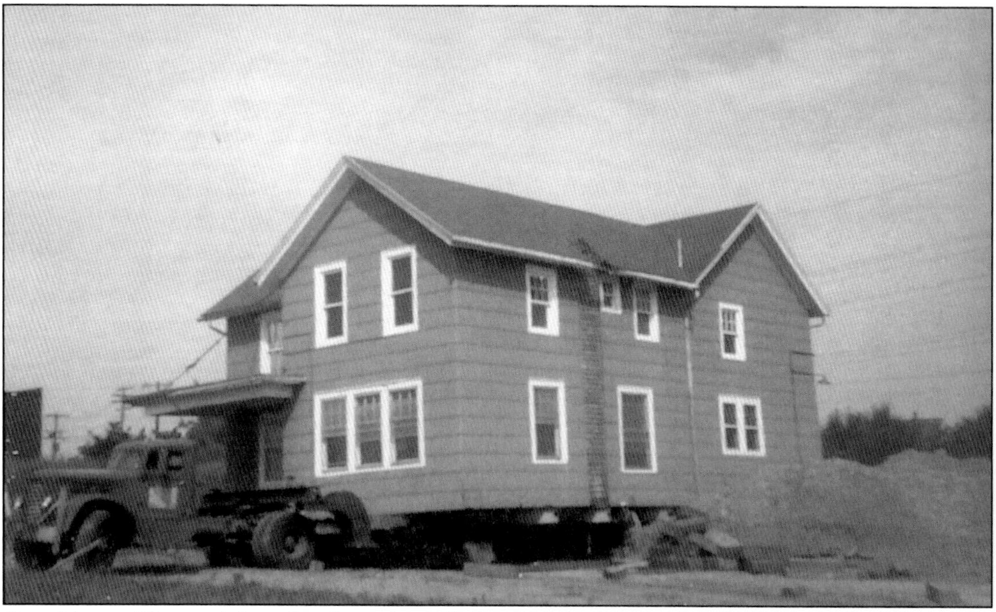

OLD TOWN HALL. After the fire of 1965 destroyed town and village offices, town offices were relocated in the former American Legion home, 287 East Avenue, until the new town hall was built. Edward "Bud" Hendershot Jr. then purchased the former legion home, once the Tyler-Luffman property, moved it down the hill, and opened it as rental apartments at 281 East Avenue. Clio Lodge, Free & Associated Masons, then erected their new lodge hall on the house site.

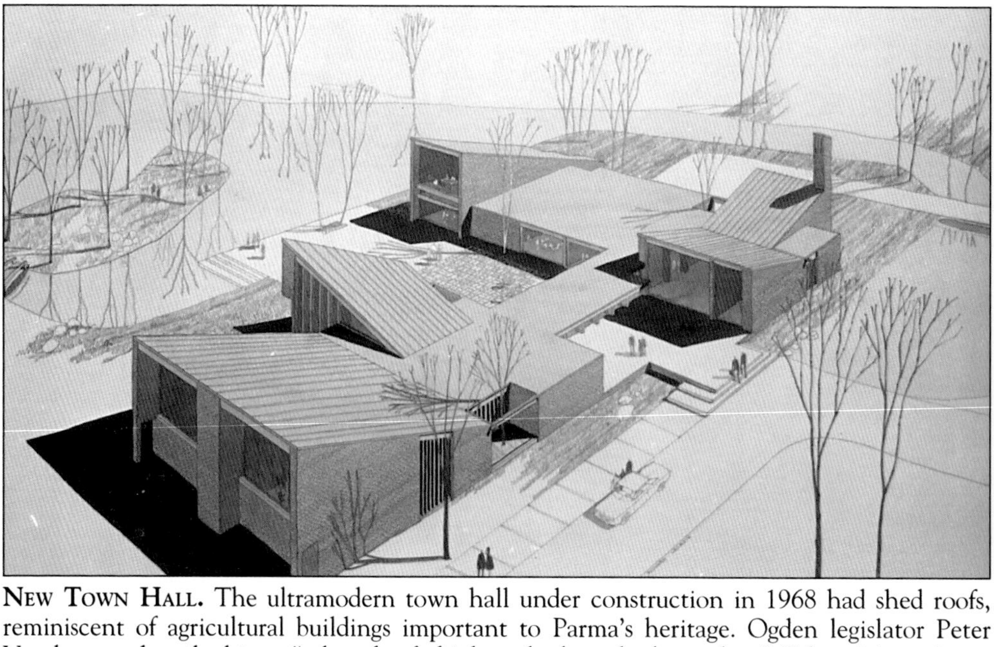

NEW TOWN HALL. The ultramodern town hall under construction in 1968 had shed roofs, reminiscent of agricultural buildings important to Parma's heritage. Ogden legislator Peter Vandertang described it as "a bunch of chicken sheds pushed together." Hilton Mayor Larry Gursslin, asked by a reporter to describe the new post office, replied, "It looks like a horse barn to me." Soon, a hitching post appeared on the lawn by the new post office; and every year at Easter, children hunt for and find chicken eggs on the town hall grounds.

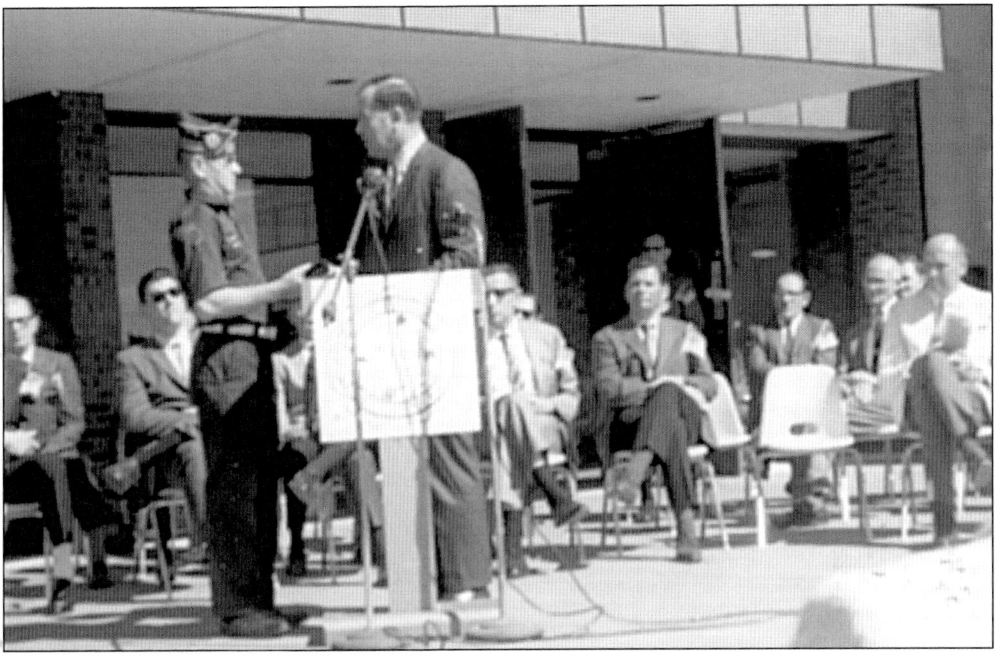

Hall Dedication. At the town hall dedication in 1970, Congressman Barber B. Conable Jr. (right) presents Legionnaire Art Harmer with an American flag. Seated at the far right is Supvr. John F. Jennejahn Jr., a Korean War veteran chosen in 1999 as one of Hilton's distinguished graduates. Dignitaries seated include town board member Victor Anderson; county legislator John Hoff; Hon. James E. Powers, state senator; and town board members Robert Ingham and Vernon Pickett.

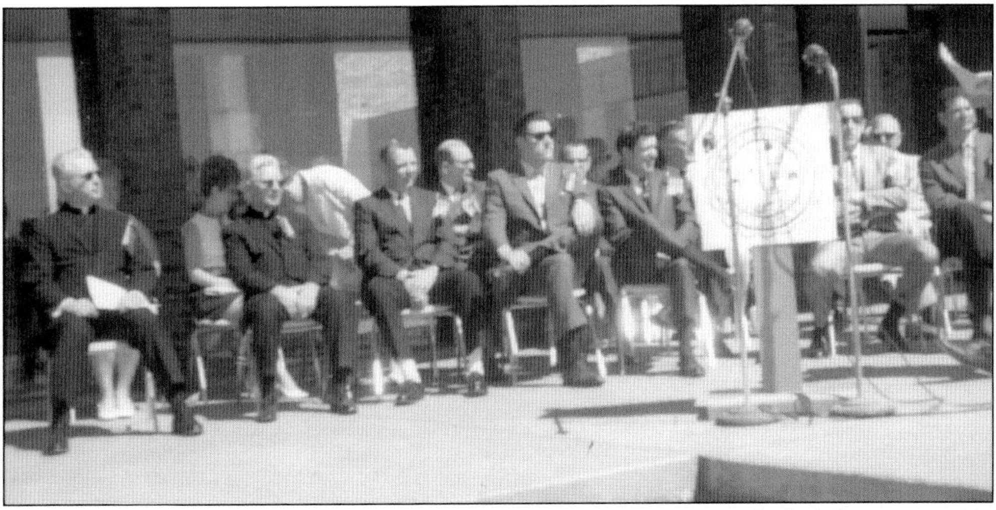

More Dignitaries. Among the dignitaries attending the 1970 town hall dedication are Fr. Chester M. Klocek; deputy town clerk Barbara DeHollander; Mayor Douglass Hurlbutt; town board member Victor Anderson; county legislator John Hoff; James Scott, of the assessor's office; and county legislator Edwin Foster. Foster, designated a distinguished Hilton Central graduate in 1999, began the planning and funding for the new town hall before going on to become president of the Monroe County Legislature. Five Foster brothers served in World War II.

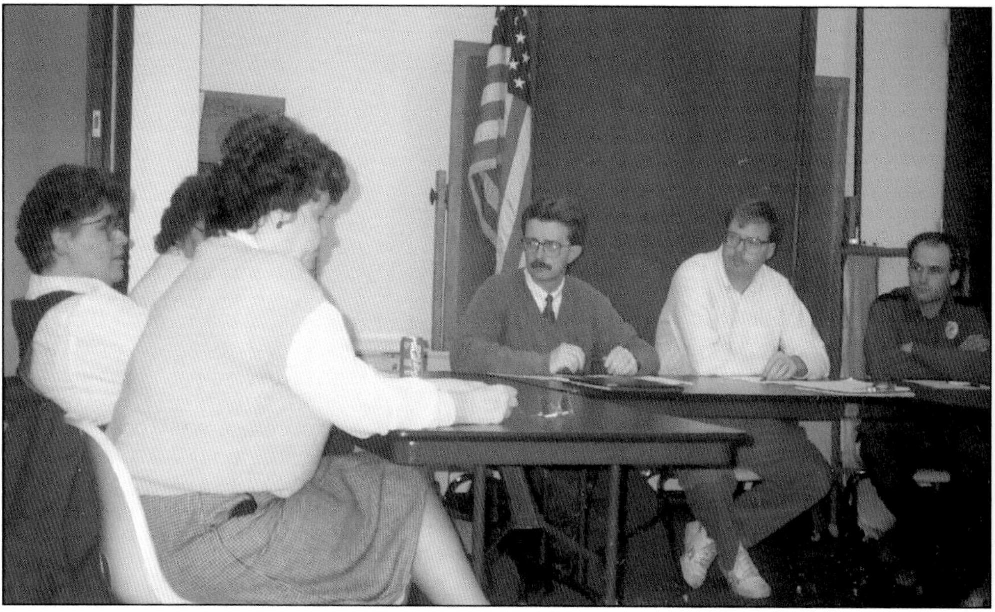

Staff Meeting. Discussing public needs and services at Parma Town Hall in 1992 are, from left to right, town clerk Elsie Webster; librarian Sue Henderson; Supvr. Rick Lemcke; recreation director Steve Fowler; and dog warden Patrick Kenny. Lemcke is an officer of R.M. Landscape Inc., which he and Mike Lemcke began in 1973, after taking over the Braemar nurseries of the 1950s.

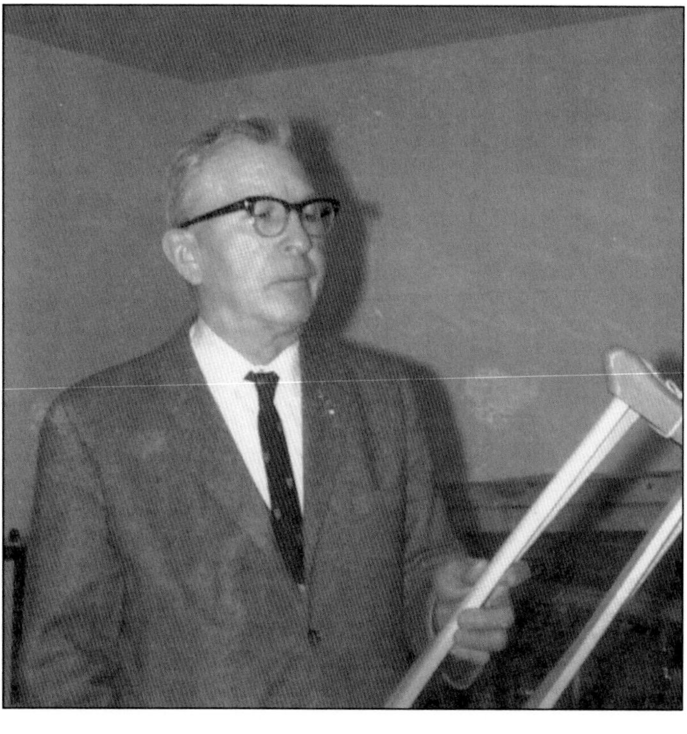

Equipment Available. Town clerk William B.D. Watters supervised the operation of the Lions Club Loan Closet at the town hall, dispensing medical equipment without charge when needed by convalescents. Known for his concern for others, Watters requested that the new town hall be accessible to the disabled. The 1990 Americans with Disabilities Act, an important legacy of President George Bush's administration, requires public accommodations for physically challenged Americans, and has vastly improved facilities for persons with disabilities.

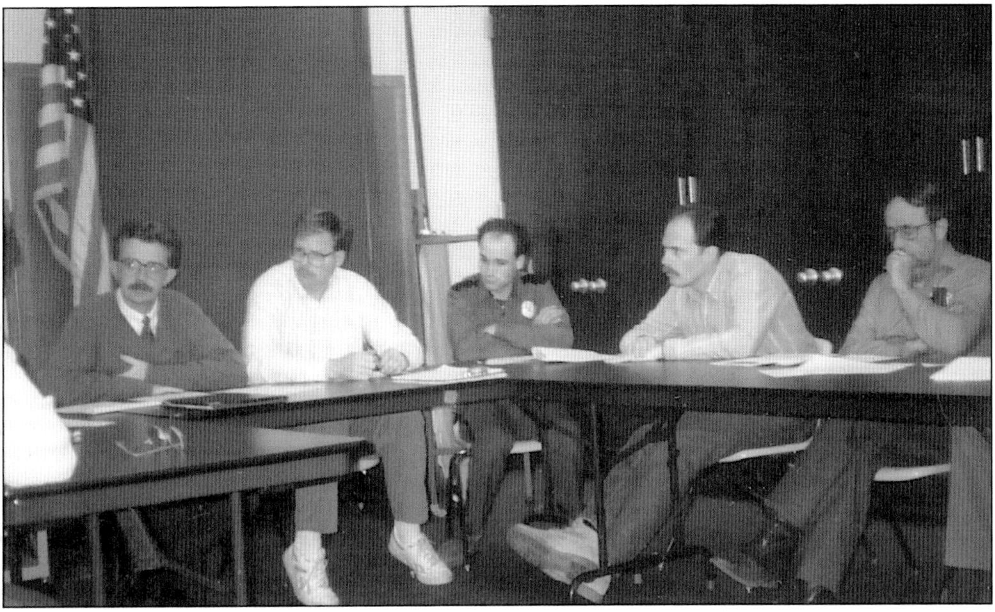

Staff Meeting Continues. Pictured in this view of the 1992 staff meeting at Parma Town Hall are, from left to right, Supvr. Rick Lemcke; recreation director Steve Fowler; dog warden Patrick Kenny; assistant building inspector and emergency management coordinator Jack Barton; and commissioner of buildings and grounds Joseph Reinschmidt. The Kenny family have operated Willowcreek Farms, 5377 Ridge Road, since 1978. The farm specializes in brown eggs, beef, fresh vegetables, and auction services.

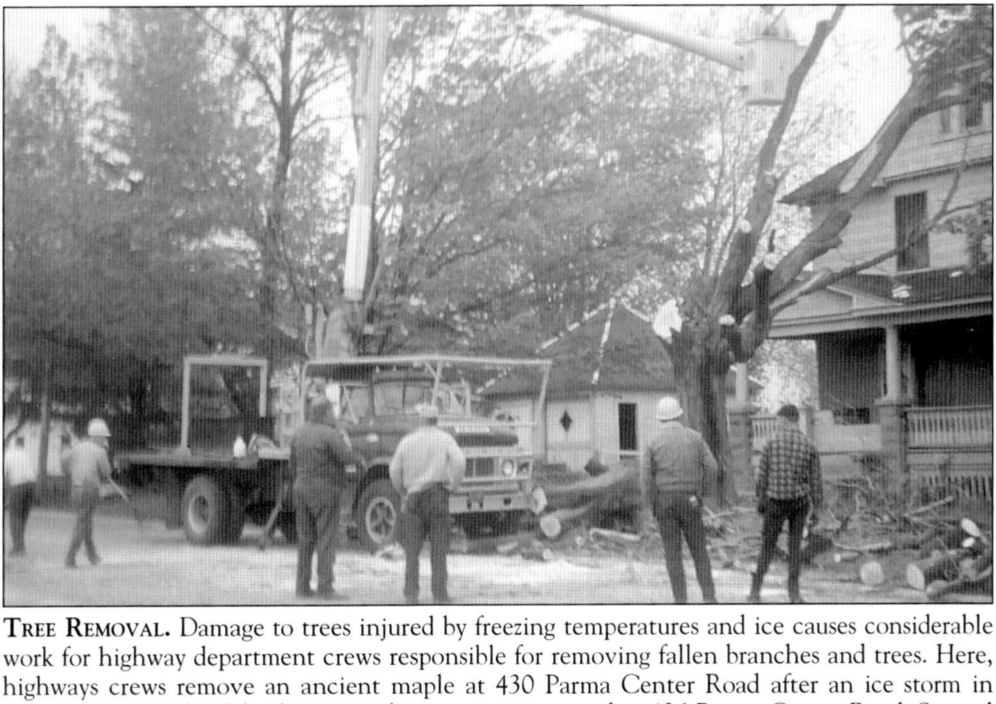

Tree Removal. Damage to trees injured by freezing temperatures and ice causes considerable work for highway department crews responsible for removing fallen branches and trees. Here, highways crews remove an ancient maple at 430 Parma Center Road after an ice storm in 1981, utilizing federal funding. Another tree was removed at 436 Parma Center Road. Several hundred others were badly damaged by the storm.

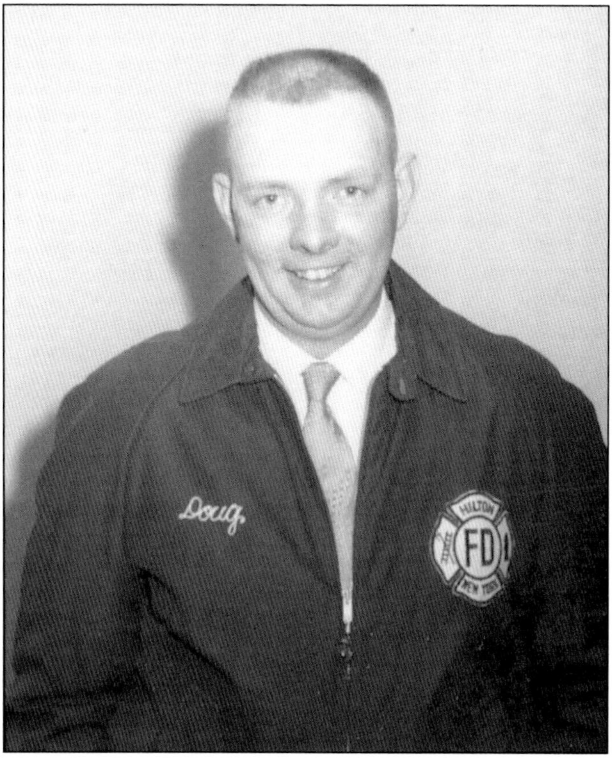

Mayor Hurlbutt. Douglas Hurlbutt, a descendant of the Wright family, served as village mayor when the village offices were at 24 Main Street. Hilton's former high school on Henry Street was later converted into offices, a senior center, and a community meeting place. Hurlbutt is the last to operate a local home delivery service, the Hilton Dairy. Another Wright descendant, Kathleen Tenny, recently endowed a shelter for homeless animals. Albert Hazen Wright became a noted Cornell University professor and author.

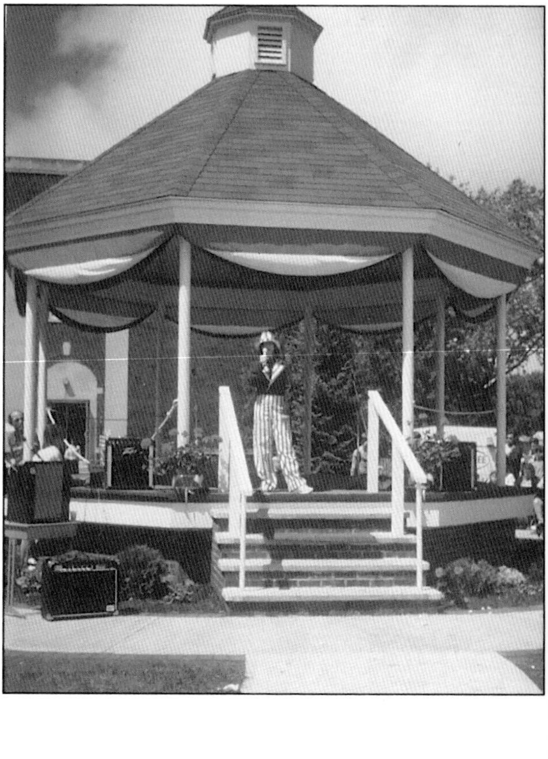

Gazebo. Richard "Big Foot" LaForce wore Uncle Sam duds for this photograph at the Centennial Gazebo near the village offices. The brick base of the gazebo was the work of Rosario "Ross" Albano, who also worked on the brick sign and flowerpot at the high school, a shrine at St. Leo's, a sign at Northwood School, the veterans' monument, the new town hall, and the Hilton Fire Department headquarters. Summer crowds enjoy band concerts at the gazebo, and winter spectators enjoy its twinkling lights and caroling programs during the holiday season.

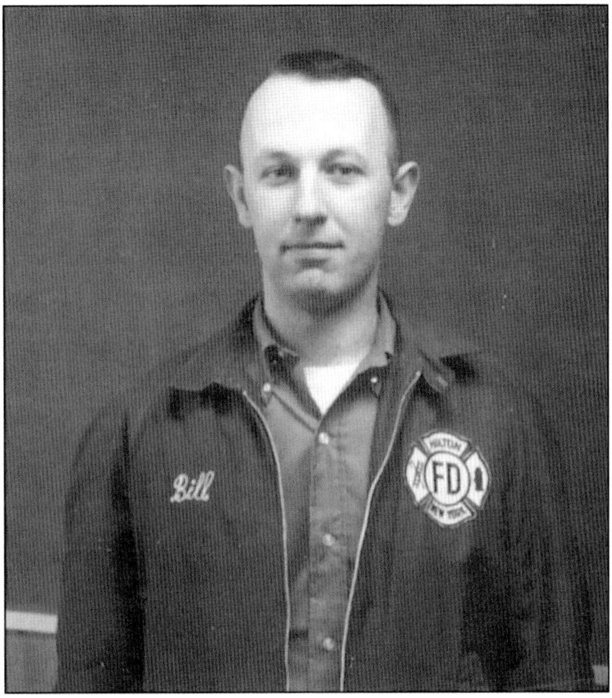

Mayor Carter. William Carter, named for his grandfather, is following in the footsteps of his father, Mayor Henry "Hank" Carter (1952–1967). In his first year of office, William Carter quickly won recognition for his progressive outlook.

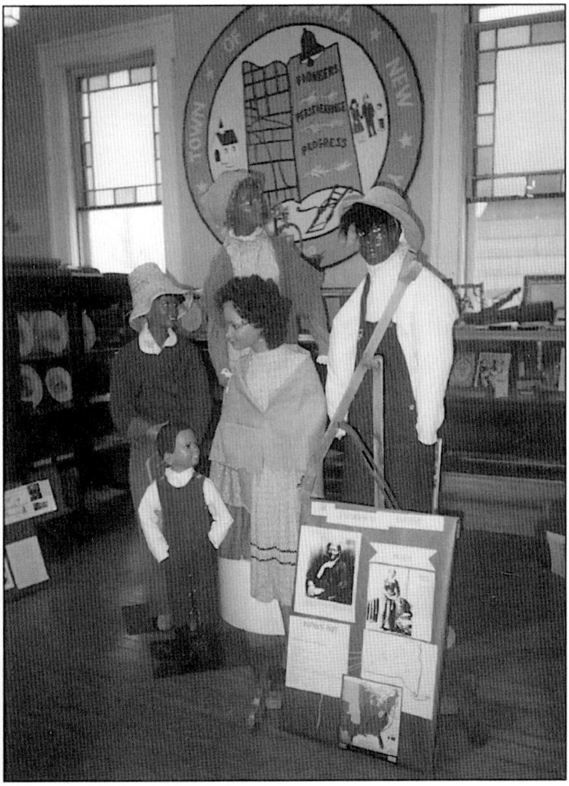

Escaping Slaves. Mayor Frank Pickett, instrumental in the installation of sewers for the village, was a descendant of the Gideon Archer family, whose home atop Hilton Hill sheltered homeless slaves. Parma's several Underground Railroad stations and local efforts for African-American emancipation are remembered in a display at Parma Museum. Some of Parma's 250 men in military service sacrificed their lives in order to save the Union of free states, and several were never heard from again.

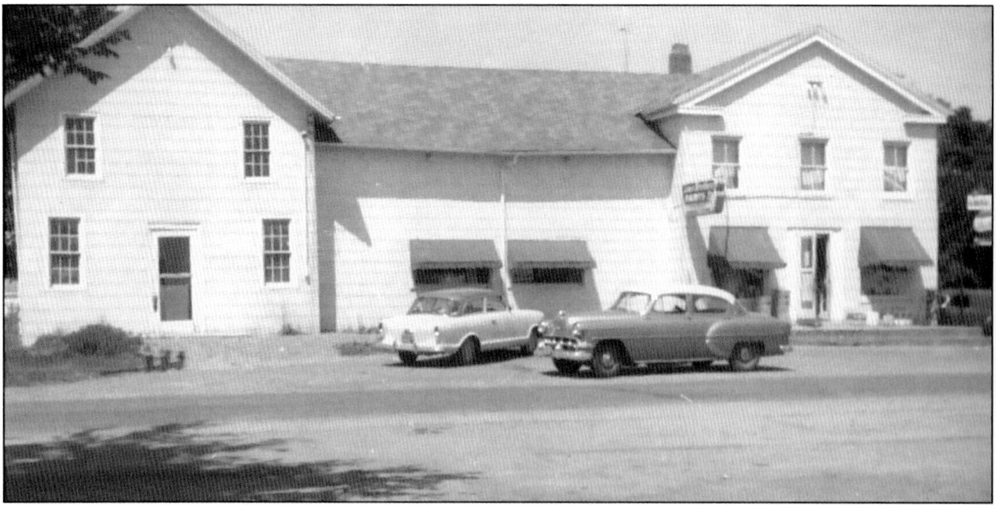

General Store. Supvr. Isaac Chase Jr. and his storekeeper brother-in-law, town clerk Chauncey Knox, were documented participants in the Underground Railroad movement—an eyewitness once saw slaves hiding in the basement of Knox's general store at Parma Center. Rumors persist that a tunnel led from the store to the nearby coffin shop of local undertaker William Burritt, and then on to Burritt's home, where coffins were stored in a rear addition. Town board meetings were held in the store until Knox loaned money to finance the erection of a Presbyterian church just west of the store in 1831; it became the town hall in 1847.

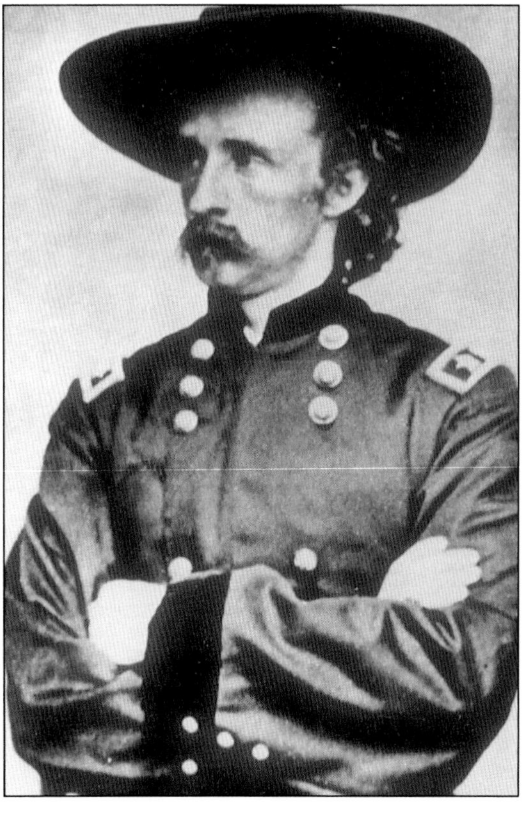

George Armstrong Custer. Many local Civil War soldiers served in the 8th New York Volunteers, a cavalry unit, under Gen. George Armstrong Custer. Darren Custer, a personable relative of the general, now operates Darren's Automotive; his mother, Ferne Custer, once ran a popular Main Street restaurant. Parma's highest ranking Civil War officer was Maj. Joshua Palmer, buried at Parma Corners, one of only six officers with a monument marking the place where he fell on the Gettysburg battlefield, near Culp's Hill.

SOLDIER MCCARTY. Harry McCarty's cameras are now part of the photographic collection at the Parma Meetinghouse Museum. Eastman Kodak Company, where many local residents have been employed, produced a folding camera during World War I that could be carried in a soldier's pocket. McCarty and his brother Fred both served in the army during World War I, and his son, Harry McCarty Jr., served in the army at a later date. After World War I, veterans John Crook and Herman Worden became Parma supervisors and John Harlan Cooper managed the local Rochester Gas & Electric Company office.

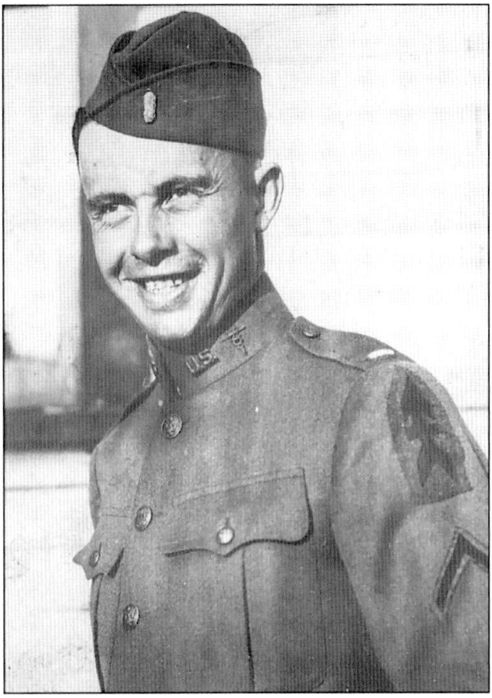

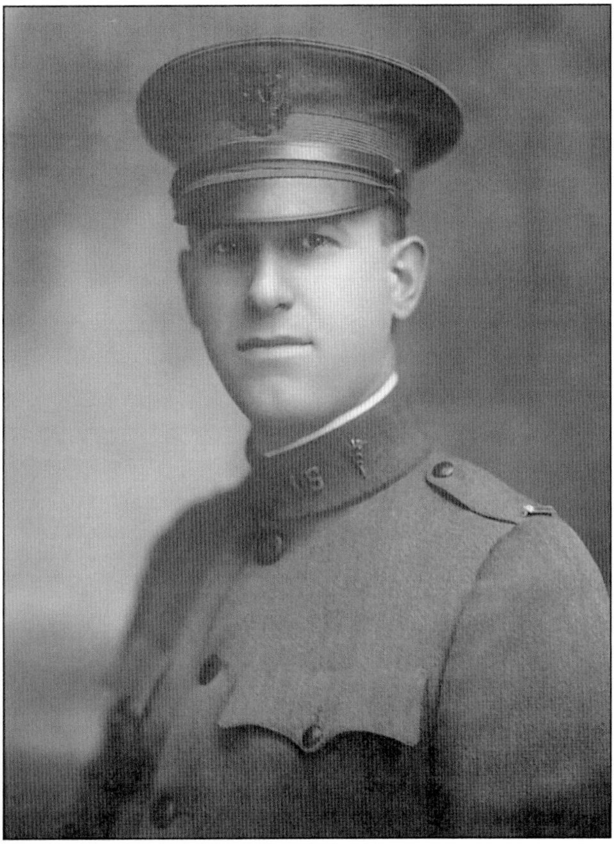

SOLDIER LENHART. Dr. Charles Lenhart, later a summer resident in Parma, provided medical services to the army during World War I, as did Dr. Fred McCarty. Lenhart later invented and patented special hospital equipment and developed a new method for clotting blood that saved many lives, bringing him worldwide praise. He was a Fellow in the American College of Surgeons, a member of the International College of Surgeons, and chief of surgery at Park Avenue Hospital.

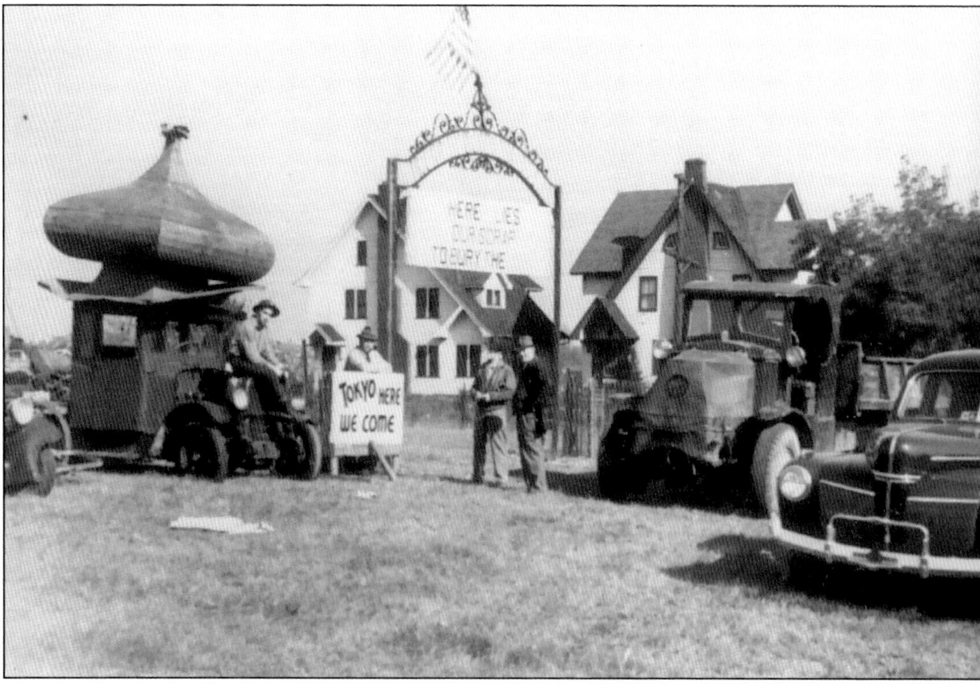

ANYTHING GOES. Citizens everywhere collected scrap metal to aid the war effort during World War II. In Irondequoit, a cemetery fence and a church's onion tower adorned the highway department's 1942 scrap pile. Donors hoped that, melted down into reusable metal, the scrap would be recycled into bullets and bombs to fight Japanese and German enemies.

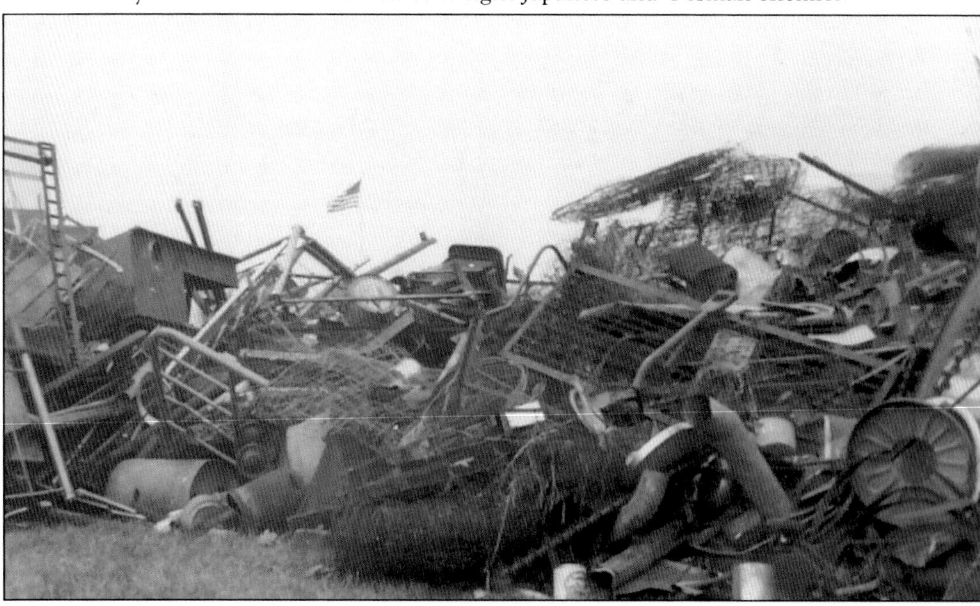

SCRAP METAL DRIVE. On the home front, metal cans were saved, washed, and flattened; razor blades, cigarette foil, and even silk stockings were collected for recycling. As scrap metal piles accumulated at several sites, town board member Charles Tubb Sr., a World War I veteran, used his milk trucks to haul loads of salvage. Cigarettes, chocolate, mayonnaise, sugar, egg, fats, and nylon stockings were scarce, but victory gardens helped to feed the folks at home.

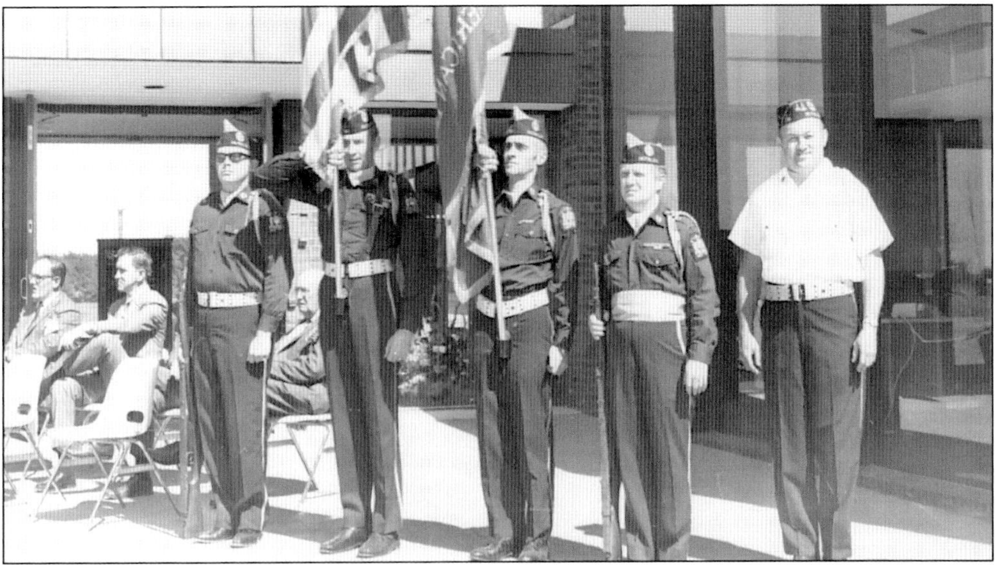

Honor Guards. At the 1970 dedication of the new town hall, local veterans were represented by honor guards at the town hall's flagpole. Parma's three veterans' organizations are Ferris-Goodridge Post 330, Trimmer Road; Hiscock-Fishbaugh Post 788, Hilton; and the Veterans of Foreign Wars 6105, Peck Road. Town clerk Arthur Kirchgessner, a World War I veteran, began flying a flag at town hall in response to a lady's 1969 request.

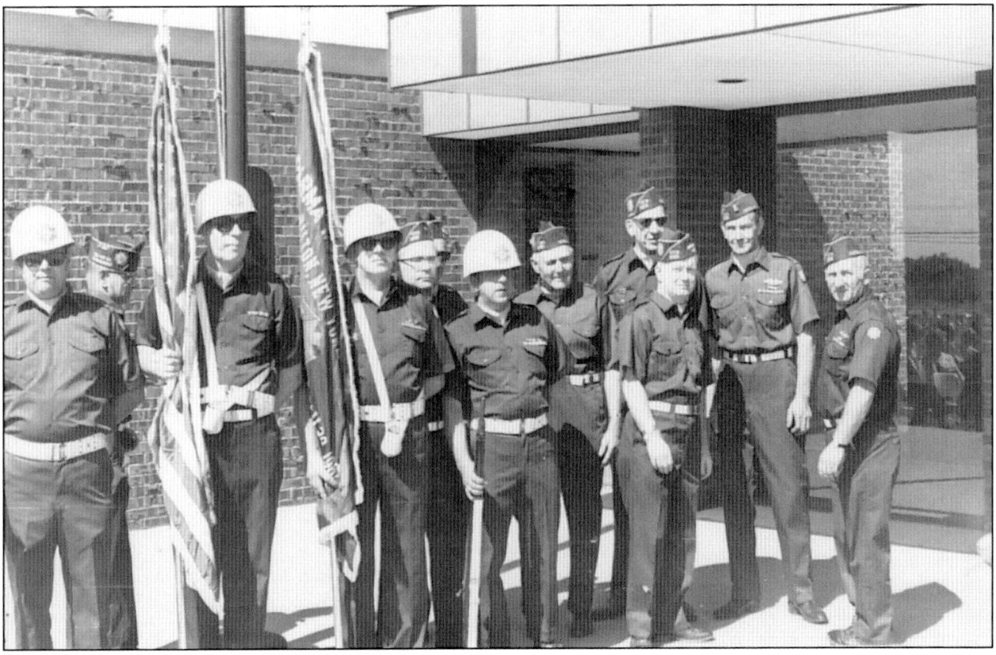

Veterans. Alvin Neal earned the Distinguished Flying Cross and Robert Graupman, the Silver Star. In front of the town hall a smaller flagpole and a monument honoring all veterans was solemnly dedicated on Memorial Day in 1975. The granite monument was the gift of Hilton-Parma Memorial Post, Veterans of Foreign Wars, and Hiscock-Fishbaugh Post, American Legion. Town engineer William C. Larsen designed the memorial base, using clinker firebricks that matched those of the town hall's walls.

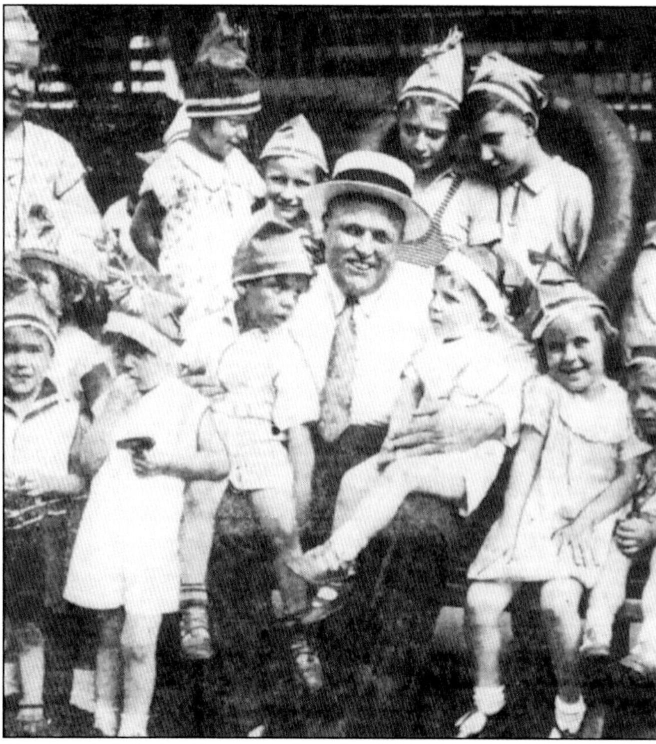

SHERIFF SKINNER SURROUNDED. One of Hilton High School's most renown graduates was Albert W. Skinner, a beloved law enforcement officer. When he was running for sheriff on the Republican ticket in 1937, he took time out from campaigning to continue a practice begun in 1924, supervising the annual picnic for children at St. Joseph's orphanage. Surrounded by children, the popular bachelor turned on his famous smile, as well-known as that of a later friend of his, Gen. Dwight D. Eisenhower.

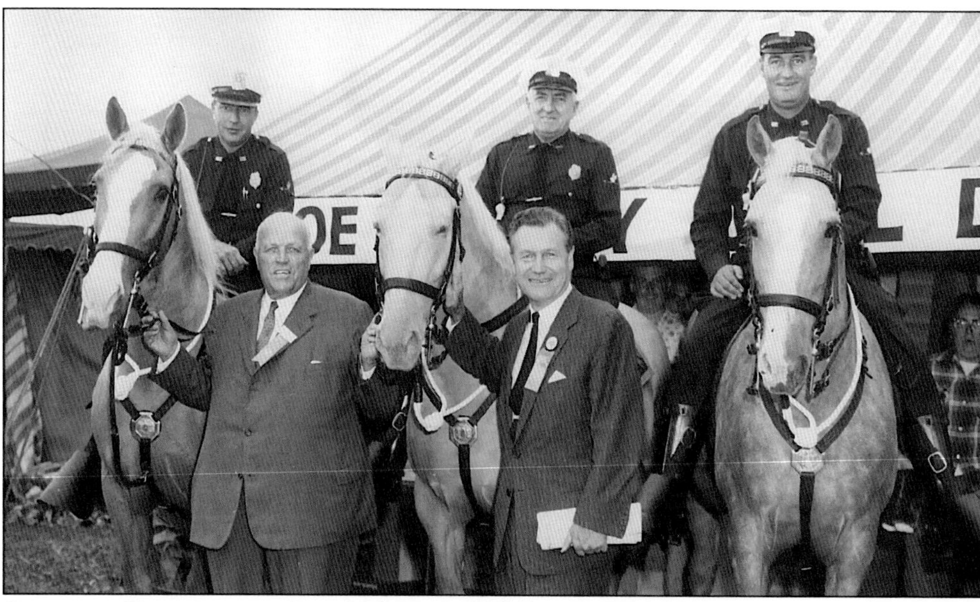

GOVERNOR ROCKEFELLER. Gov. Nelson Rockefeller (front right) admires the palominos of Sheriff Albert Skinner (front left) at the Monroe County Fair. On horseback, from left to right, are Deps. John Howlett, Packy McFarlen, and H. Barton When funds for a mounted patrol and a rescue boat were unavailable, Skinner personally bought two horses and a 16-foot rowboat and trailer. His first two handsome steeds were purchased from the circus troupe of Troop D, New York State Police. Skinner's horses were enthusiastically greeted at parades and other public events.

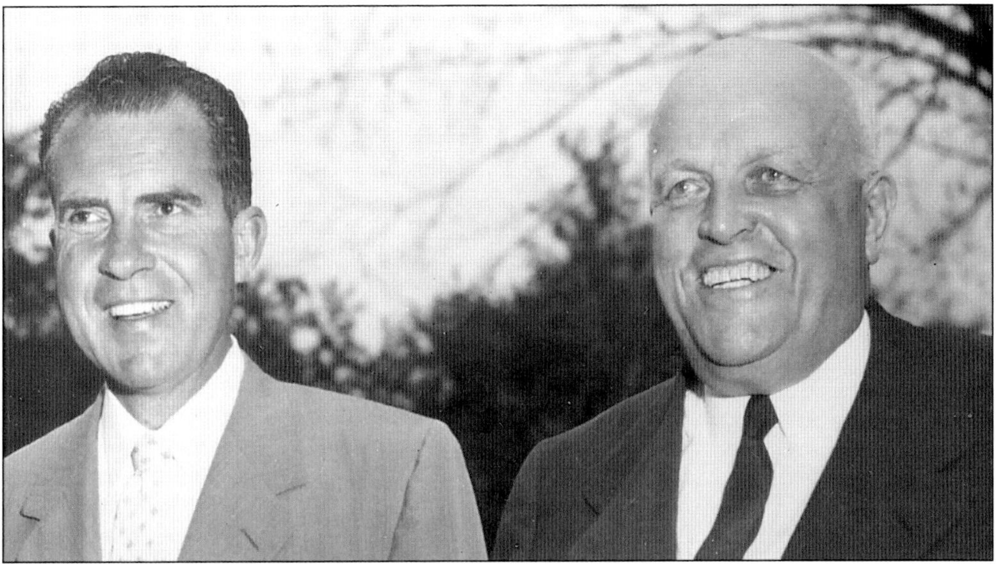

President Nixon. Pres. Richard M. Nixon (left) visited here in 1971 during the Monroe County sesquicentennial. Prominent Republican Sheriff Albert Skinner (right) was among those greeting Nixon. Nixon called Skinner "the big man." When Skinner entered a room, the audience always rose to its feet in tribute to him, perpetually enjoying his conventional speech: "I'm going to stand up so you can see me, smile so you will like me, and sit down so you will vote for me!" A U.S. marshal in the Prohibition era, Skinner became a living legend with 38 years in office.

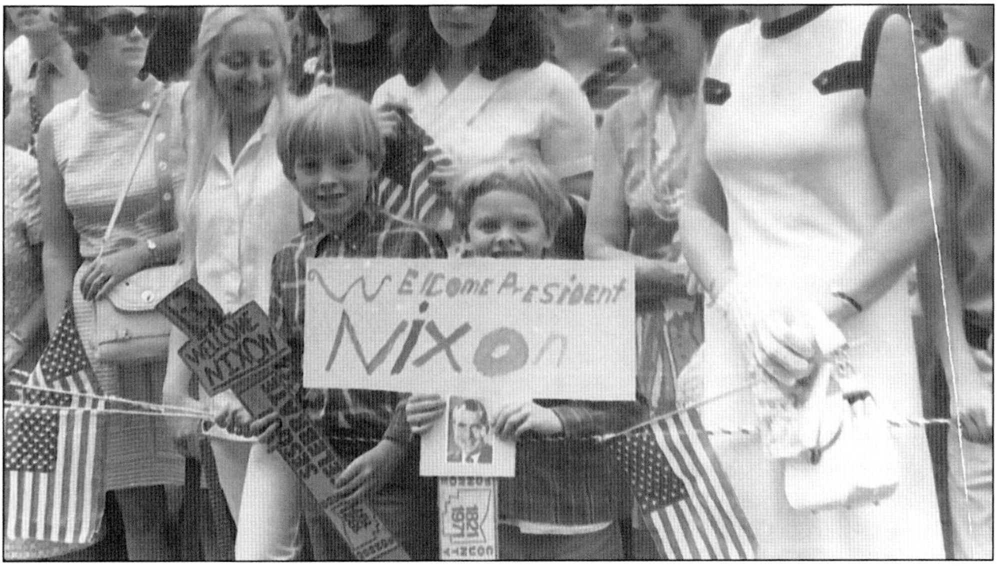

Welcome Sign. Donald and Christopher Husted were among the throng awaiting President Nixon's motorcade in 1971. Nixon's leadership successes included friendly overtures to China and Russia; the passage of Title IX, enabling women to participate in sports events; and, although not a victory, an end to the Vietnam War. He brought home the troops that Pres. John F. Kennedy and Lyndon B. Johnson had sent to prevent the spread of Communism. Nixon's unprecedented resignation from office came in 1974. In 1983, Donald graduated from the nation's military academy at West Point.

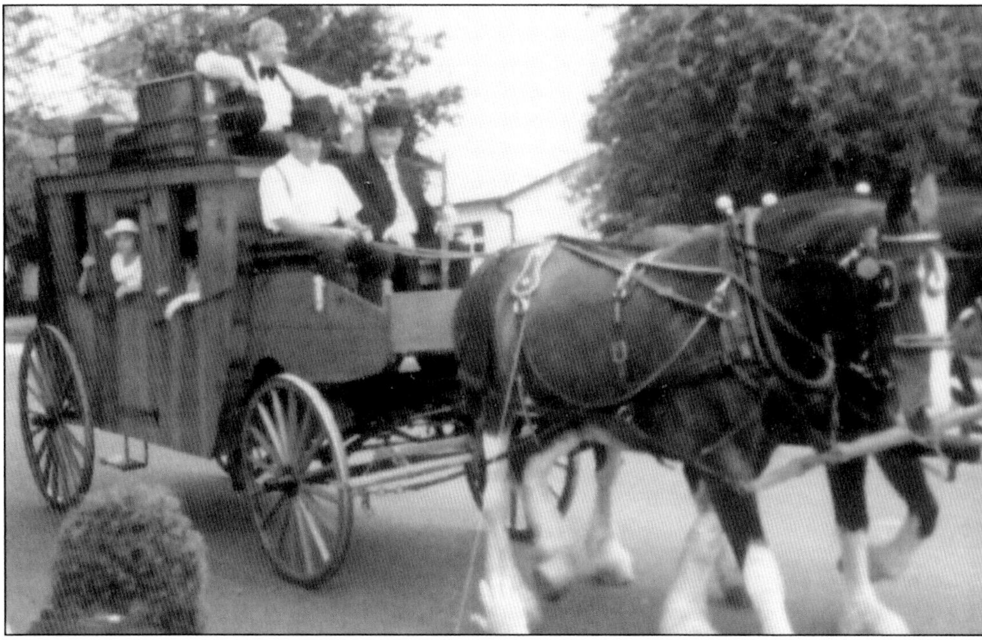

STAGECOACH. Supvr. Thomas Younker and other town officials merrily waved from Kruger's stagecoach during Hilton's centennial parade in 1985. Norman Kruger's coach replica is always a popular sight, as are his majestic Clydesdale horses. Mayor Larry Gursslin and his wife and family walked near the head of the parade in Victorian costumes. Carol Cox Gursslin was the first director of the Hilton Applefest.

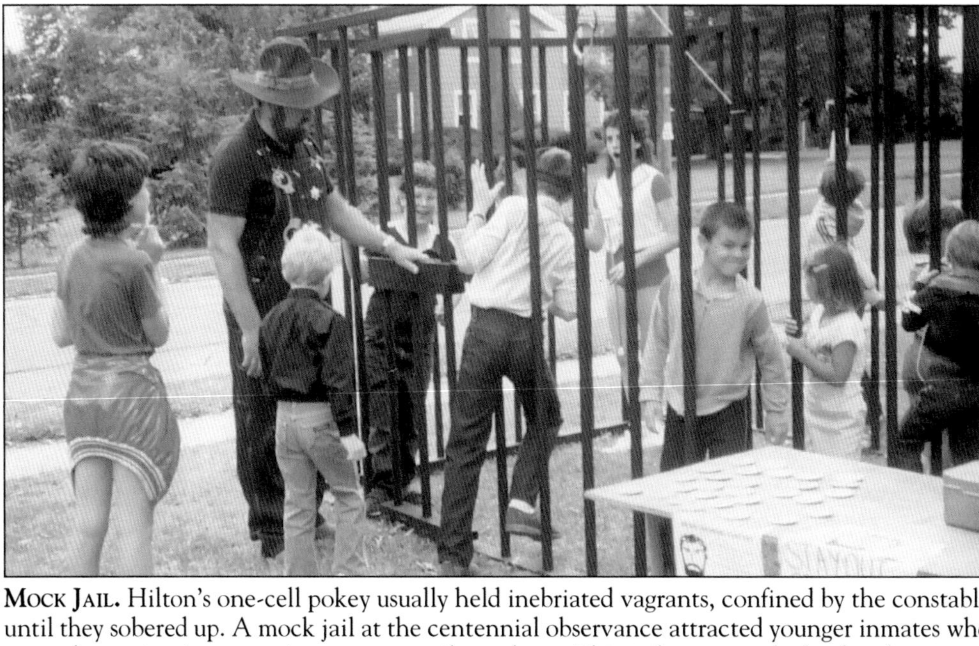

MOCK JAIL. Hilton's one-cell pokey usually held inebriated vagrants, confined by the constable until they sobered up. A mock jail at the centennial observance attracted younger inmates who seemed to enjoy incarceration—temporarily, at least. This jail was strictly for fun, but it was also a reminder that ensuring law and order is an important government service. Speeding, bad checks, dangerous pets, or other petty crimes will guarantee you a date with a Parma judge.

Five

TRANSPORTATION AND COMMUNICATION

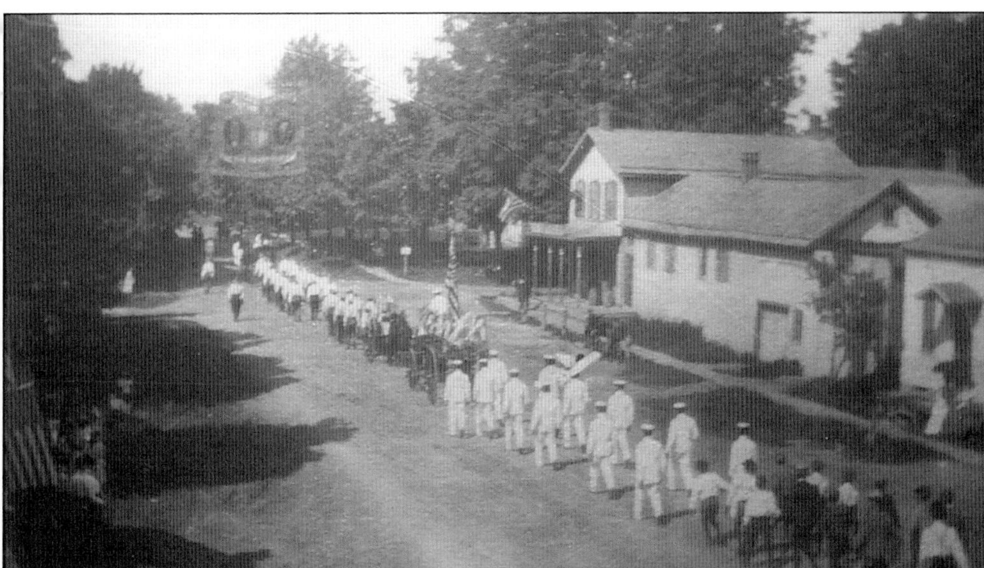

MAIN STREET PARADE. An early parade heads east on Main Street, passing the Merritt Block's drugstore and upstairs print shop and houses long gone, while shadows at the left reveal the outlines of business places on the north side of the street. As the fire department's three companies pass beneath a political banner, board sidewalks are empty and only a few parade watchers lean against hitching rails. The Merritt Block burned in 1903. By then, the coming of a railroad had spurred the growth of the little village and provided fruit growers with an opportunity to ship out their produce. The Industrial Revolution changed the employment picture, too, offering job opportunities for men and women that had not existed in the 19th century, when most businesses were family operations employing only relatives.

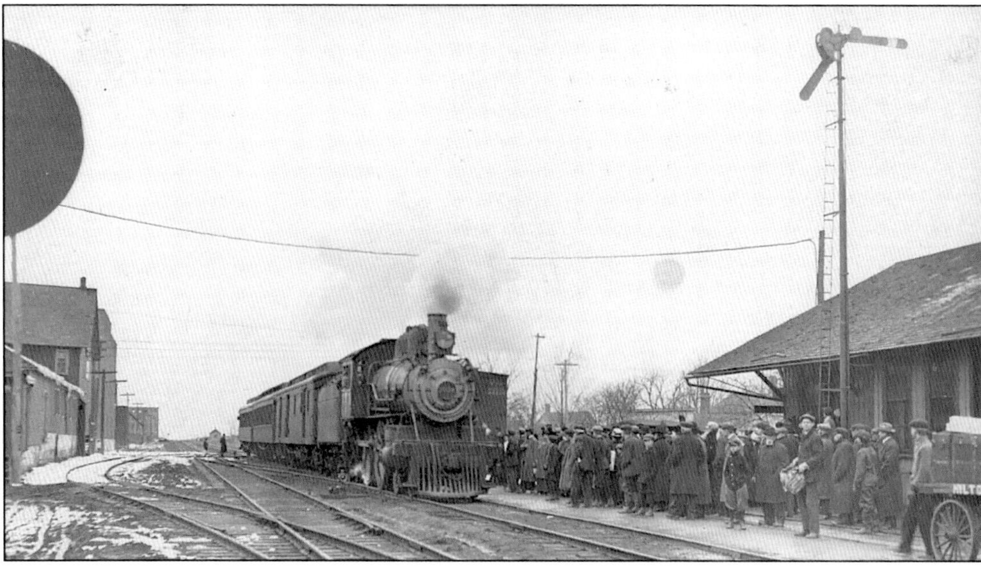

TRAIN AT DEPOT. Nicknamed the Hojack, the Lake Ontario Shore Railroad from Oswego to the Niagara River later expanded into the Rome, Watertown & Ogdensburg Railroad. It was originally scheduled to pass through Parma Center; however, Supvr. Charles Efner persuaded officials to run the line near his Main Street store, ensuring the growth of the village. Train watching was such a popular event that crowds gathered at Parma Station to watch trains go by, carrying mail. This photograph dates from 1913.

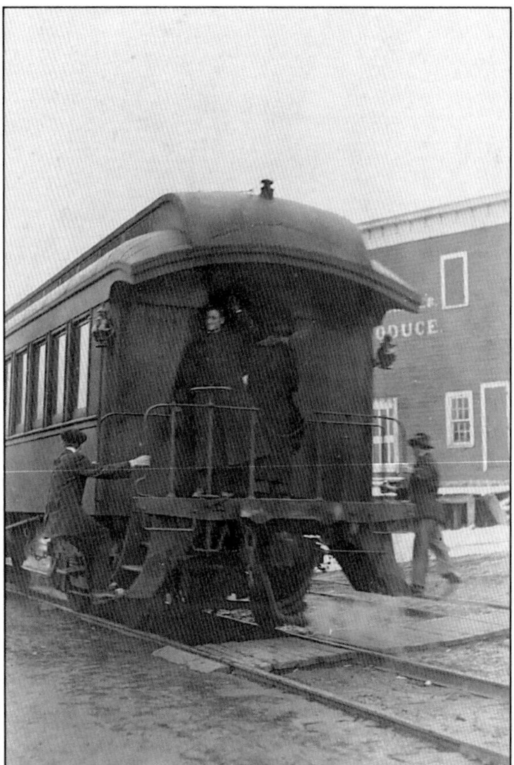

TRAIN CABOOSE. A big huffer-belly train with a cowcatcher was an exciting sight to see, as was this train caboose passing by Clapper's fruit warehouse, in a photograph taken by Harry McCarty. A rough crew came to town to build the railroad, and drunken vagrants became a problem once trains were running. A jail was located in the rear of Clapper's warehouse until the Dunham's Corners school was relocated beside the tracks and converted into a fire hall, village hall, meeting rooms, and jail. (McCarty photograph.)

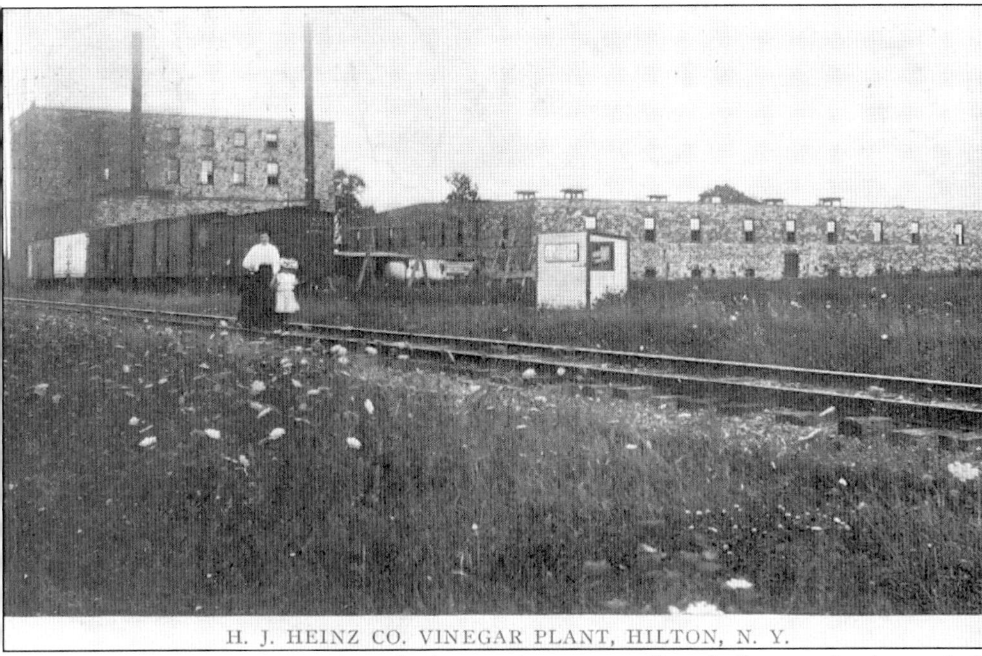

HEINZ PLANT, 1909. Inside a later lockup in the newer village hall, a single electric bulb dangled from the ceiling over one cot, which usually accommodated a tramp or an alcoholic stowaway brought by the railroad. Once, several dead tramps were found inside a locked boxcar. Others were killed while asleep on a trestle near the village. Farmers saw a hobo jungle near the west side of the Heinz plant when they hauled loads of apples, cabbages, cucumbers, peas, or tomatoes there in the 1940s.

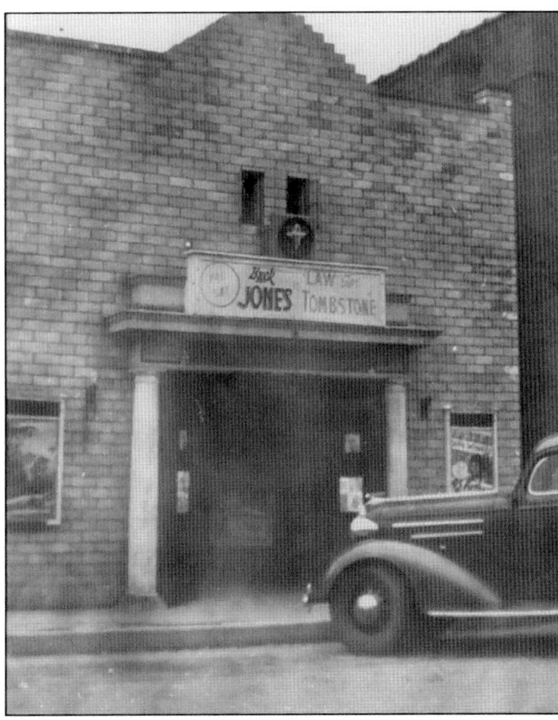

HILTONIA THEATER. From December 6, 1913, until March 1956, Main Street's Hiltonia theater showed news, cartoons, and motion pictures. These movies featured actors such as Clark Gable, Greer Garson, Walter Pidgeon, Jane Withers, Shirley Temple, Doris Day, Joseph Cotton, Gene Autry, and Roy Rogers. Jay Silverheels, who later became Tonto in the *Lone Ranger*, was attending high school in Rochester when Buck Jones's movie *Law in Tombstone* played in Hilton. At the time, no one expected that movie actor Ronald Reagan would become one of America's most popular presidents. (Tyner photograph).

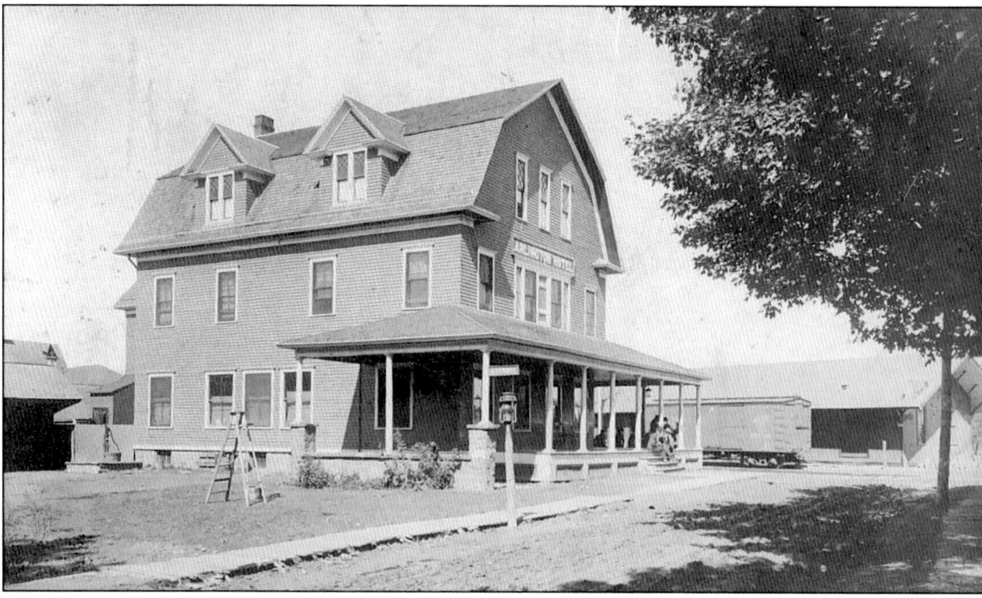

Arlington Hotel. The 1897 Arlington Hotel was decked out in bunting for patriotic events, such as the Fourth of July or the public reception to welcome home World War I veterans. The hotel served terrific fish dinners on Fridays. Its popular rail-side bar was operated for many years by the Skinner family. George Edelman Sr.'s new Arlington on Main Street featured steak dinners and wonderful pies made by his wife, June. Edelman was responsible for the erection of a gigantic American flag nearby.

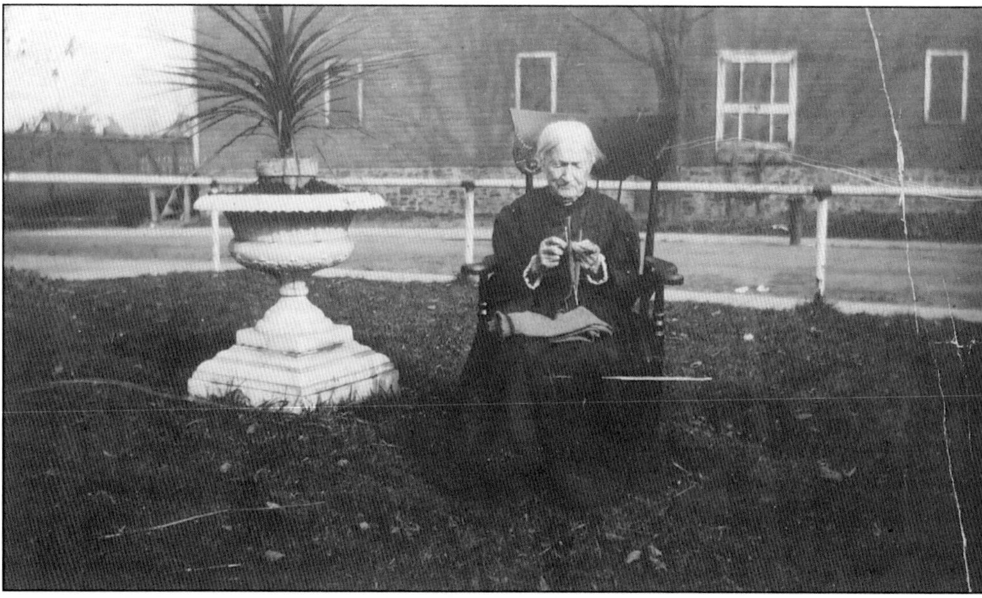

Woman in Yard. A lady believed to be the first woman of German birth to live in the village is shown here knitting in the yard of the Arlington Hotel, beside a Victorian flower urn. Behind her is visible Philo B. Clapper's produce warehouse, where apples and beans were sorted, graded, and packed for shipment. To provide more parking space, Hilton Baptists demolished a warehouse beside their church in 1961 and tore down the Arlington in 1967.

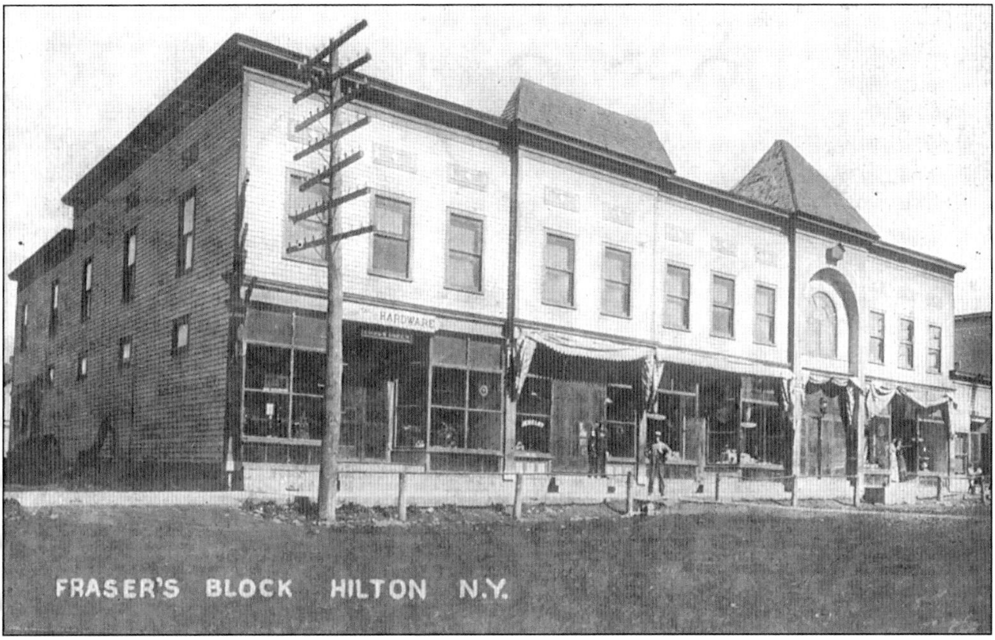

FRASER BLOCK. Canadian-born Evan Fraser supervised crews laying tracks through the village in 1876 and later returned to open a store with his brother, A.E. Fraser. Frasers' Store, the largest of its type in western New York, was rebuilt after the first block was destroyed by fire, and offered all sorts of merchandise, including furniture and buggies. It even had a bank. A post office addition later became Vernon Elzey's barbershop, and then Clyde Robillard's Jewelry & Watch Repair store, before the block burned in 1965.

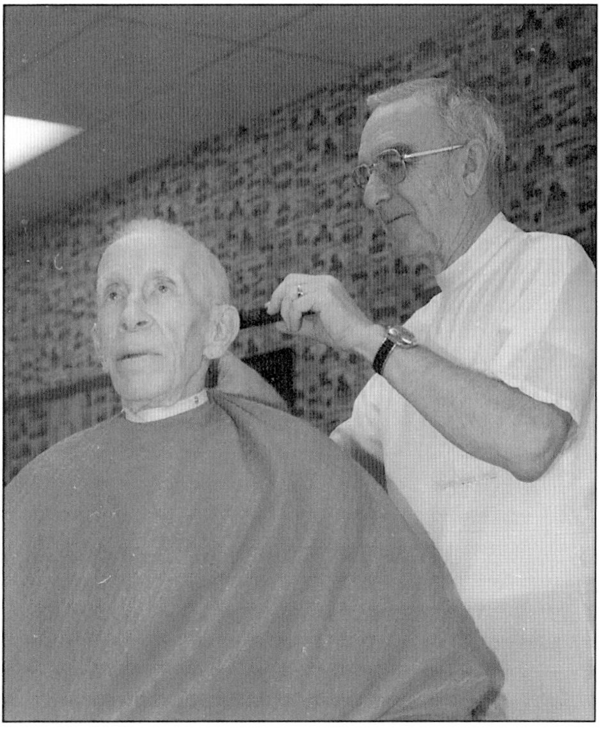

BARBERSHOP SCENE. Barber Al McMann gives Hy Burritt a special haircut in a photograph taken by Denny Wright. Still fondly remembered is Burritt's great sense of humor, especially the time that he found that someone's outhouse had been moved to Main Street by Halloween pranksters. That morning being All Saints' Day, Burritt soberly entered the privy, left something behind, pulled up his pants, and went on his merry way.

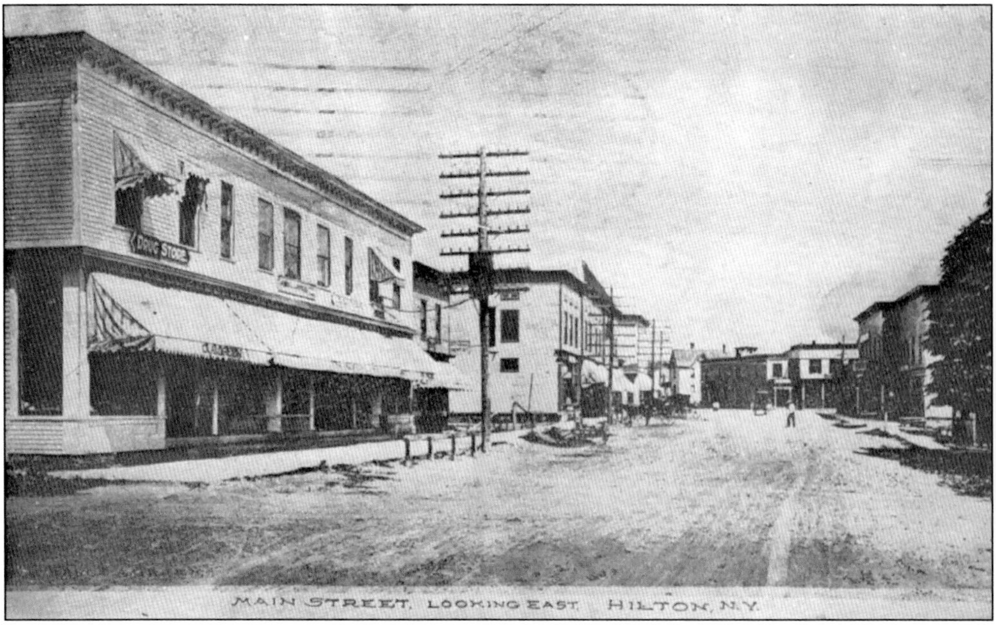

GREEN BLOCK. O.A. Green built more structures in the village than any other individual, and he and his daughter, Violet Green Wayne, eventually owned almost all of the structures that burned down along Main Street. After Green married Ferne Burritt, he joked that if he had a son he would name him Paris Green after a green insecticide and wood preservative. Steep steps led upstairs above Green's drugstore to Cooper's printing shop and the telephone company office.

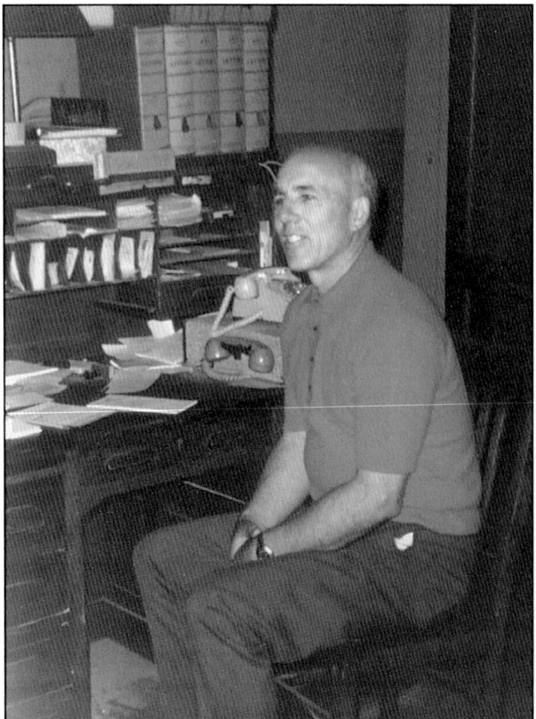

C. HARLAN COOPER. Charles Harlan "Trudge" Cooper was the third generation of his family to operate the printing business begun in 1897 by John E. Cooper and continued by his son Charles Sr. A navy veteran who survived the Pearl Harbor attack, young Cooper learned the trade at the Rochester Institute of Technology. Cooper's *Hilton Record* had more than 1,200 subscribers when sold to Arthur Perry, publisher of *Suburban News*. Cooper continued to operate a printing business in Sebring, Florida, until his retirement on August 1, 1999.

ORANGE GREEN. Orange Arthur Green was once incorrectly identified in a Ripley's *Believe It or Not* newspaper feature as Orange Apple Green. He was a quiet, modest, and usually serious man, perhaps best known for his drugstore's high prices, but was willing to smile at lame jokes such as providing itching powder for a newlywed couple's bed. When his daughter Violet joined him in the drugstore business, she became one of the country's first women pharmacists. Green served as a village president and fire chief.

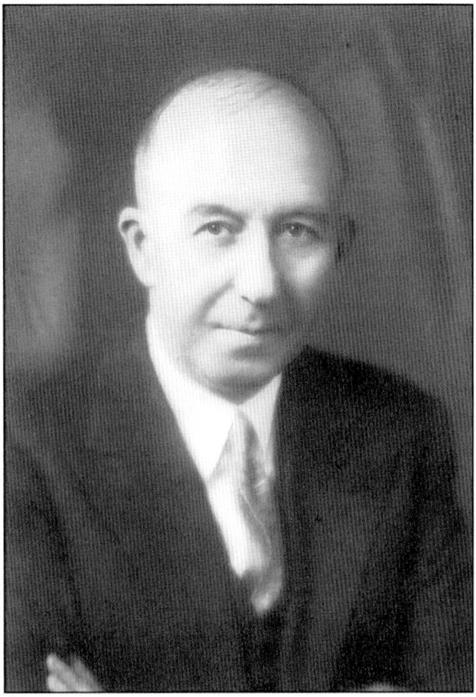

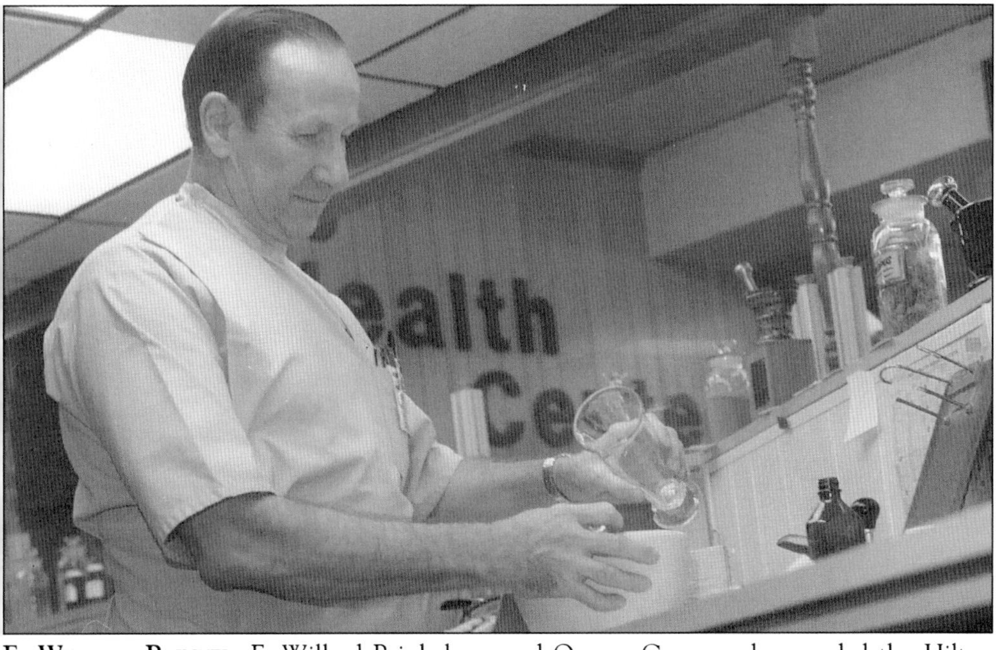

E. WILLARD BRINKEL. E. Willard Brinkel succeed Orange Green and expanded the Hilton Pharmacy as a Rexall drugstore, adding a variety of merchandise. Always affable, Brinkel became a popular community leader. Denny Wright's photograph of Brinkel preparing a prescription evokes happy memories of a respected druggist and friend. As did Green, Brinkel had the pleasure of seeing a descendant, David Brinkel, also become a pharmacist. Note the apothecary bottles from Green's drugstore in the background.

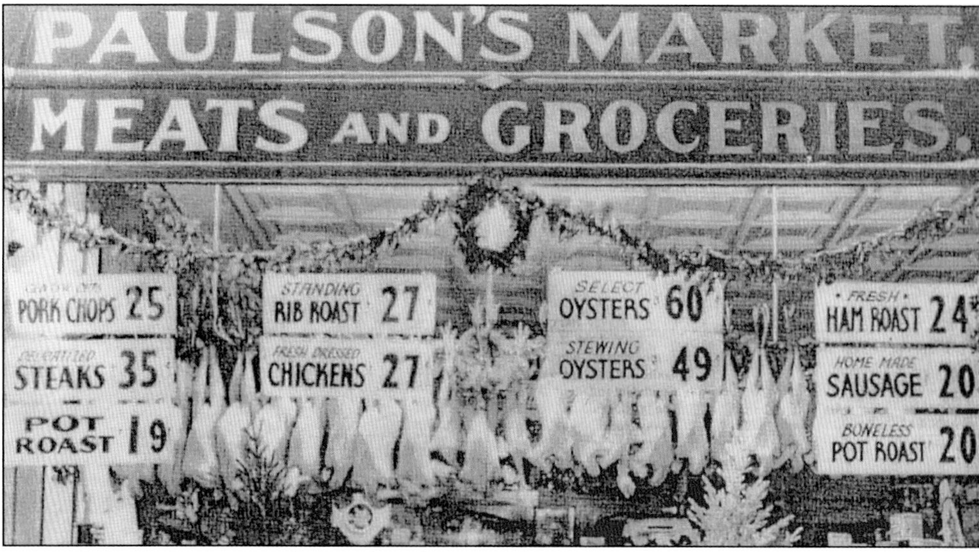

MAIN STREET VIEW. In the mid-20th century, downtown buildings included the 1904 Fraser Block, the 1904 Curtis Block, the 1912 Fisher Block, the 1895 Flatiron Building, and Opperman's 1896 store. The post office moved into the Fraser Block in 1945. The 1916 Green Block included Paulson's market, owned by D.A. Paulson and his wife—and intrepid meat-cutter—Elva Baxter Paulson; Oreb and Hazel Kenyon's Hart Store; Hank Smith's barbershop; and the Panaritis family's Hilton Candy Kitchen, which offered delectable food, homemade candy, and free advice from Nick Panaritis, who allowed "no loitering."

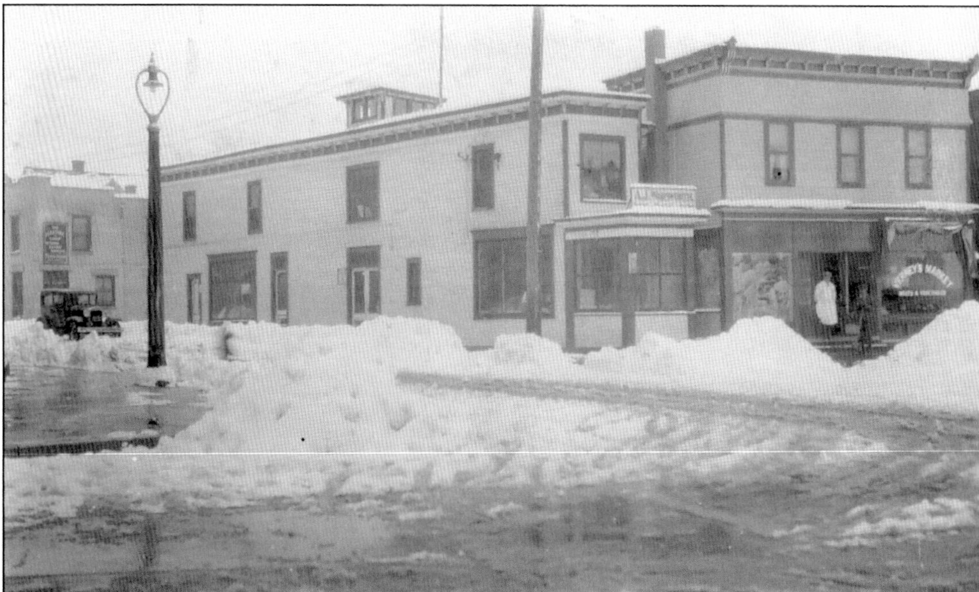

OPPERMAN BLOCK. Henry Opperman, a German merchant, owned two buildings at numbers 1 and 7 South Avenue. His cousin, Adolph "Otto" Wolf, ran the family grocery business for many years. Kathy Wolf, granddaughter of Adolph and Erma, became a nurse practitioner and charter member of Hilton Central's Hall of Fame, in part for her services during the Persian Gulf War. In this photograph, Raymond Verney's meat and vegetable market occupies the 1896 Opperman Block.

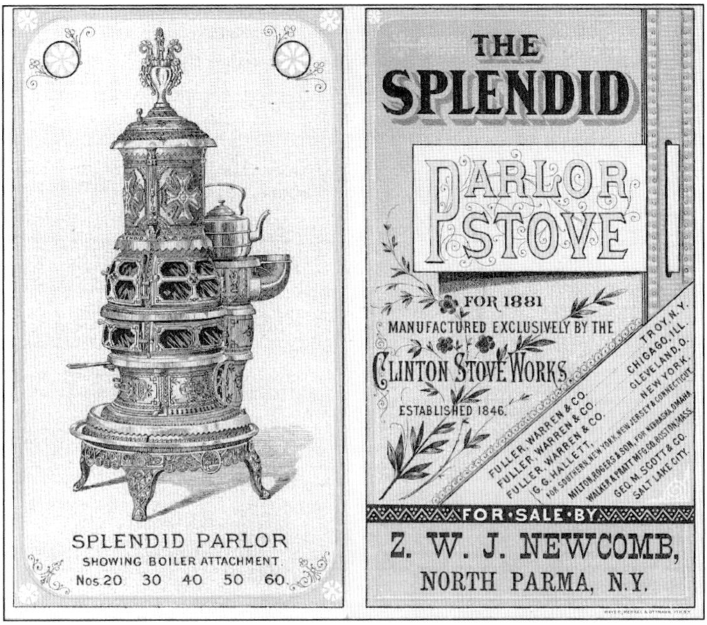

Newcomb's Stoves. Canadian-born Zela W.J. 's hardware store was an important local business place. Newcomb's son, William V. Newcomb, became Hilton's mayor, and Newcomb's great-grandson, Hon. Peter McCann, became a Monroe County legislator. The advertisement shown here is from the late 1890s. A beautifully crafted copper teakettle made by Newcomb survives today, demonstrating the tinker's talent.

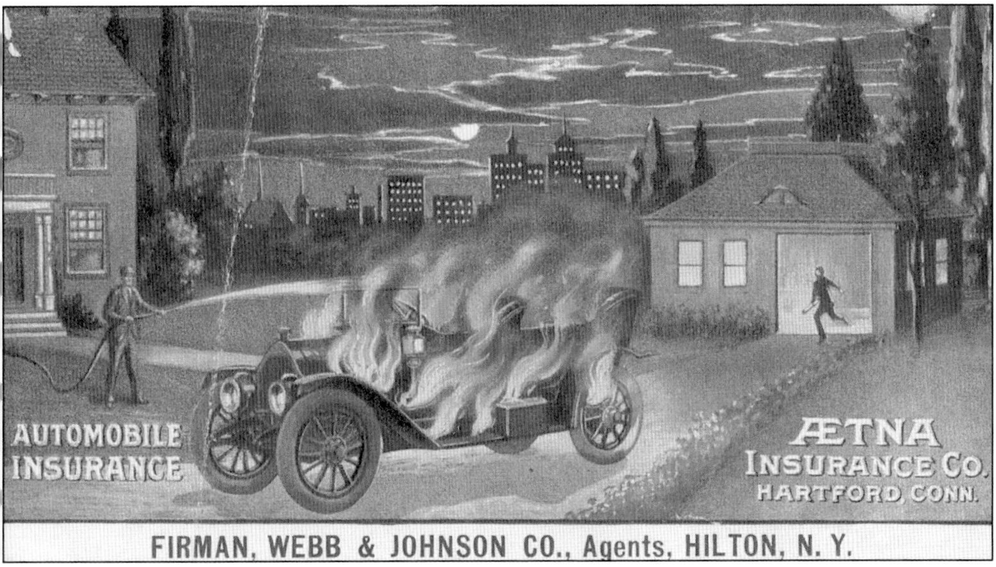

Firman's Insurance. The constant threat of fires and the coming of automobiles brought a need for better roads and better insurance coverage. Since 1921, insurance services have been offered on South Avenue by the firm now known as the Newcomb-McCann Insurance Agency. The business is located in the brick building that Henry Opperman built in 1913 between his grocery store and the hardware store that then was the oldest business block standing. Fires from 1874 to 1910 had taught builders not to erect wood-framed buildings.

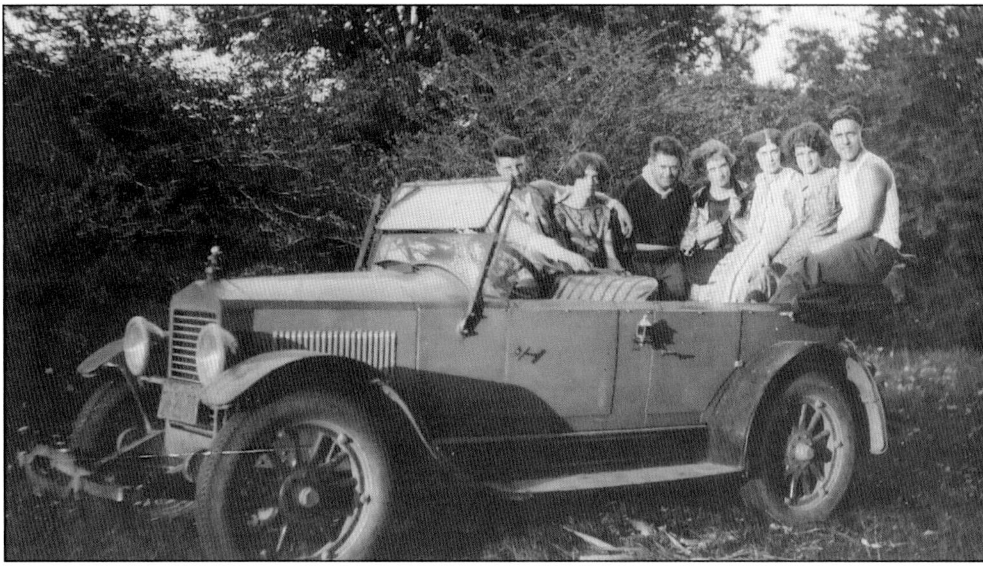

Early Automobiles. Harry McCarty's love for automobiles is evident in many of his photographs, including the above one of local teenagers in a rumble seat. Below is a charming 1915 photograph of two young girls in a Ford horseless carriage. The Ford Motor Company produced more than 15 million Model T touring cars from 1909 to 1927. Black vehicles were not made until 1914; the earlier colors were gray, red, blue, and green. Note the clotheslines behind the Ford—indispensable in the days before electric dryers.

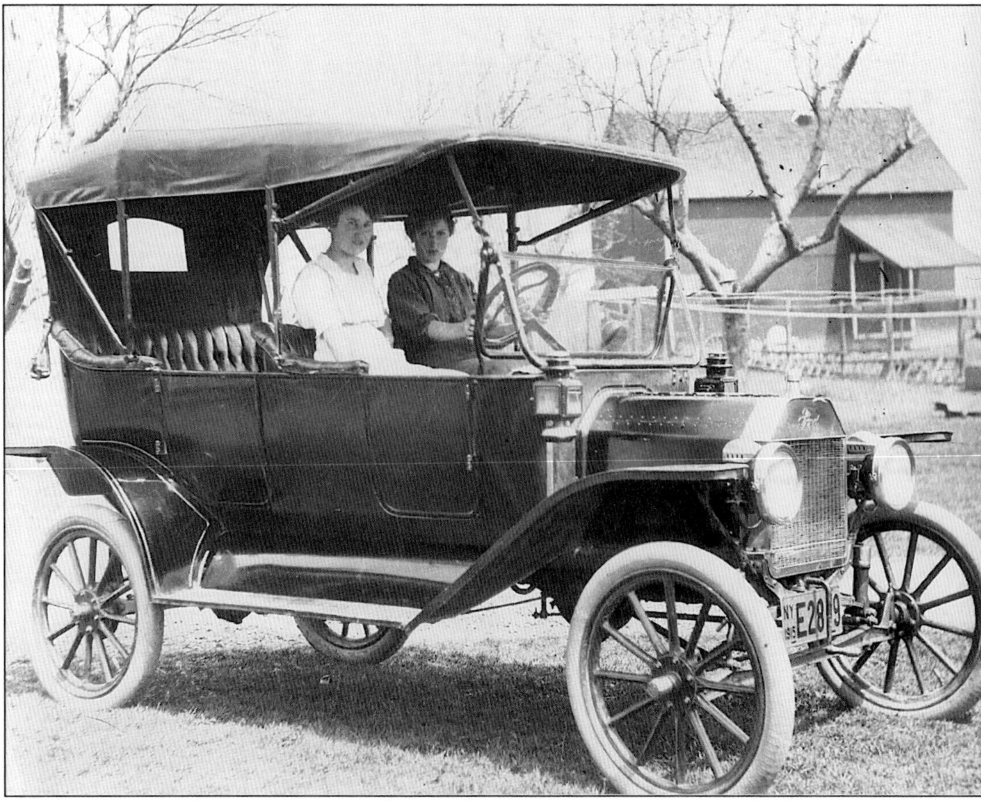

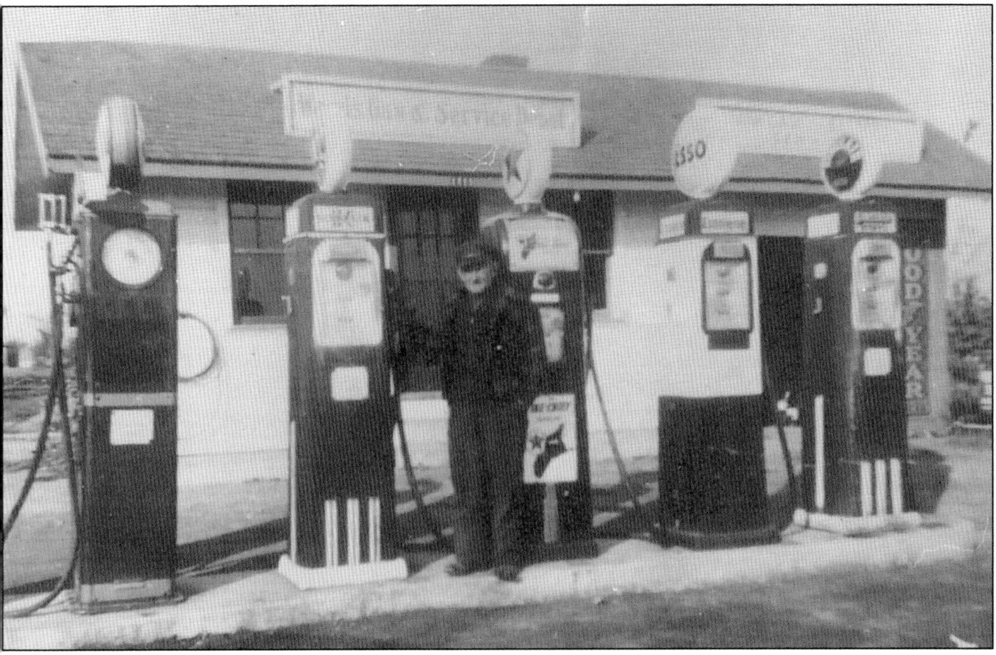

Ward's Gas Station. Supvr. Myron Roberts, a Wright family descendant, chaired the project to build hard-surfaced roads throughout Monroe County. Because the newfangled heavy automobiles required both good roads and special care, gas stations and repair garages soon sprouted at many intersections. Denny Wright operated one at Parma Center that was euphorically dubbed Ward's Gas & Service Depot after its owner, Ward Cox. After Wright took a Kodak job, Cox ran the station for many years, offering grease, gas, oil, snacks, euchre games, tobacco, political news, and local gossip. If he liked you and you asked politely, Cox would give you a free glass of sulfur water, smelling like rotten eggs, but probably a healthful drink. Otherwise, you had to buy soda pop. Holding aloft a bottle of cherry or grape soda, Cox would dramatically repeat his favorite Teetotaler's phrase: "Look not upon the vine when it is ripe or when it glistens in the glass."

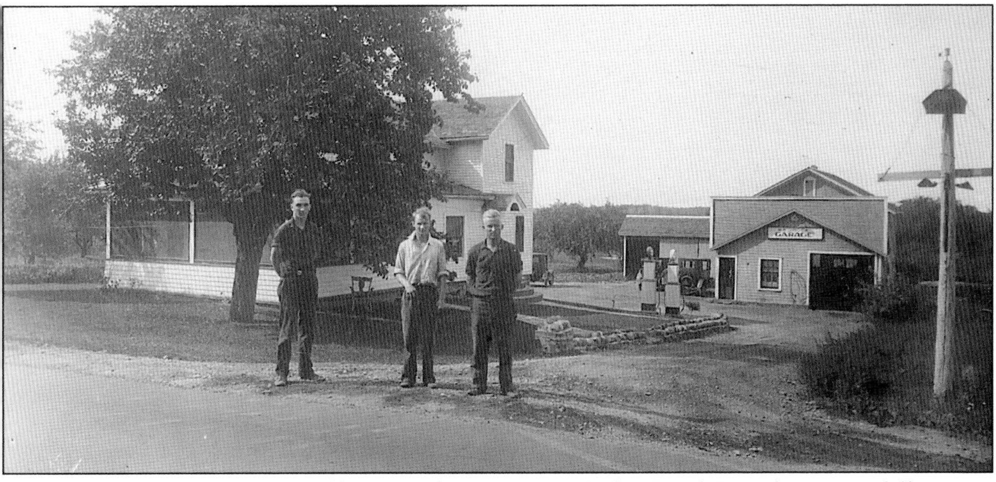

Willis Dimock's Station. Willis Dimock's garage on Ridge Road West became a full-service repair shop. In this photograph, founder and owner Bill Dimock stands at the right. The business is still going strong.

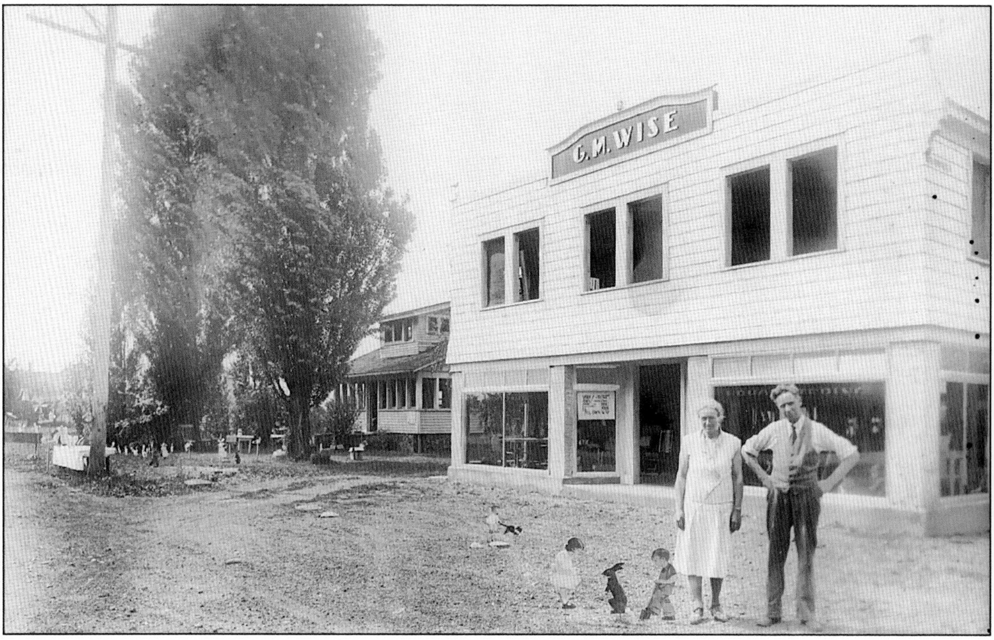

MINOR WISE'S SHOP. Cartoon lawn ornaments embellish G. Miner Wise and Lulu Webster Wise's lawn on Ridge Road West at Parma Corners, a well-traveled road dating back to 1804. After a fire hit his furniture and upholstery shop, he continued to repair and reupholster chairs and sofas in his home next door, despite his advanced age. The house was crammed full of overstuffed furniture in various stages of disrepair, awaiting Miner's tender loving care. Ridge Road is still Parma's busiest highway.

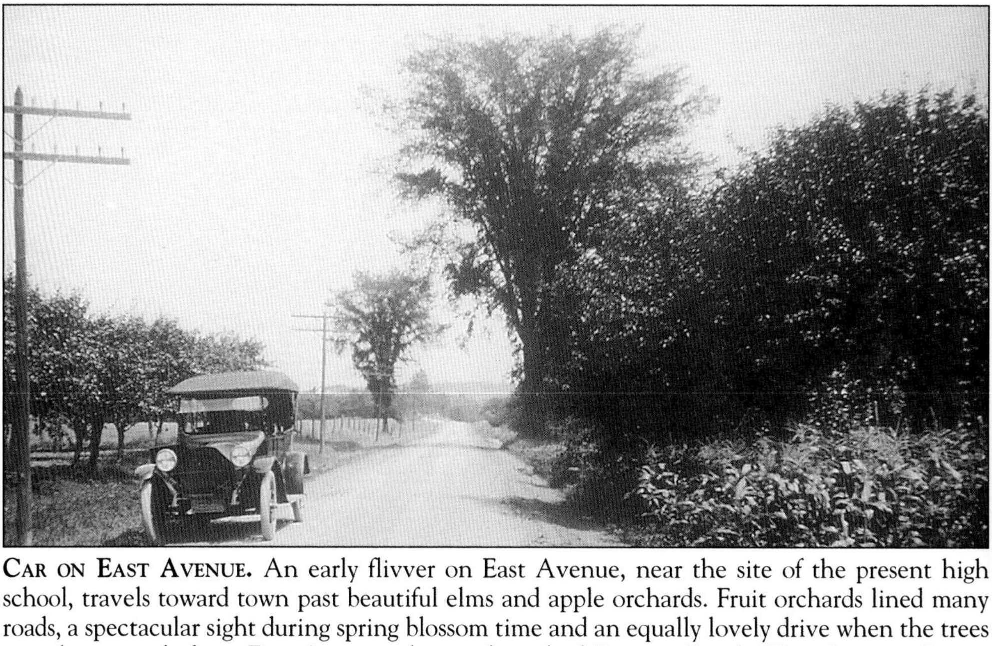

CAR ON EAST AVENUE. An early flivver on East Avenue, near the site of the present high school, travels toward town past beautiful elms and apple orchards. Fruit orchards lined many roads, a spectacular sight during spring blossom time and an equally lovely drive when the trees were heavy with fruit. East Avenue, the south end of Bennett Road, West Avenue, Parma Center, the west end of Peck Road, Manitou Road from Ridge to Latta, Hinkleyville, Bailey, and Clarkson-Parma to Parma Center Road date back to 1807.

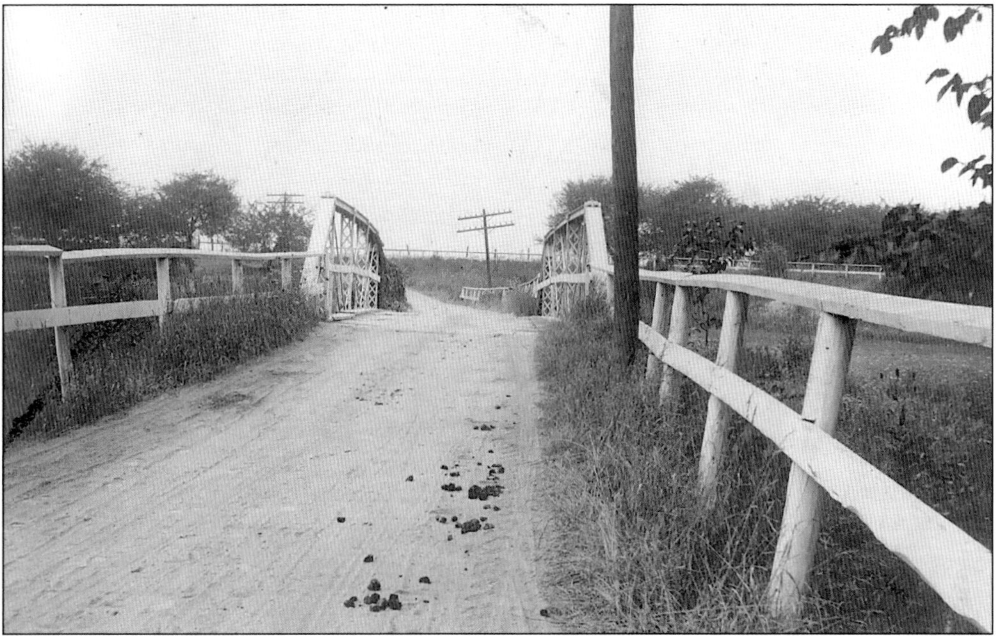

WILDER ROAD BRIDGE. This August 11, 1919 photograph shows that a horse had recently passed over the Wilder Road bridge. Bezaleel Atchinson built a mill that never worked well, just across the creek from the present Burger Funeral Home. Also in the vicinity was the mill of William Colf, or Cole, an area landmark. It stood opposite the present high school athletic field, off Bennett Road. The "lost" VanWormer cemetery is nearby on the former property of Harley "Tug" Bigler.

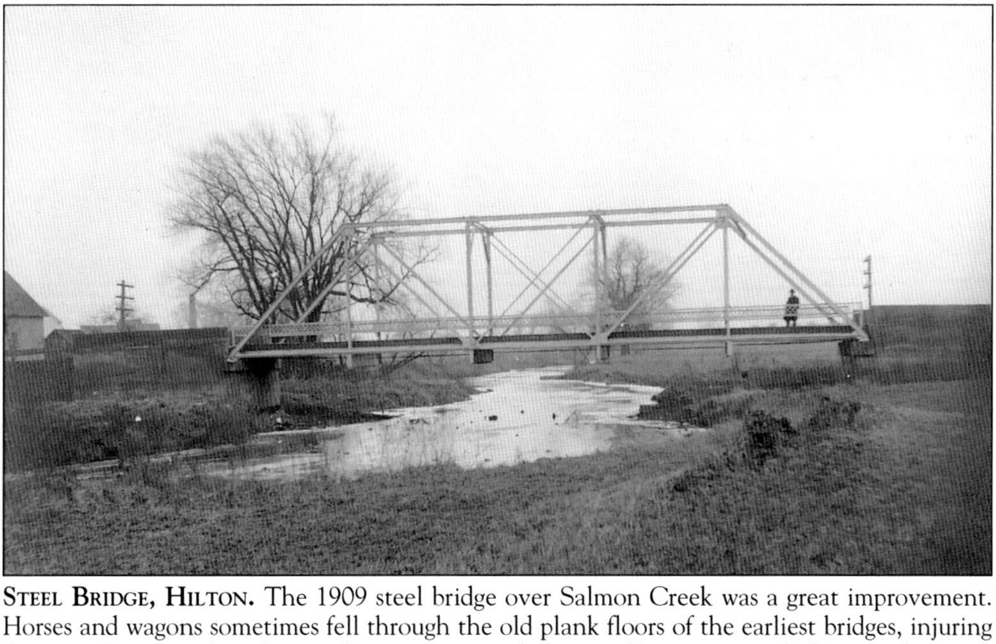

STEEL BRIDGE, HILTON. The 1909 steel bridge over Salmon Creek was a great improvement. Horses and wagons sometimes fell through the old plank floors of the earliest bridges, injuring drivers or horses and resulting in lawsuits against the town of Parma, town clerk's records reveal. While repairs were being made to an earlier bridge in 1871, an unfortunate accident killed a Mr. Crane and injured Sylvanus Buell. Buell sued the town.

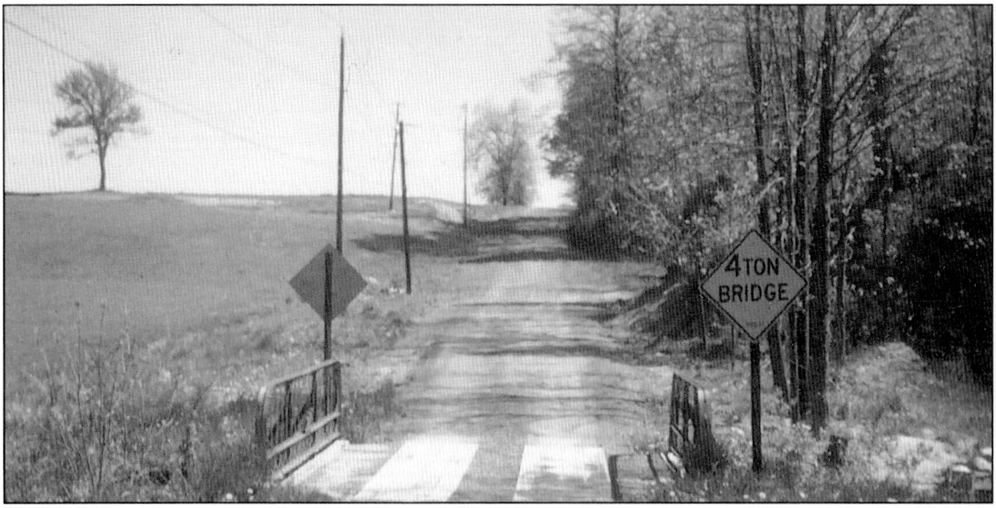

Sleepy Hollow. The road that crosses the creek near Monroe Chemical was named after the Draffin family but is better known as Sleepy Hollow Road. When it was laid out in 1814, it provided a shortcut for farmers hauling grain or lumber to the mills beside the waterfall on Salmon Creek. The south end of Draffin Road and the north end of Bennett Road were still unpaved in the 1950s. Note the cement steps in the picture below, possibly used as a horse block for those wishing to fish or picnic by the 1868 bridge. The horses shown here belonged to John and Betty Cushing, who built at Sleepy Hollow after their home was demolished to allow construction of an Arco station. Their earlier home stood on the site of the Parma Center's first house built in 1809, the Odell family's big barns, and a stone building used as a town clerk's office by Chauncey Knox. In the early 1900s, the Odells had more fruit trees than other Parma horticulturists. Guerdon Odell was a skillful fruit grafter.

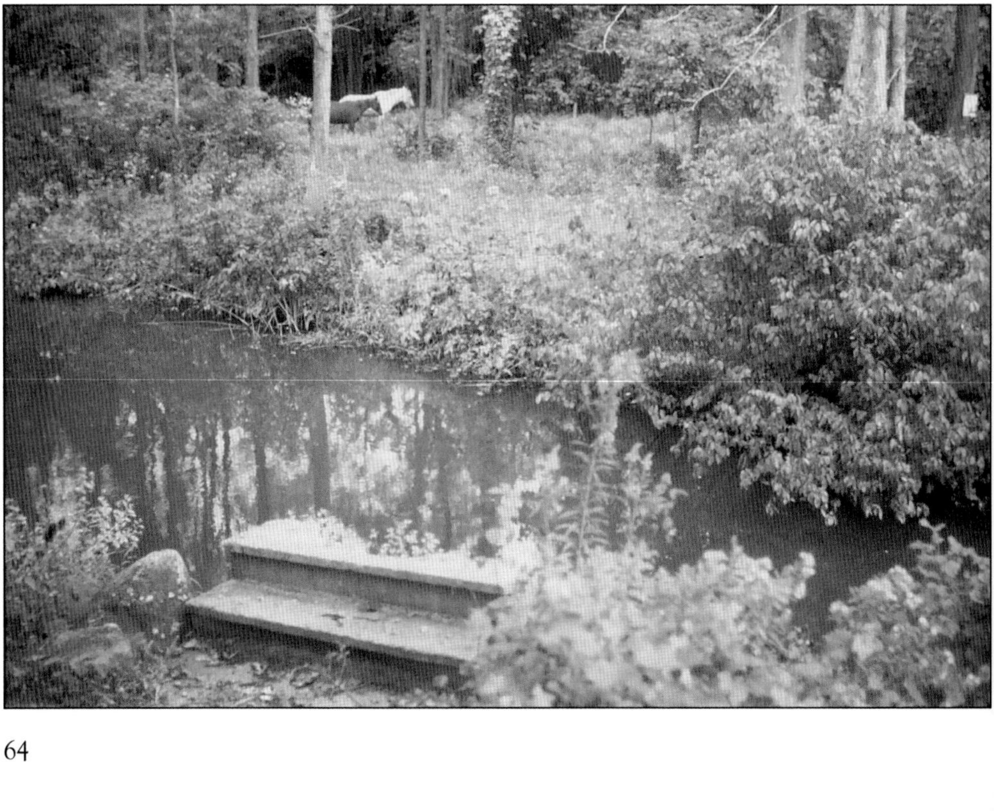

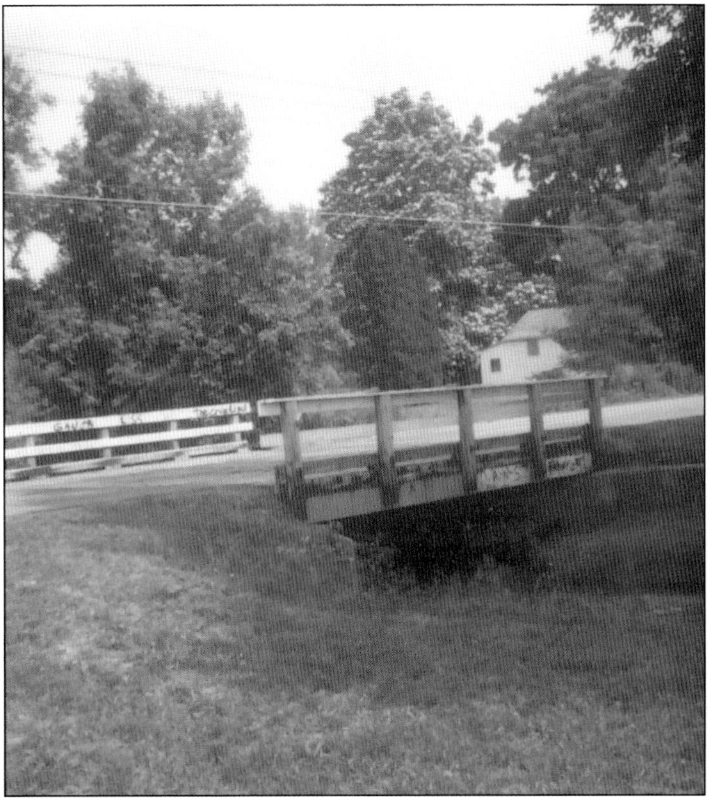

Dean Road Bridge. Although Parma Highway Supt. Anthony Schalk and his family lived nearby, the Dean Road bridge over Northrup Creek was the last old-time bridge in Parma to be replaced. It still had a strong plank floor when replaced, long after the era of wooden bridges had ended. In early times, the road was called Coffee Road and Curtis Road, after area land owners. Dean Road dates back to 1799, when the first roads were surveyed. It followed a part of the Canawaugus Indian trail, as did Peck and Spencer Roads.

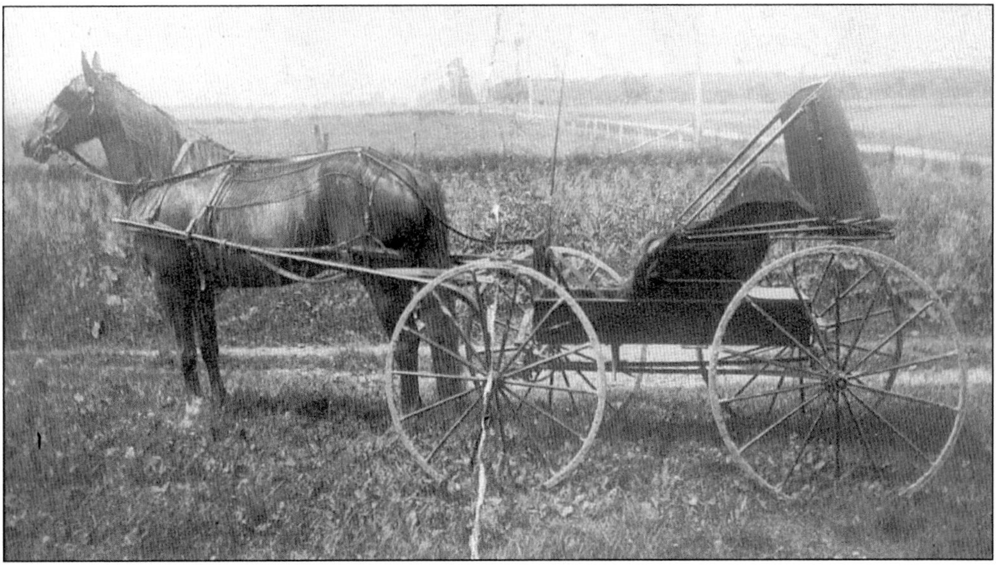

Carriage in Hoosick. This early photograph shows William and Emma Wilcox's buggy on a dirt country road believed to be Manitou Road in Hoosick. The Wilcox family lived on the Greece side of Manitou, near the home and office of Dr. Samuel Beach Bradley. The office was later relocated across the road for use as a storage shed. The local pronunciation for Manitou, a Native-American spirit god, is Man-a-toe (Westerners pronounce it Man-ah-two). The road was so named because it led toward Manitou Beach.

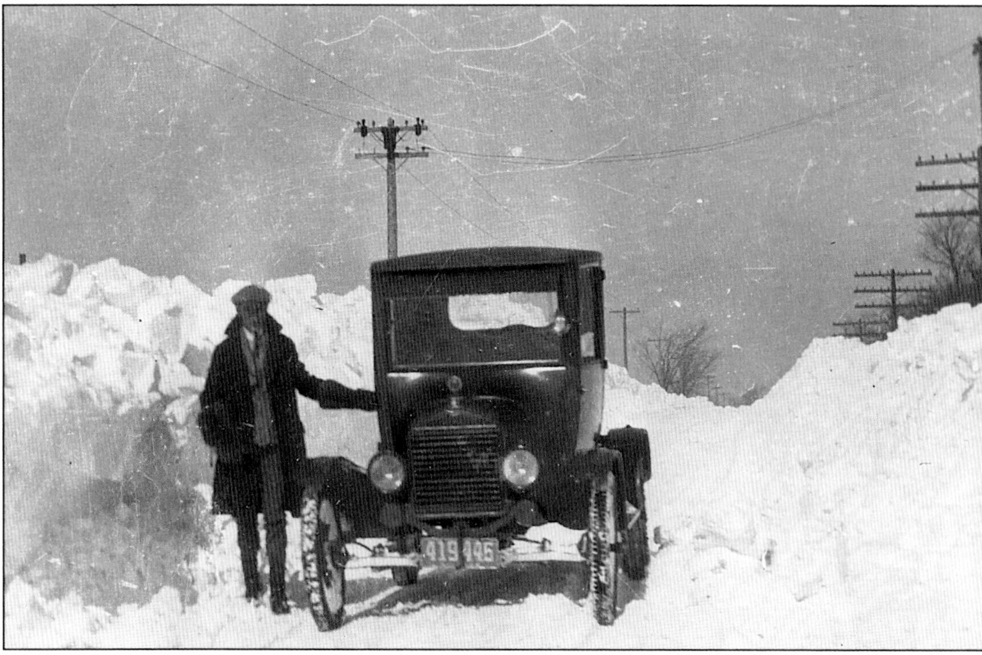

Snowstorm in the Cut. Getting through the cuts, or dips, where roads pass over creeks near Parma Center was a harrowing task. Fred Stevens is believed to be the motorist in this Harry McCarty photograph, taken when snowbanks were about 6 feet high. With visibility limited by swirling snow or fog, driving was truly treacherous. Dr. Charles Keller Sr. once struck pedestrian Nelly Quinlan in the Route 259 south dip, injuring her hip so badly that she was crippled for life.

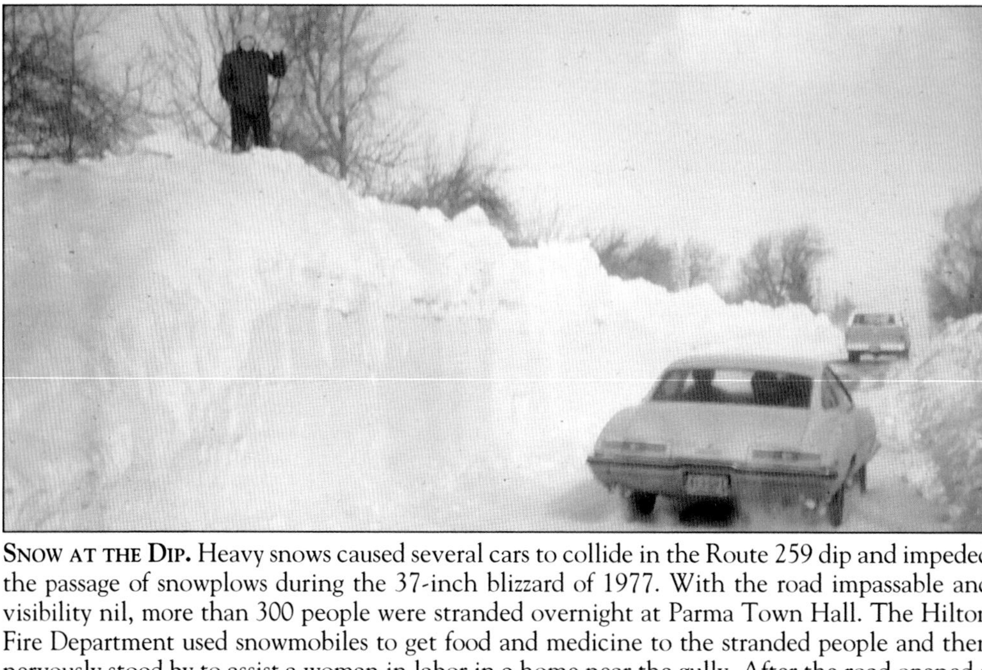

Snow at the Dip. Heavy snows caused several cars to collide in the Route 259 dip and impeded the passage of snowplows during the 37-inch blizzard of 1977. With the road impassable and visibility nil, more than 300 people were stranded overnight at Parma Town Hall. The Hilton Fire Department used snowmobiles to get food and medicine to the stranded people and then nervously stood by to assist a woman in labor in a home near the gully. After the road opened a day later, Brian Husted happily demonstrated the depth of the snow.

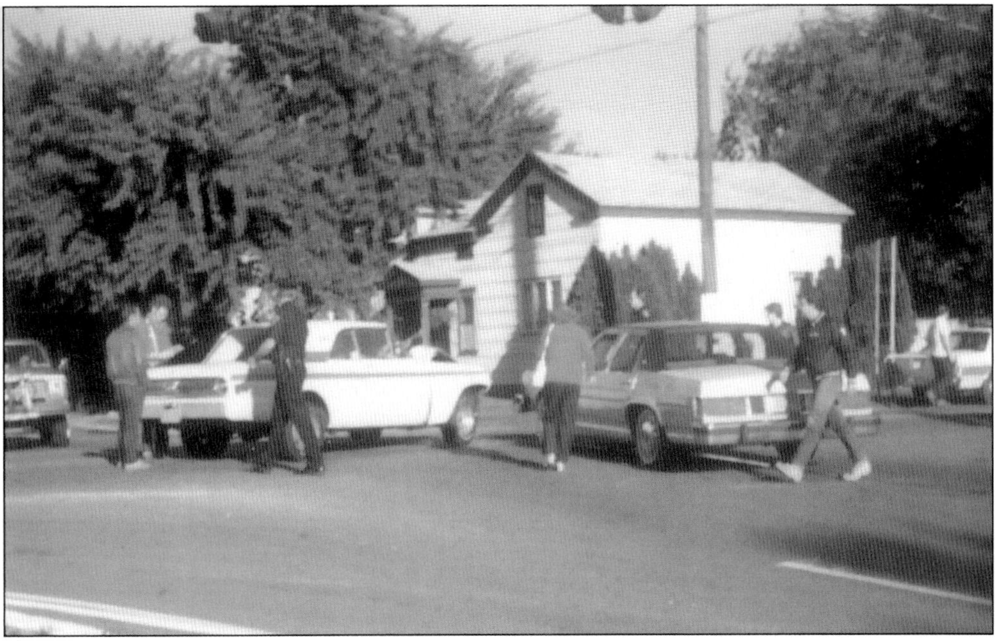

Accident Scenes. Pictured here are two scenes of a 1986 accident at the intersection of Routes 18 and 259 at Parma Center, one of many at that location, usually caused by a car on Parma Center Road failing to stop for the through traffic on the main road, Route 259. The bloodcurdling sounds of squealing brakes and colliding vehicles were so frequent that the intersection acquired the nickname Collision Corners. Unfortunately, Parma Town Board's repeated requests for a traffic light were rejected by state officials, and the community lost highly respected resident Roger Meyer in a fatal motorcycle-car crash there. That tragedy prompted a petition drive for a stoplight, which was supported by residents, merchants, firemen, and politicians.

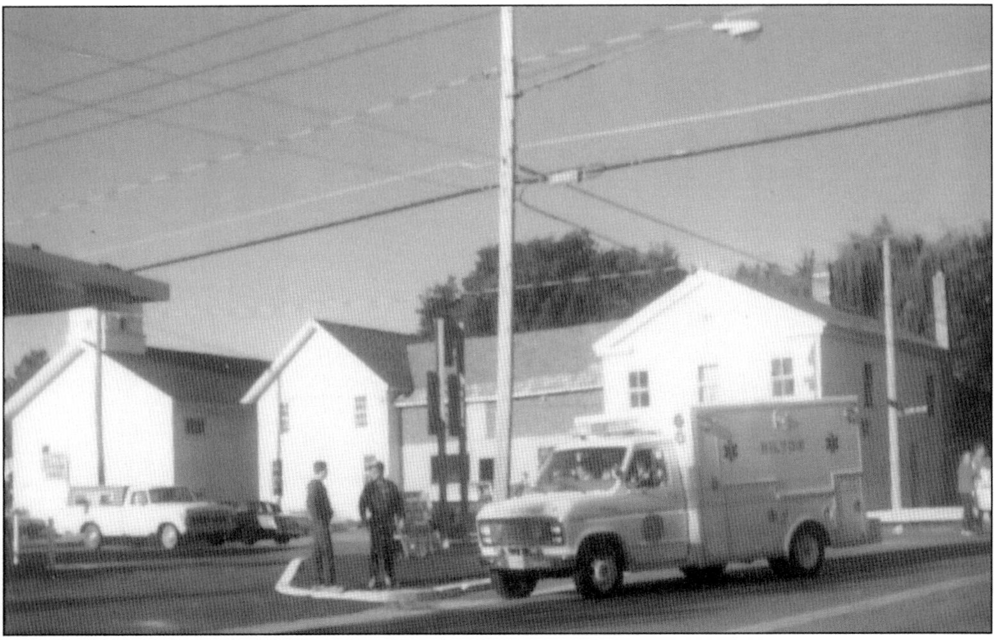

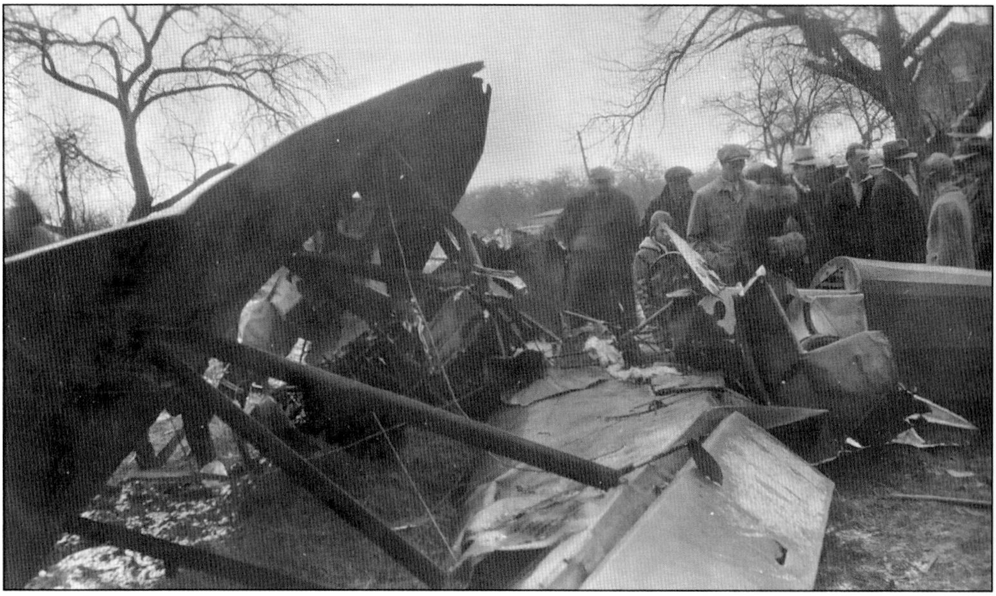

PLANE CRASH. The pilot escaped without serious injuries when this small plane crashed in fields north of Parma Center Road in the 1930s. McMann's barn, visible at the right, is no longer standing. Only a few local residents owned their own private planes at that time. Airplane travel was considered a status symbol, and best clothes were worn because flying anywhere was a remarkable occasion. The age of flight began with the Wright brothers' flights during Pres. Theodore Roosevelt's administration. People began watching the skies. On at least two occasions, local residents reported seeing mysterious lights—were they flying saucers or UFOs or something else? As the century neared its end, people watched the Hale-Bopp comet. (Harry McCarty photographs.)

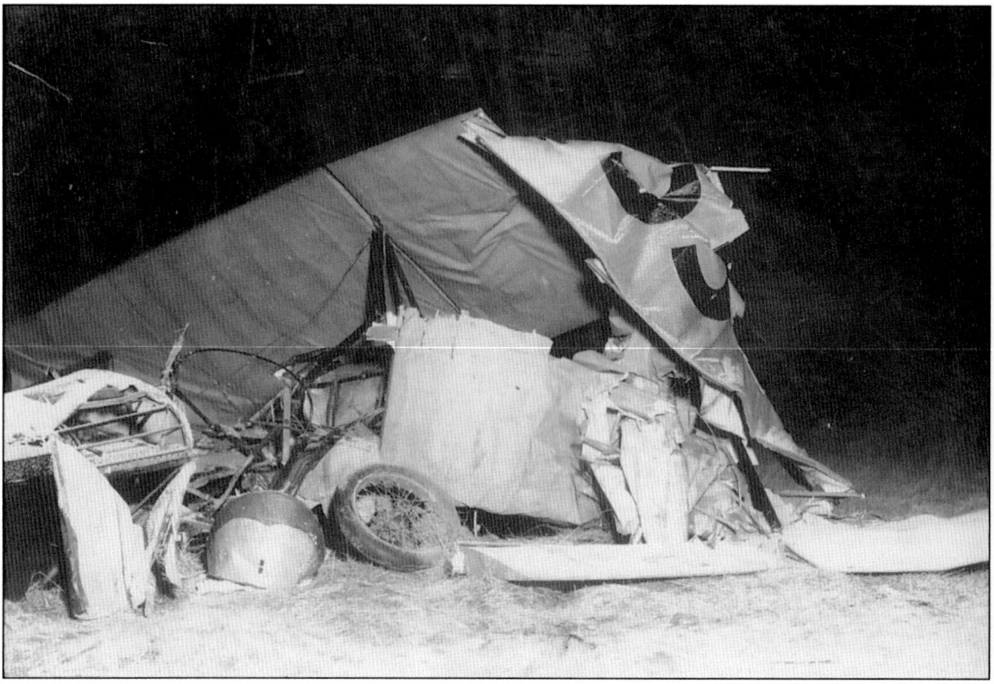

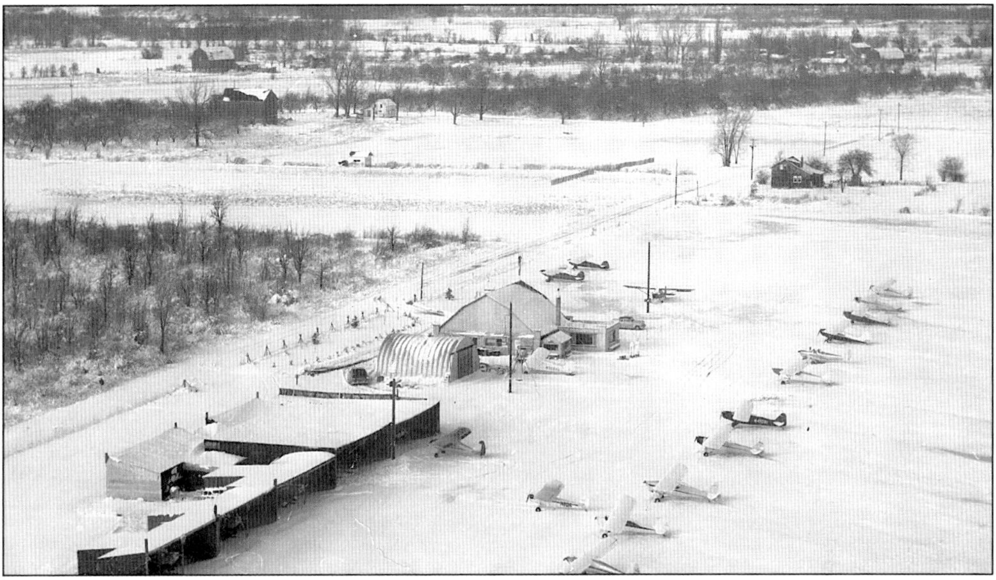

HILTON AIRPORT. Hilton Airport opened on Draffin Road in 1944 and soon became a popular site for fly-in breakfasts. The airport had private hangars for a few local planes, and owner Harold Silloway held events there. Silloway and his family moved into the nearby Draffin homestead. With a love of flying and great inventiveness, Silloway built small planes for his grandchildren and made himself a bright yellow Italian touring car, which he often drove in local parades.

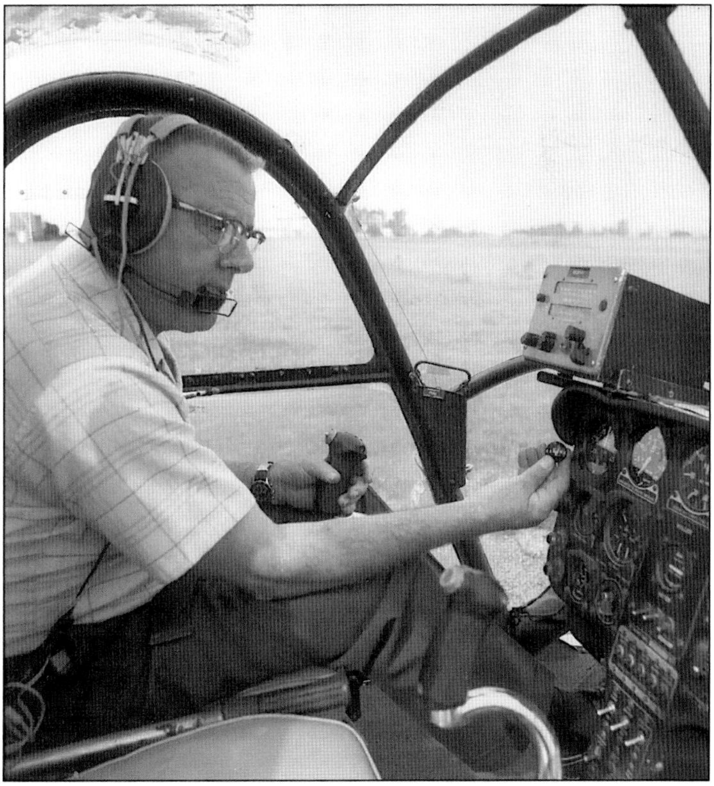

HELICOPTER. Harold Silloway had the first helicopter based in the local vicinity. As a result, he was sometimes called upon by the sheriff's office for surveillance aid or to transport badly injured auto crash victims to area hospitals, demonstrating the importance of mercy flights. Eventually, these flights resulted in the Canandaigua-based helicopter service that now makes over 400 mercy flights annually.

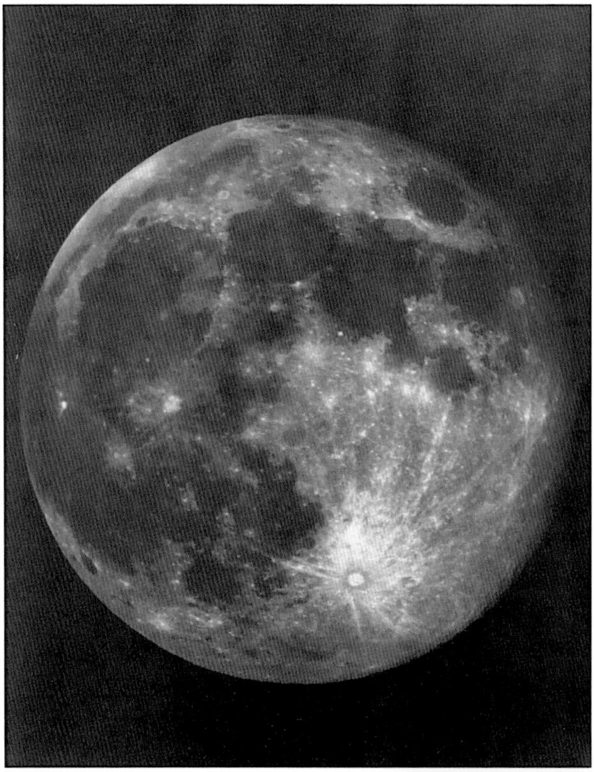

Moon Shot. Harold Silloway developed and manufactured a cutting oil at his Cool Tool firm, Monroe Chemical, that he believed went to the moon. His oil was purchased by the federal government for use on early rocket flights. The sky was never the limit for Silloway, nor for photographer Denny Wright, who took this moon shot through a telescope set up during the summer of 1977 near the present loading dock of today's Hilton Post Office.

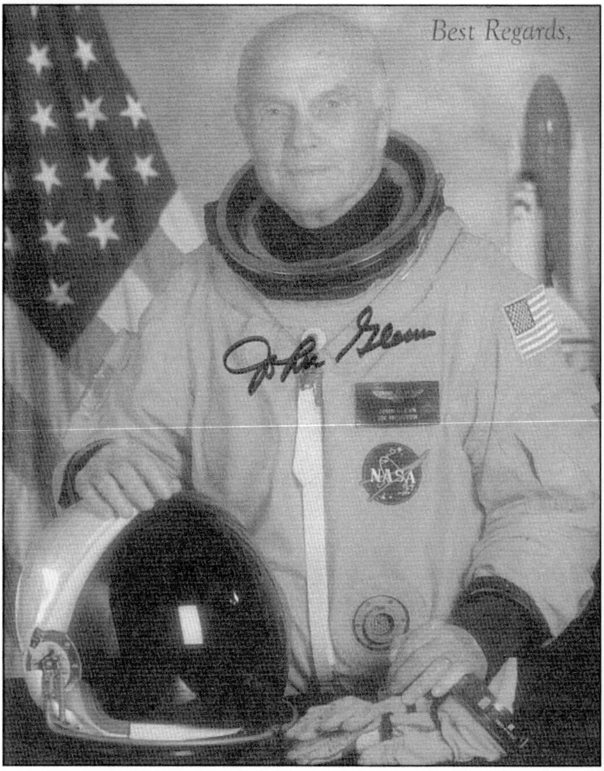

John Glenn. The exploration of outer space, begun under Pres. John F. Kennedy, soon brought reality to the fanciful Buck Rogers stories that kids once read at Parma No. 1 School. Neil Armstrong and Edwin "Buzz" Aldrin walked on the moon in 1969. Sen. John Glenn, 77, became the oldest astronaut in space in 1999.

Six

Schools and Churches

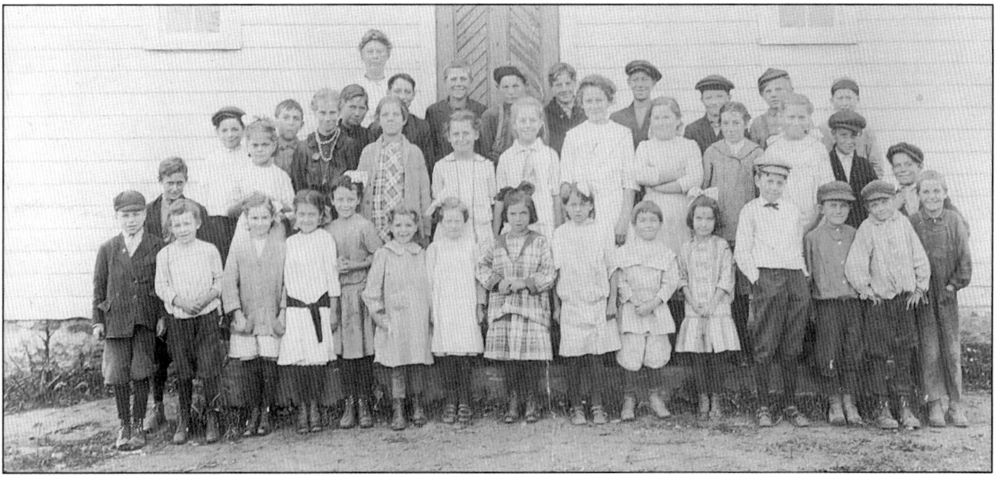

Parma Center School. This photograph of the Parma No. 1 District School is the only one known to exist showing the schoolhouse's brick-and-wood façade. The little schoolhouse was built in 1849–50 with a wooden porch and cloakroom. Standing in front of teacher Lois Baxter McCarty are her students in grades one through eight. They are, from left to right, as follows: (front row) Elmer Hall, Albert Murrell, Alice Tyo, Virginia Stoffel, Sarah Murrell, Emily Hunn, Alice Hall, Libbie Kerwin, Irene Carter, Howard Cox, Consulo Stoffel, Leonard Twentyman, George Decker, Joseph Chismar, and William Hunn; (middle row) Louis VanDorn, Elizabeth Roberts, Rose Hunn, Bertha Klemma, Avis Vanderbeck, Ethelyn Butcher, Ethelyn Vanderbeck, Rose Glenn, Eliza Kerwin, Blanche Roberts, Ed Conklin, and Ellsworth Stoffel; (back row) Horace Murrell, Charles Kerwin, Philip Hoyt, Paul Ingraham, Ephraim Hunn, Weston Pickett, Chester Mauer, Sydney Marshall, Arthur Welch, Mike Chismar, and Fred Glenn. Avis Vanderbeck Blair, Elizabeth Roberts Watters, and Blanche Roberts Newsome became teachers at Hilton. A 1915 sandstone addition modernized the school facility into a two-room building with a small upstairs room, where Pearl Veness and other leaders held 4-H meetings. After centralization of schools in 1949, the building became the Milton Rayburn family's home.

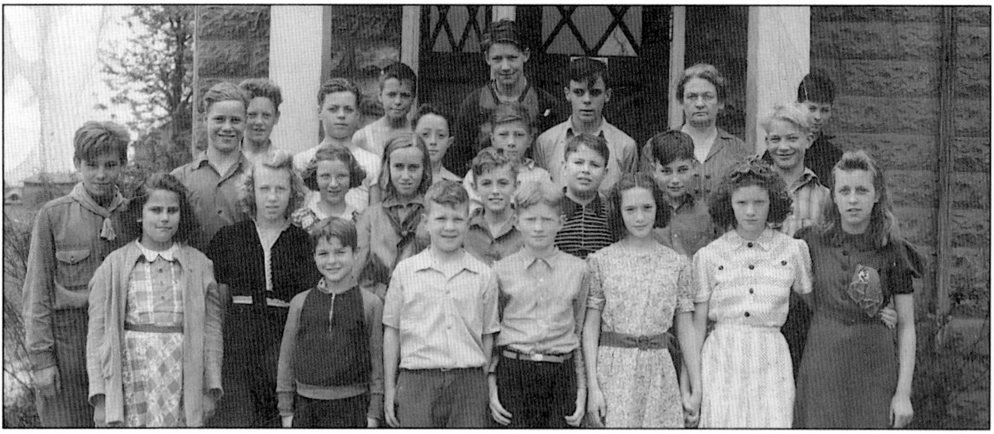

Grades Five to Eight. Mary Taber's class at Parma No. 1 District School in 1941 included, from left to right, the following: (front row) Ethel McCumber, Blanche Williams, James Blodgett, Donald Kasper, Leland Helfrich, Dorothy Blodgett, Marian Helfrich, and Frances Burns; (middle row) Hoyt or Burns (?), Robert Kasper, Ethel Derosia, Phyllis Ainsworth, Norman Wright, Harry McCarty, Lyndon Anderson, and Gordon Feil; (back row) Robert Casper, John Derosia, Charles Miller, LaVerne "Bear" Hoyt, Al Lowden, Ralph Ingraham, Dixie Miller (?), Vincent Burke, teacher Mary Taber, and Levi Derosia.

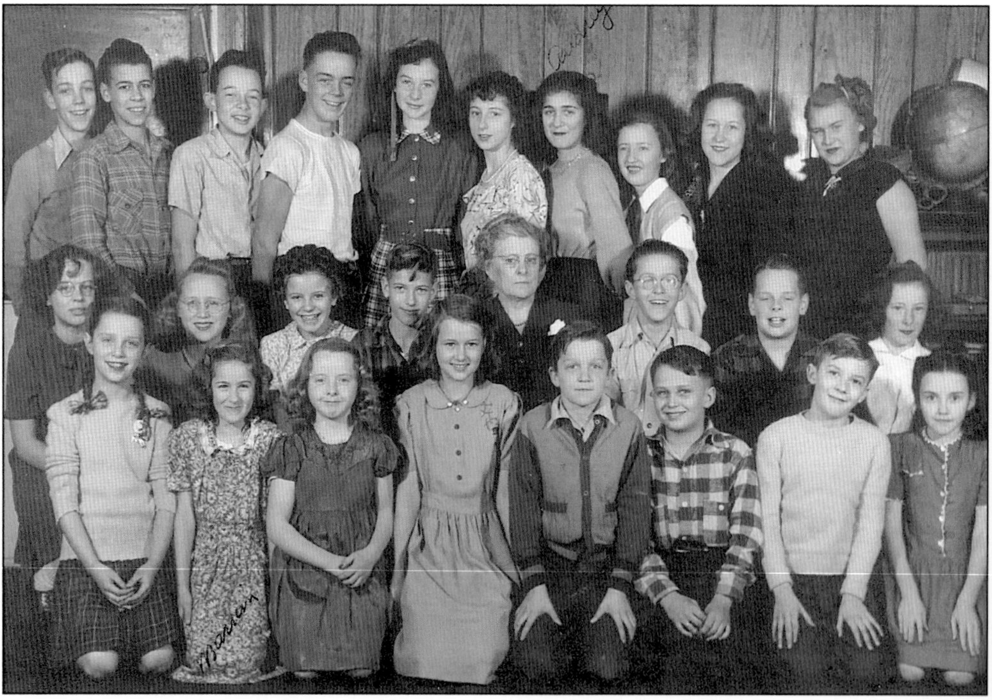

Class of 1948. One of the last classes at Parma No 1 District School was the Class of 1948. They are, from left to right, as follows: (first row) Dixie Miller, Marian Derosia, Patty St. George, Gladys Stevens, John Miller, Gerry LaDue, Tommy Coyle, and Priscilla Tyner; (middle row) ? Schultz, JoAnn McKenzie, Pauline Morse, Roger Decker , teacher Mrs. Fowler, Dick Miller, Kenny Spears, and Dorothy Blodgett; (third row) Paul Hermance, Edward "Crow" Stevens, Fred Tyrell, Donald Hermance, Norma Tyrell, Peggy Balough, Audrey DeRosia, Jean Radford, Shirley Blodgett, and Noreen McKenzie.

OLDEST SCHOOL. At Parma Corners is the oldest school building now existing in Parma: No 3 District School. The district's 1810 frame school, the little brown school, was encapsulated with brick in 1861 instead of being torn down. In this charming photograph, arms and legs are modestly covered, young boys are wearing suit jackets and knickers, and girls are wearing plaid dresses or pinafore aprons.

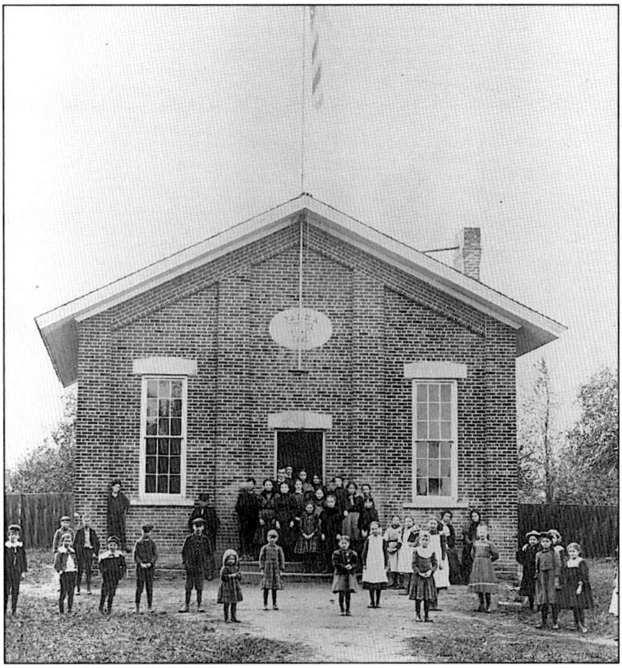

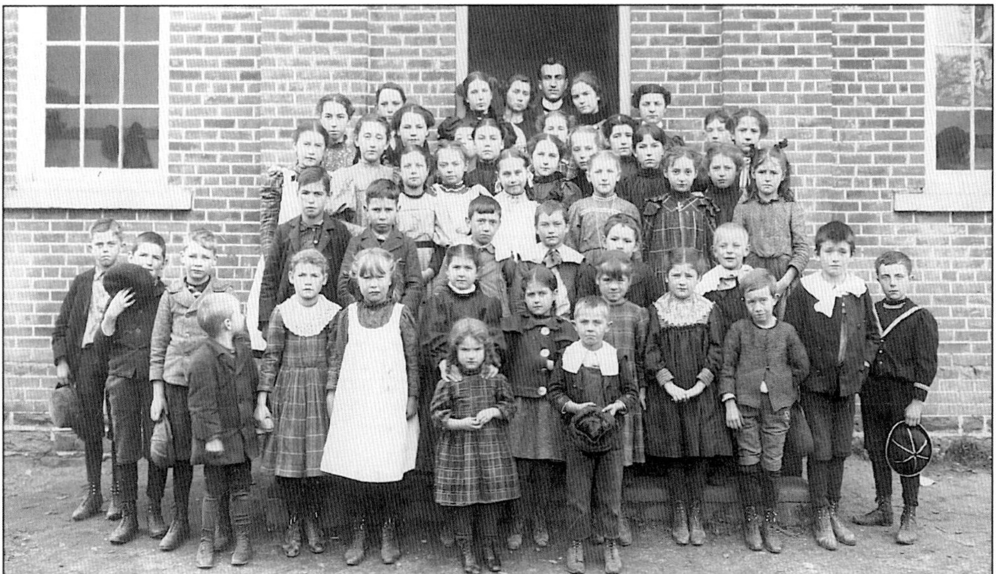

PARMA NO. 3 STUDENTS. The following are names of students at Parma No. 3 District School, in no particular order: Eva A. Houghtlin, Raymond Wood, Emma E. Peck, Lena A. Sigler, Alice T. McCue, Florence Breckenridge, J. Fosmire, Fannie A. Houghtlin, Alice I. Carney, Ira C. Lankton, Hattie E. Lankton, Myra L. Cox, Mabel F. Wheeler, Bertha M. Peck, Mary Duffey, Ella E. Wood, Frank R. Wilder, Julia T. Carney, Will Hewitt, Florence J. Smith, Gladys B. Collins, Ethel Whitney, Alice Croft, Ida M. Baldwin, Catherine A. Carney, Julia Duffey, Harry Peck, Boyd Fosmire, Will Wood, Charles Croft, John Wilder, Frank Ring, Glenn F. Corley, John Duffey, Grover Tracy, George Hewitt, Maurice Hewitt, Almira Cork, Adella Smith, Etta Smith, Clara Hewitt, Mabel Carney, Helen Wood, and Guy Corley.

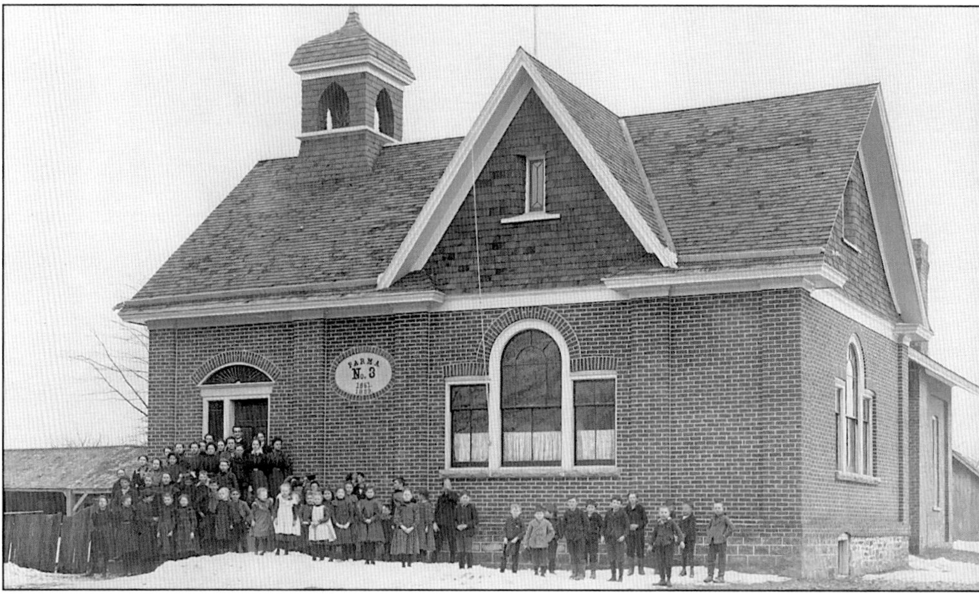

TWO-ROOM SCHOOL. A $2,500 brick addition to its north side in 1899 converted Parma No. 3 District School into a two-room school. By then, it had 65 pupils. Note the horse sheds to the left of the school. The building was used for instruction until 1953, when it was closed and its pupils were sent to Spencerport. The Parma Baptist Church purchased the building for $1 on December 1, 1953. It was converted into a recreation center.

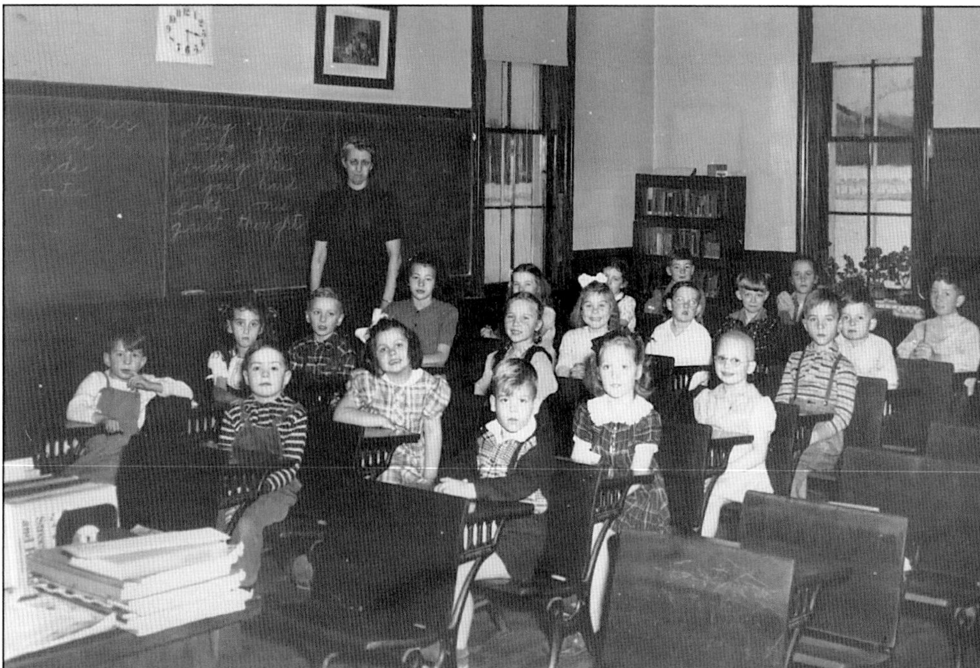

SCHOOL INTERIOR. This photograph shows a classroom at Parma No. 3 District School. When Mr. Hockbruckner fell while repairing the school bell in 1938, the town paid $14 to cover his hospital and doctor's expenses. However, when two schoolteachers shocked district residents by marrying, the wife was forced to resign so as "not to set a bad example for the students."

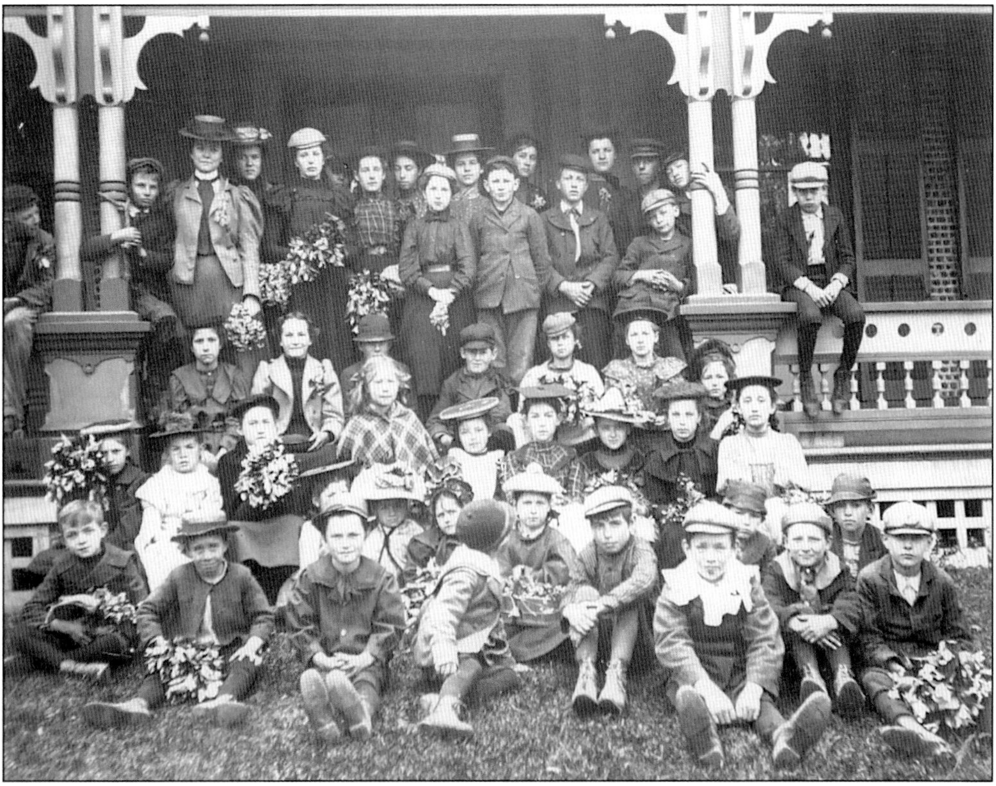

ARBOR DAY. Posing in 1889 at the Eastlake Victorian porch of Tracy's cobblestone home are students of Parma No. 3 School District. On this Arbor Day field trip, the class visited Tracy's nearby woods and picked wildflowers. In those days, people wore their best clothes into the woods—one girl here even wore a shawl. The ornate porch has long since been removed and Tracy's majestic Greek Revival cobblestone manor is now owned by the Slavic Pentecostal Church, a congregation of immigrant Russian Christians.

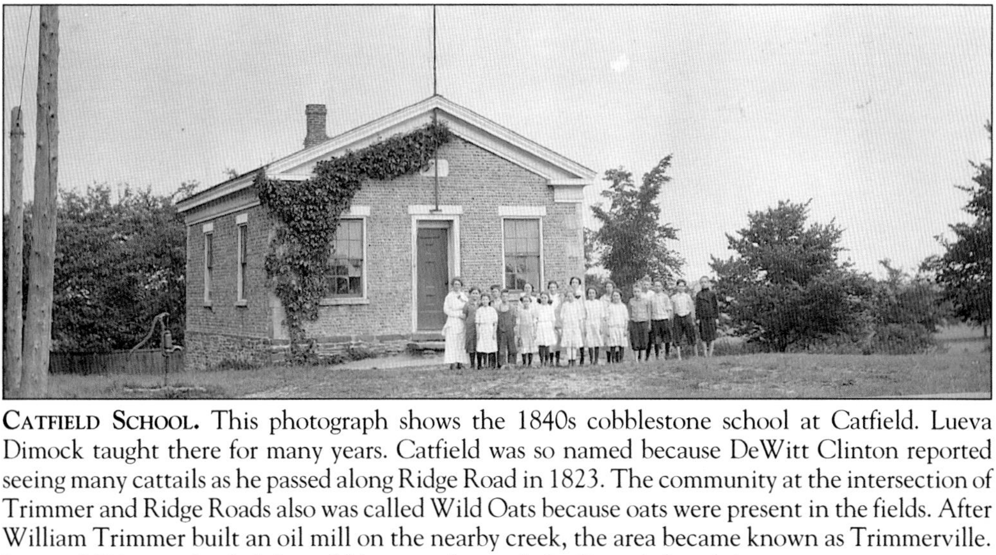

CATFIELD SCHOOL. This photograph shows the 1840s cobblestone school at Catfield. Lueva Dimock taught there for many years. Catfield was so named because DeWitt Clinton reported seeing many cattails as he passed along Ridge Road in 1823. The community at the intersection of Trimmer and Ridge Roads also was called Wild Oats because oats were present in the fields. After William Trimmer built an oil mill on the nearby creek, the area became known as Trimmerville. Leonard Trimmer hauled the cobblestones from a Lake Ontario beach by ox cart.

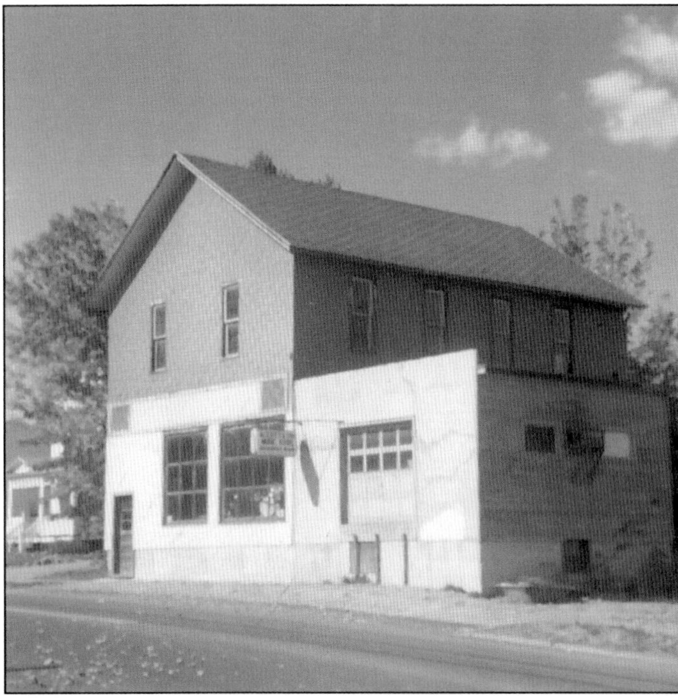

DUNHAM'S CORNERS SCHOOL. This two-room grade school, Dunham's Corners District No. 4 at the intersection of Henry Street and West Avenue, was purchased by the village of Hilton and moved to its present location on East Avenue, where it became a village hall, jail, fire hall, and meeting place. In the upstairs meeting room, plays were held, the Parma Grange met, and St. Paul's Lutheran Church was organized. Later, the building housed business firms, including Harmer's appliance store, frozen food lockers, and Ciciohotti's music store.

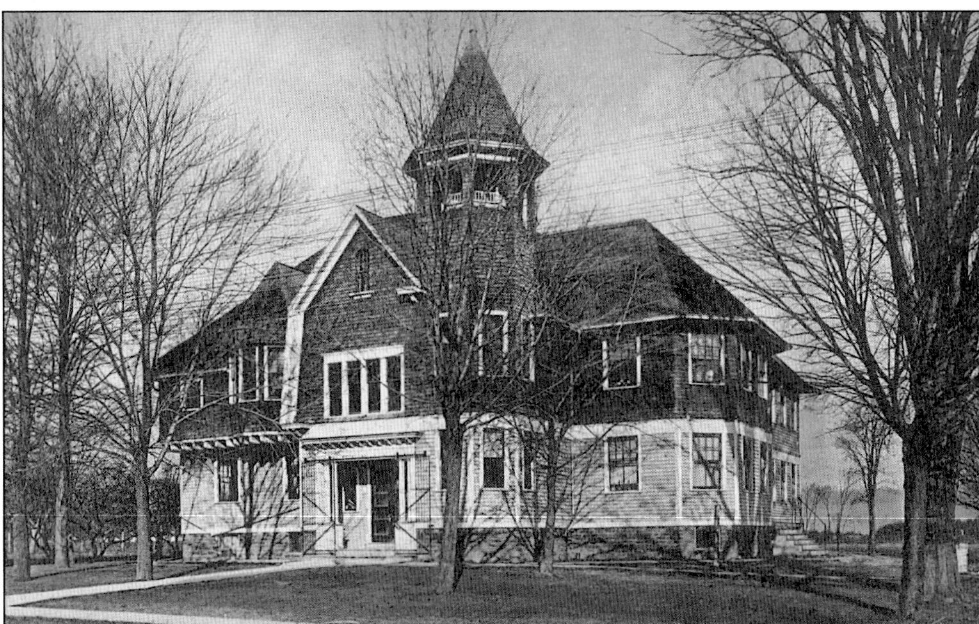

OLD HIGH SCHOOL. The 1892 high school was near the present site of the Centennial Gazebo. After a new high school was built in 1930, the building was more or less recycled. Myron Roberts purchased the old high school and Denny Wright helped him dismantle it. Ward Cox purchased many salvaged parts from Roberts, reusing them to build a restaurant and apartment house at 1217 Hilton-Parma Road. Hilton Methodist Church built a new kitchen on its parsonage from other lumber salvaged from the school. Cox later added that parsonage kitchen to a house he built in the 1940s behind his gas station at 1215 Hilton-Parma Road.

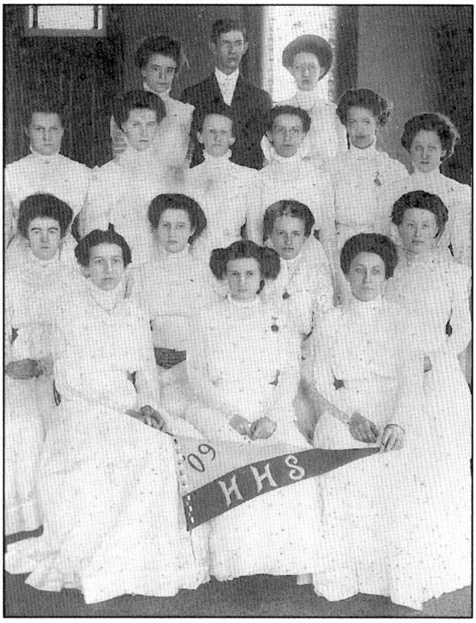

Hilton High Class of 1909. Alumni records list members of the Hilton High School Class of 1909 as follows: Ruth Archer, Ethel Bennett Horrex, Fred Buell, Mabel Clapper Wayne, Mildred Cooper Klock, Mabel Corbin, Rose Curtis DuColon, Mabel Garrison Corbin, Harry Emerson, James Hawes, Ruby Hubble, Mae Mills, Ruby Odell Stevens, Alice Northrup, Gladys Tenny Wayne, Ada Wood, and Fay Wright. Dresses similar to those worn in the photograph may be seen at the Parma Meetinghouse Museum. They were called handkerchief gowns because of their lace trimmings.

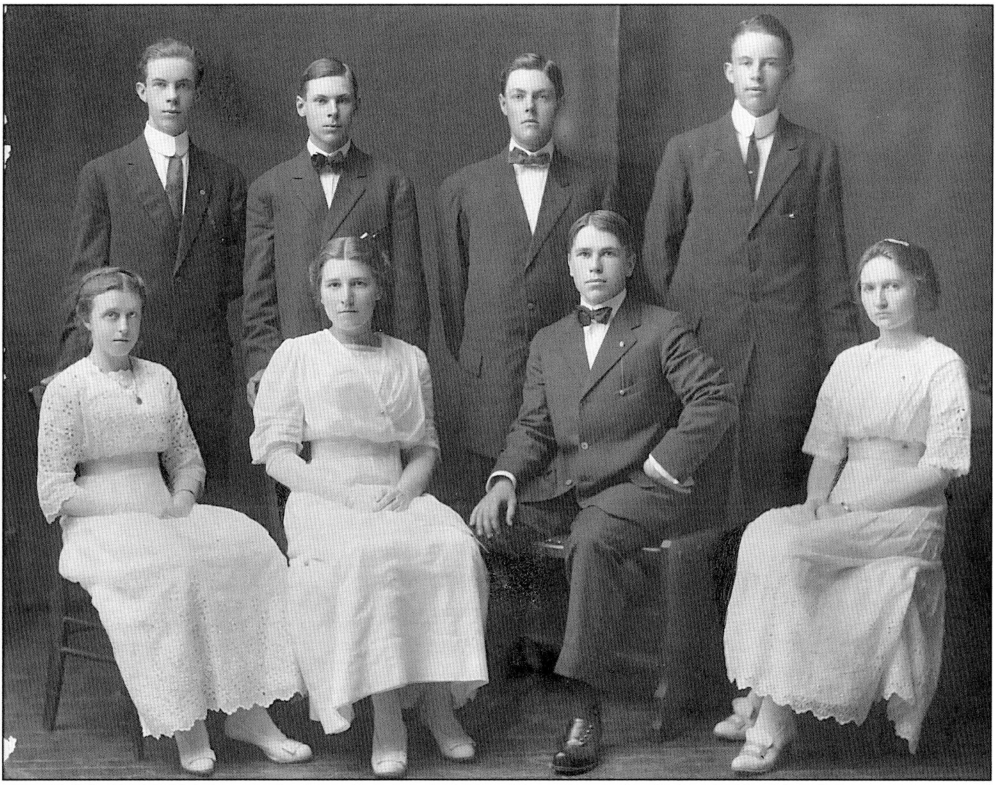

Class of 1912. Nellie Hunt Martin contributed this cherished picture of her 1912 graduating class to the Parma town historian for preservation. She identified the following girls: Francelia Holden (left), Nellie Hunt Martin (middle), and Ora Snook (right end). Alumni records listed class members as Colonel Brown, Theresa Connell, Ora Frisbee, Elton Holden, Nellie Hunt Martin, Dr. Floyd Lear, John Magee, Harry McCarty, James Pease, James Snook, and Francelia Taber Holden. Apparently, by then, young ladies were allowed to show their ankles.

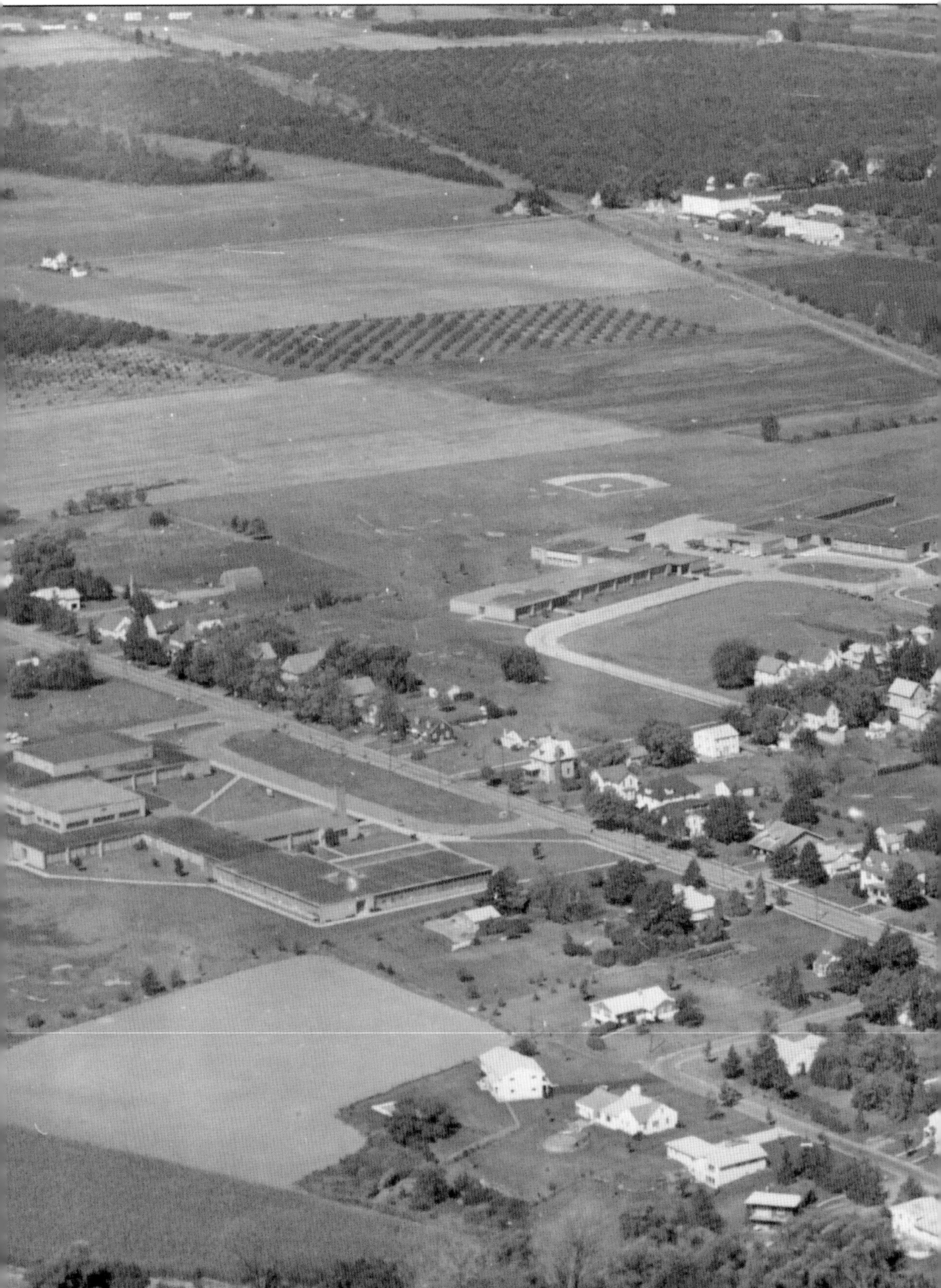

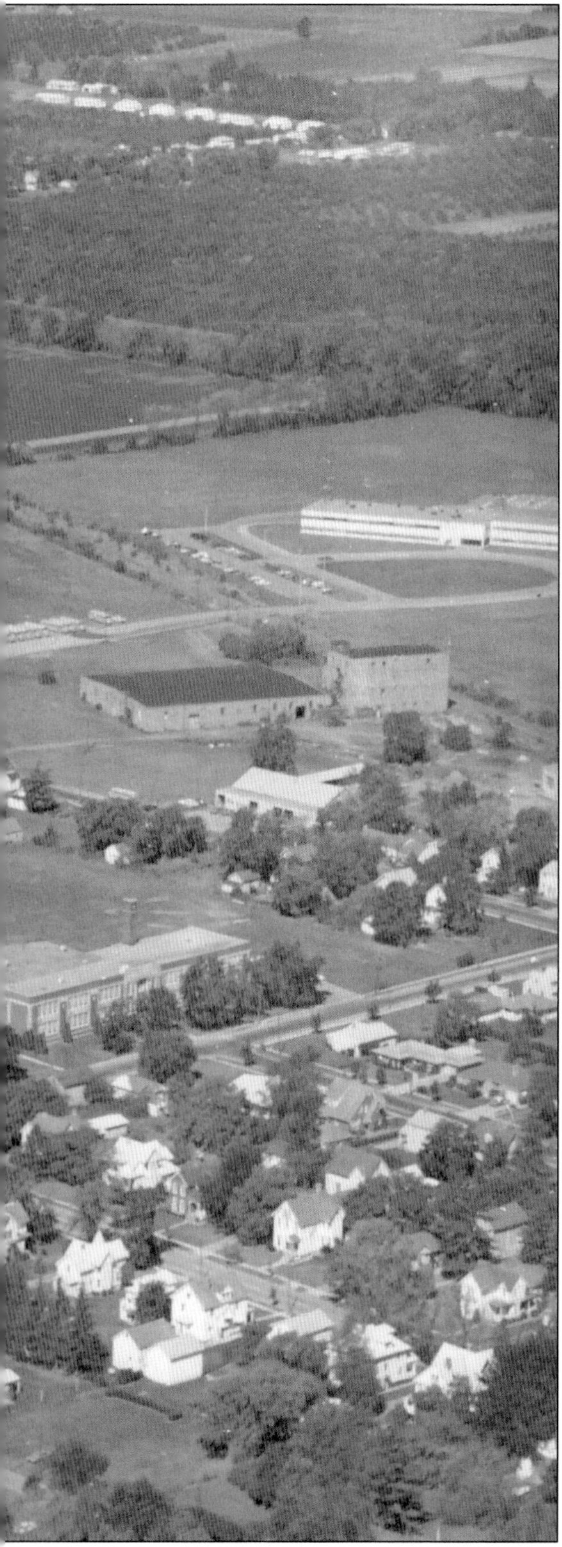

AERIAL VIEW OF HILTON. A 1960s aerial view of Hilton shows the sprawling educational facilities of its centralized system. One school is named after school board member Merton Williams. Another's name honors administrator Hazel Jenkins. The name of Jonathan Underwood memorializes an early teacher. John Douglas Klock, an esteemed school board president, was named a distinguished Hilton graduate in 1999. After centralization of schools in Parma, Hamlin, and Greece in 1949, the enrollment became one of the largest in Monroe County. Today, there are more than 4,600 pupils. Students living south of Peck Road are bused to Spencerport Central School, and a few living in the southwest corner of the town are in the Brockport Central School District.

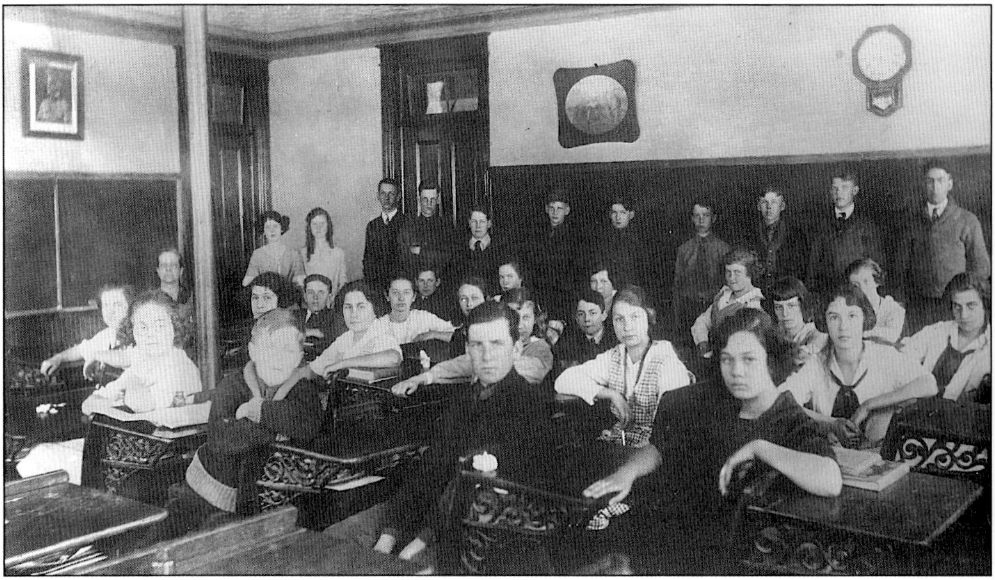

District No. 4 Class. In this District No. 4 School classroom, Ruth Blair Johnson is sitting in the second row and her sister, Inez Blair Cox, is in front of her. A third sister, Neva Blair Wright, was the mother of George Wright, recently retired head principal of Churchville-Chili Central Schools. Sister-in-law Avis Vanderbeck Blair later became a District No. 4 teacher, and was well known for her strict insistence that underachieving pupils should not be promoted. Gen. John Pershing's picture indicates that this photograph dates from the World War I era.

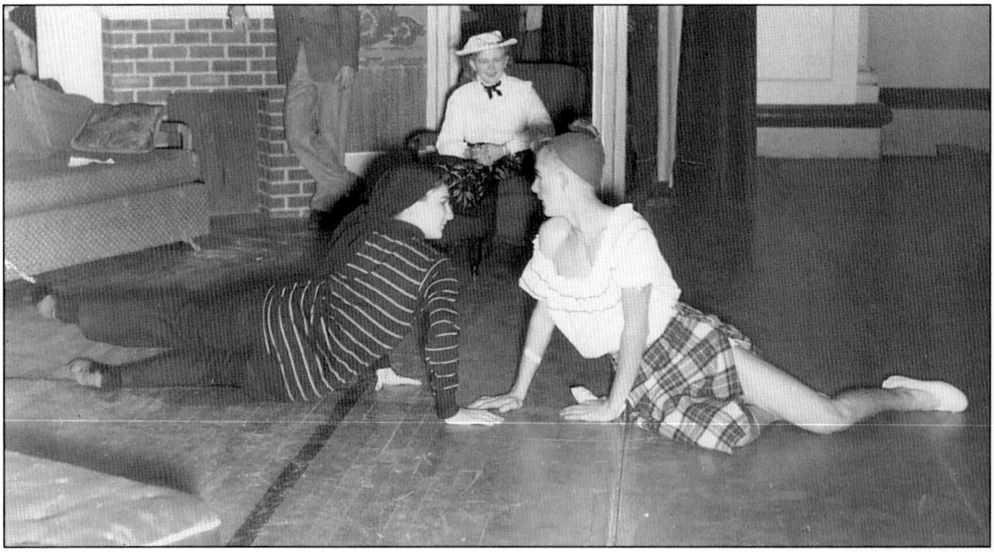

Class Play. The Class of 1949 was the last class to graduate from Hilton High School; subsequent graduations were from Hilton Central School. Later students had the advantage of musical instruction by Fred Thompson and other conductors. John L. Cieslinski encouraged adult thespians at Flour Town Theater performances. Here, in a student performance, Patty Lloyd and class president Ed Priest recreate an uproarious French Apache Dance during the senior play in 1949. Class valedictorian Shirley Cox (seated) and salutatorian Gilbert Langswager look on. One year later classmate James Pickworth Jr. was killed in Korea.

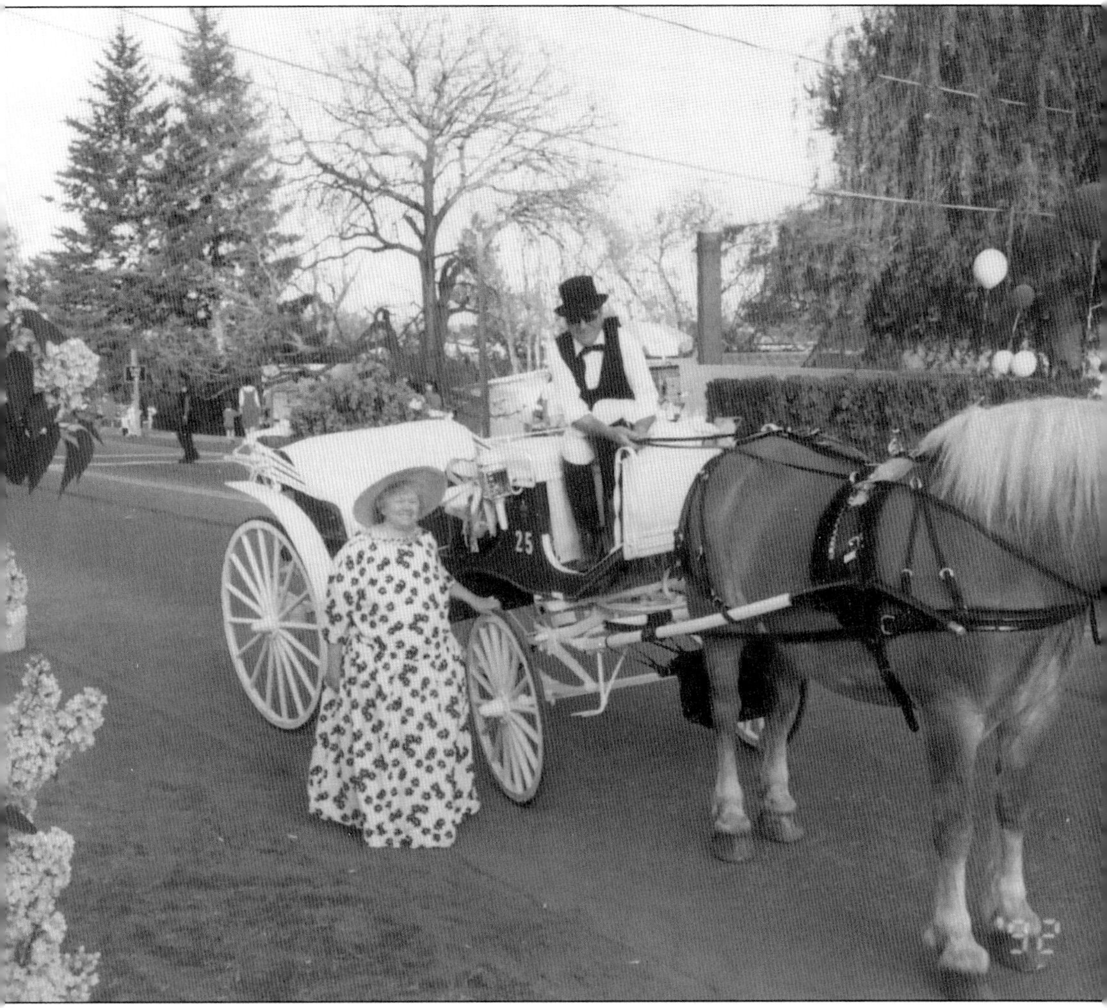

LILAC FESTIVAL. Rides through Highland Park in McCracken's wagons and Victorian carriages have been a popular feature of Rochester's annual Lilac Festival. "Rochester," the fragrantly scented white lilac at the left, was propagated by Alvan Grant, a parks director. Shown here with Lauren McCracken is Shirley Cox Husted, a historical guide for the festival. She was a charter inductee of Hilton Central's 1999 Hall of Fame. Fellow classmates Lauren McCracken and John Jennejahn Jr. were also honored as distinguished graduates. Hilton Central's school colors officially remain crimson red and white, although in the 1940s the red used was a maroon color, unlike today's bright red hue. Spencerport's school colors are blue and gold, and Parma's town colors are azure blue and wheat gold. Hilton chose gold and black for their official colors. And the town flower is—what else, the appleblossom. Hilton's Alma Mater also remains unchanged, but is seldom sung.

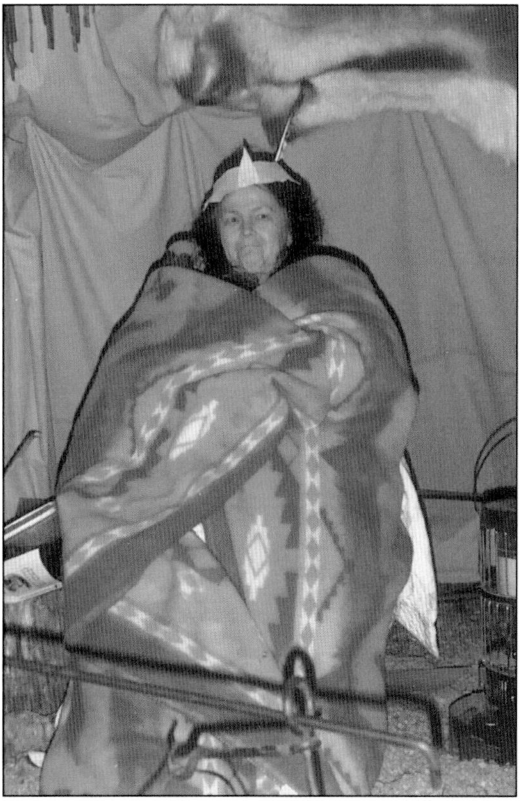

PRINCESS TALKING FEATHER. Historian Shirley Husted assumes the identity of Princess Talking Feather every October to relate Native-American legends at McCracken Farms. Students from five counties are bused to the farm to learn about their agricultural heritage and to harvest a pumpkin at the Great Pumpkin Patch. Lois McCracken demonstrates the forgotten task of pounding grain into flour by hand and Lauren McCracken explains interesting things about the animals in his farm zoo.

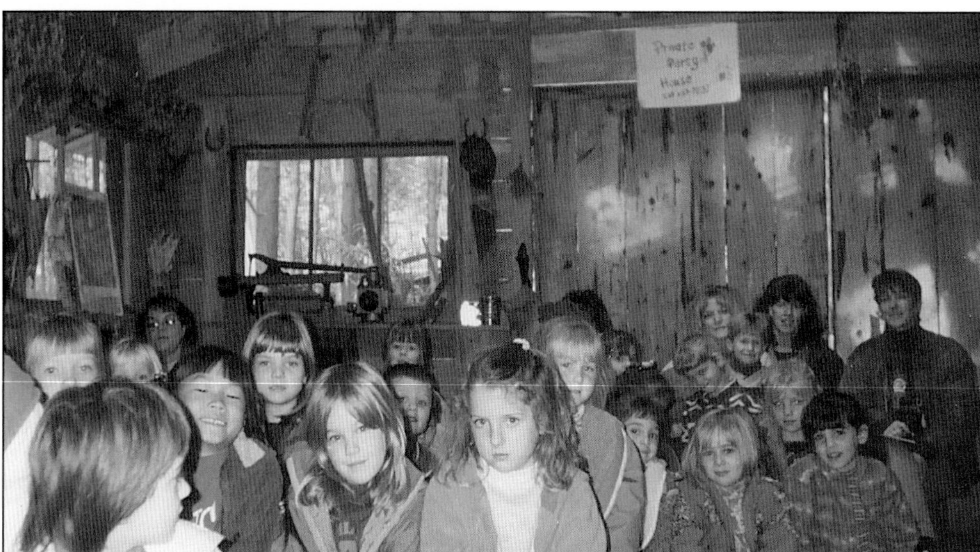

LISTENING. Burritt Road day-care children listen to Princess Talking Feather's tales, which convey a moral lesson and an appreciation for Native-American culture. An authentic Sioux tipi, maple sugar house, blacksmith shop, straw mazes, and a covered bridge are among the unusual structures in the rustic woodland village in McCrackens' Woods in Sweden, where tall sugar maples turn golden yellow in October.

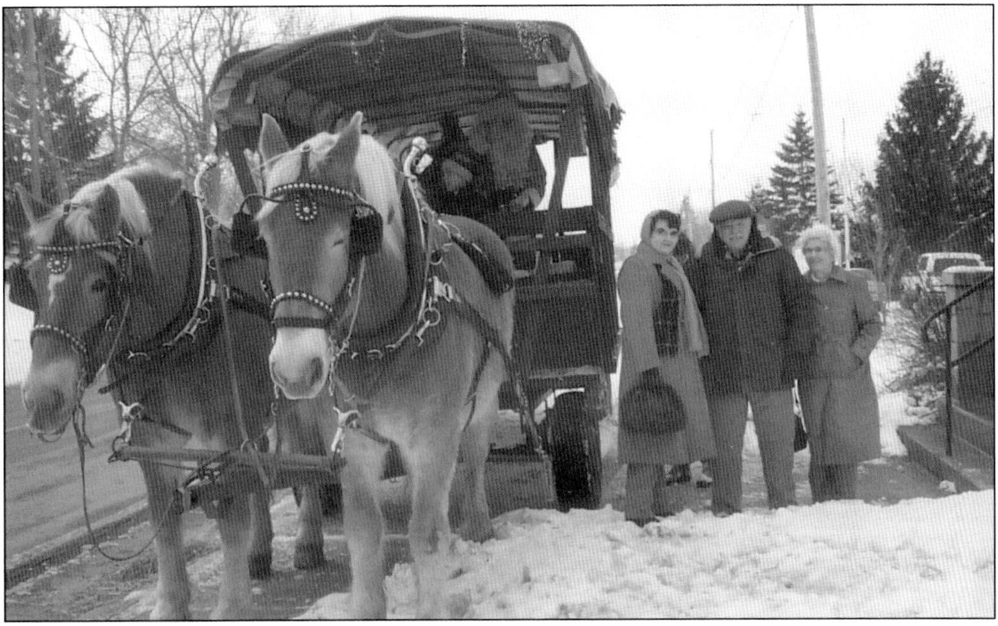

WAGON PASSENGERS. Vernon Tyner, Class of 1934, and his wife, Margaret, often come from Avoca to attend Parma Museum programs and to enjoy wagon rides drawn by McCracken's blonde Belgian horses, Dixie and Danny. With her parents is Priscilla Tyner Beeman, Class of 1955. The family cherishes fond memories of their 1830s home nearby, once the Methodist parsonage. Family member David Tyner (not pictured) of Parma Center became a graduate of the U.S. Military Academy at West Point.

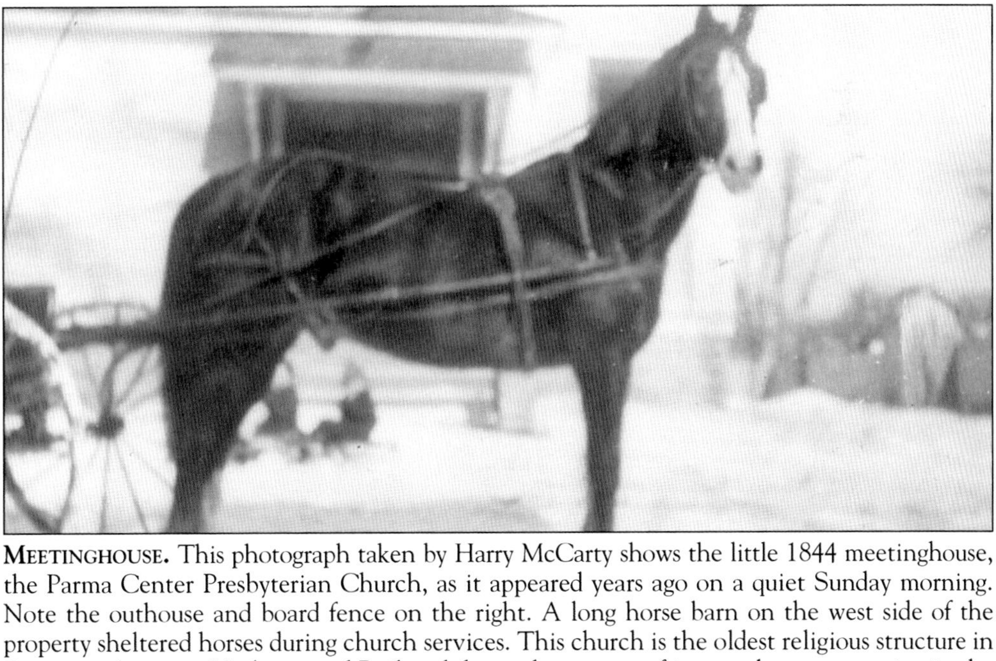

MEETINGHOUSE. This photograph taken by Harry McCarty shows the little 1844 meetinghouse, the Parma Center Presbyterian Church, as it appeared years ago on a quiet Sunday morning. Note the outhouse and board fence on the right. A long horse barn on the west side of the property sheltered horses during church services. This church is the oldest religious structure in Parma, with ties to Underground Railroad days, when many of its members were active in the Parma Antislavery Society. Sen. John Patterson, one of its 13 founders, sometimes advised Pres. Abraham Lincoln.

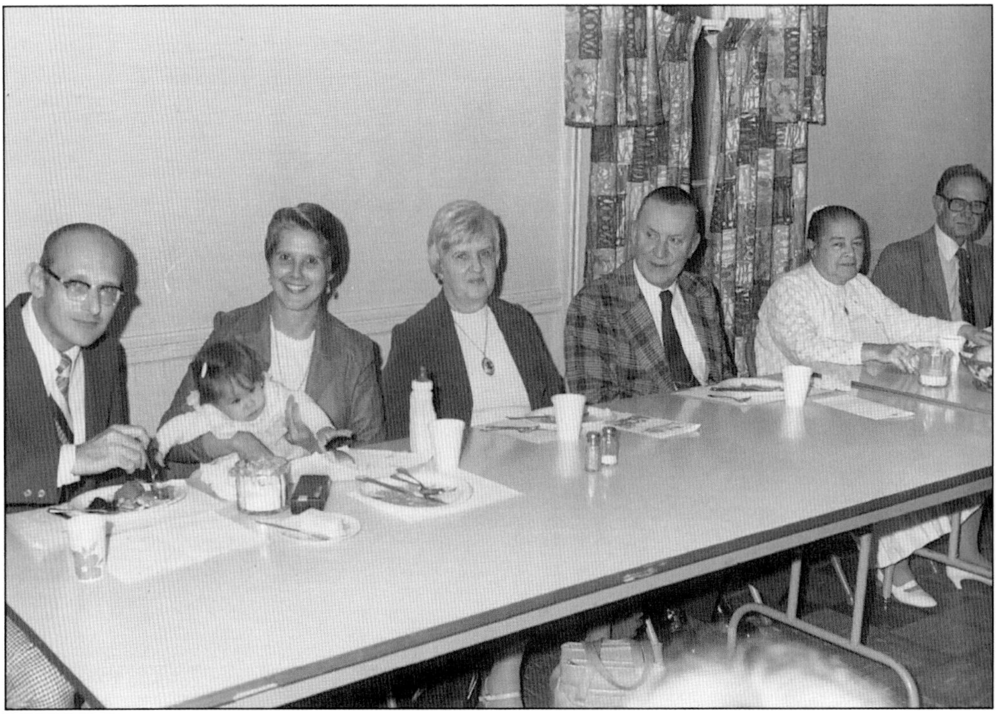

Parma Pastors. Attending the 150th anniversary celebration of Parma Baptist Church in 1982 were, from left to right, Rev. Floyd Wilder, Ruth Wilder, Mildred Bishop, Rev. George Bishop, Ruth Lloyd, and Rev. I. Vincent Lloyd. Because of its small congregation, Parma Center Presbyterian Church often had guest pastors from Parma-Greece Christian, Hilton Methodist, Bethany Presbyterian, Colgate-Rochester Divinity School, and Parma Baptist Church. One of them, Rev. George Bishop, became an air force chaplain.

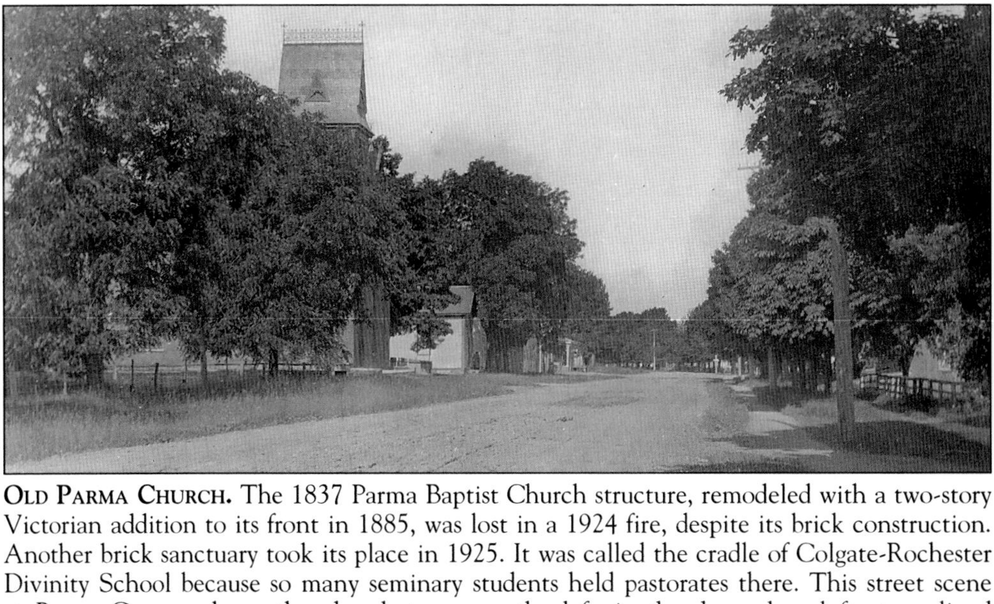

Old Parma Church. The 1837 Parma Baptist Church structure, remodeled with a two-story Victorian addition to its front in 1885, was lost in a 1924 fire, despite its brick construction. Another brick sanctuary took its place in 1925. It was called the cradle of Colgate-Rochester Divinity School because so many seminary students held pastorates there. This street scene at Parma Corners shows the church tower on the left, in the days when lofty trees lined the roadside.

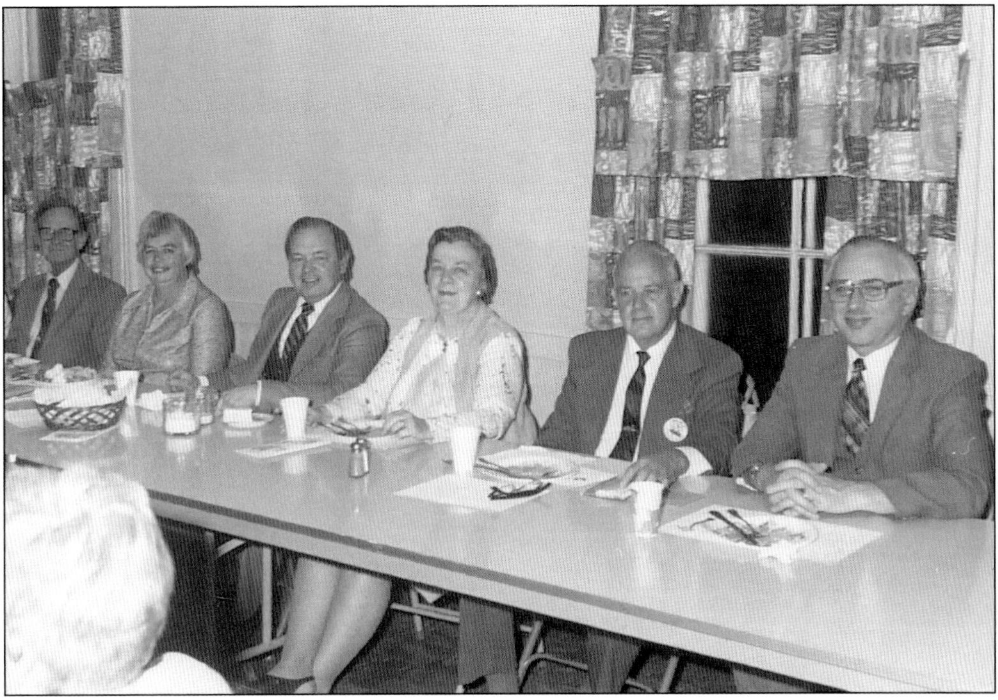

Baptist Banquet. Pastors and wives attending the 150th anniversary banquet are, from left to right, Rev. I. Vincent Lloyd, Shirley Dancer, Rev. Leroy Dancer; Kay Dickson, Rev. Albert Dickson, and Dr. Ronald Vallet. The Parma-Greece United Church of Christ had the area's first female pastor; the second one came to Parma Baptist Church.

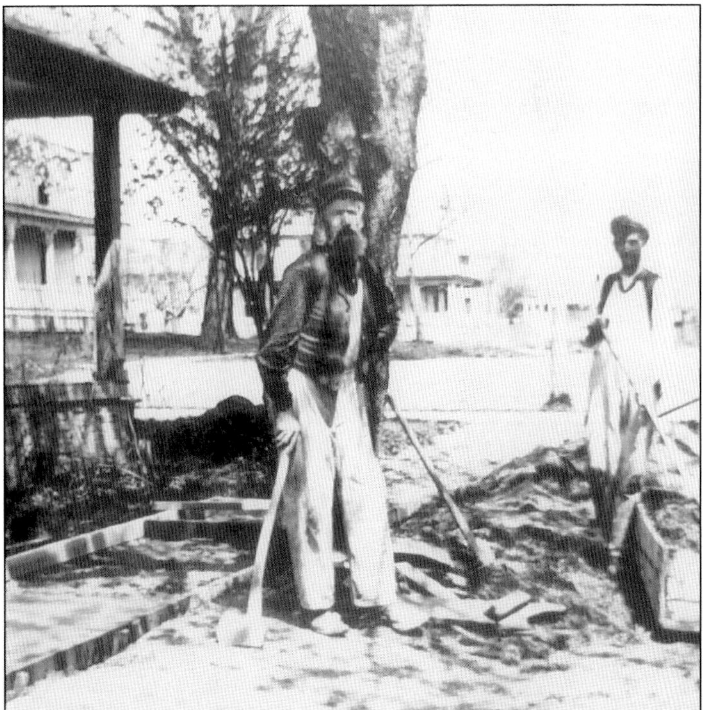

Parsonage. This photograph was taken looking north down Lake Avenue toward the Joseph Ingham house, later the Hilton Baptist Church's parsonage. Mason contractor Andrew Albiker (left) busily installs sidewalks. Hugging the railroad tracks at the right was the huge Collamer-Johnson-Rosenbaum warehouse, just north of the Baptist church, where fruit, beans, cabbages, and rags were stored. The Dunham homestead was then located on the present site of Wilson Farms.

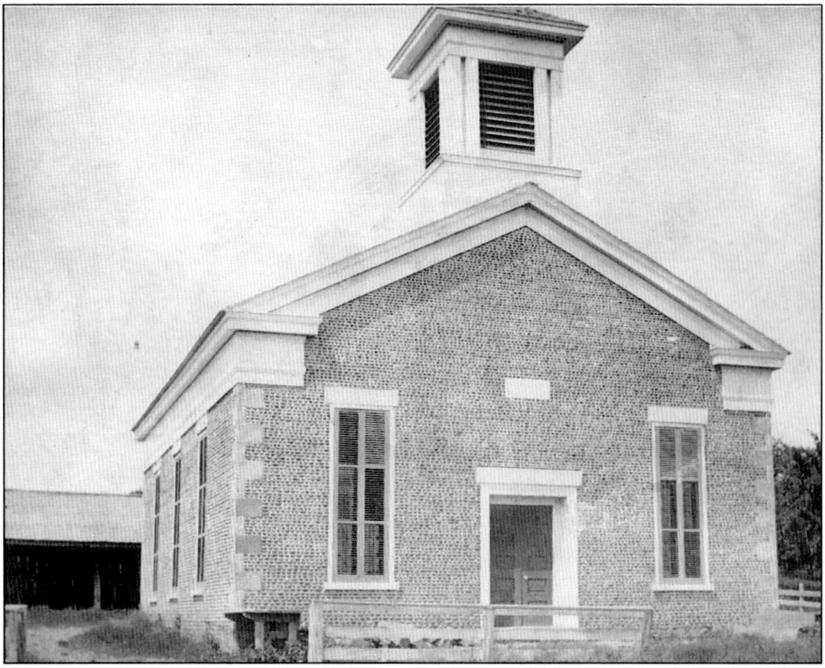

Cobblestone Church. The North Parma Methodist Church at Bartlett's Shop was allowed to crumble away after attendance became so small that a pastor said he went to the church "to preach to the four walls." The church was packed beyond capacity during Civil War days, when recruitment for the Union army was held here. The Vonds, Parma's first black family, attended this church until it united with the Methodist congregation at Hilton. Later, the Vonds attended the Baptist church where "Auntie" Vond's testimonials brought tears to many eyes.

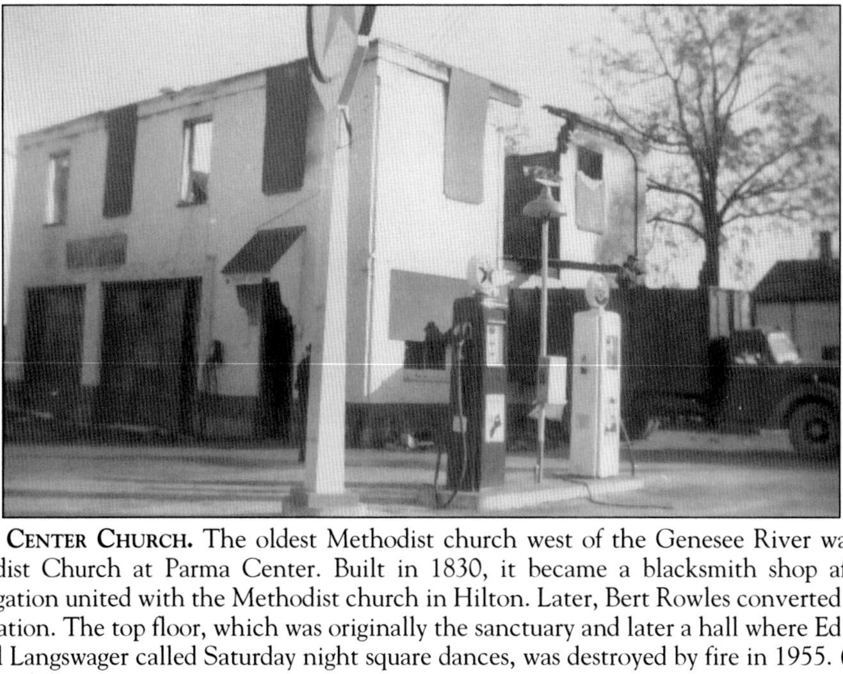

Parma Center Church. The oldest Methodist church west of the Genesee River was First Methodist Church at Parma Center. Built in 1830, it became a blacksmith shop after its congregation united with the Methodist church in Hilton. Later, Bert Rowles converted it into a gas station. The top floor, which was originally the sanctuary and later a hall where Ed Marks and Gil Langswager called Saturday night square dances, was destroyed by fire in 1955. (Tyner photograph.)

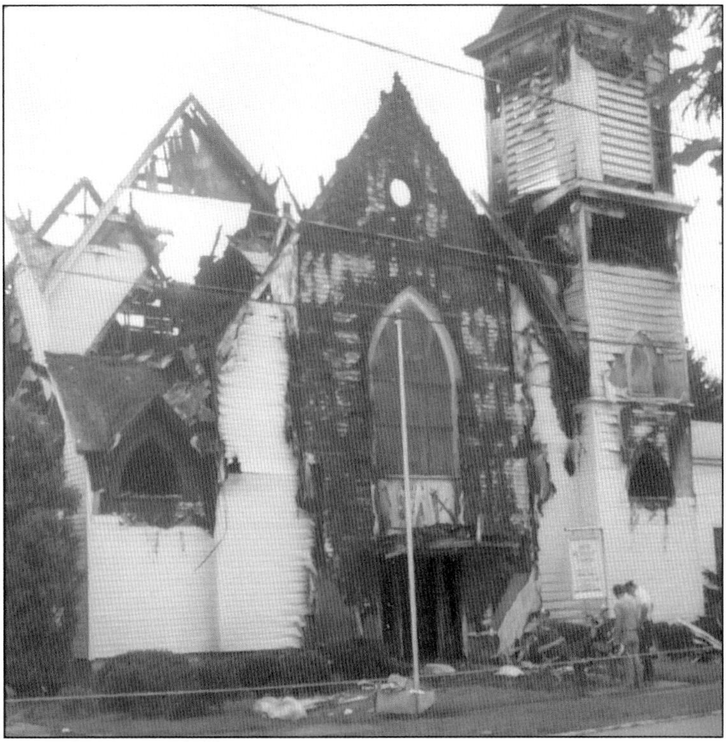

Church Fire. Fire destroyed Hilton Methodist Church in 1981. Fortunately, many of the stained-glass windows, including the beautiful center front Madonna window, were saved. The fire was set by two young men trying to conceal a theft. The pair were imprisoned but given reduced sentences because of the church's request for forgiveness. One of the pastors of this church was Rev. Raymond Draffin, a descendant of a local family.

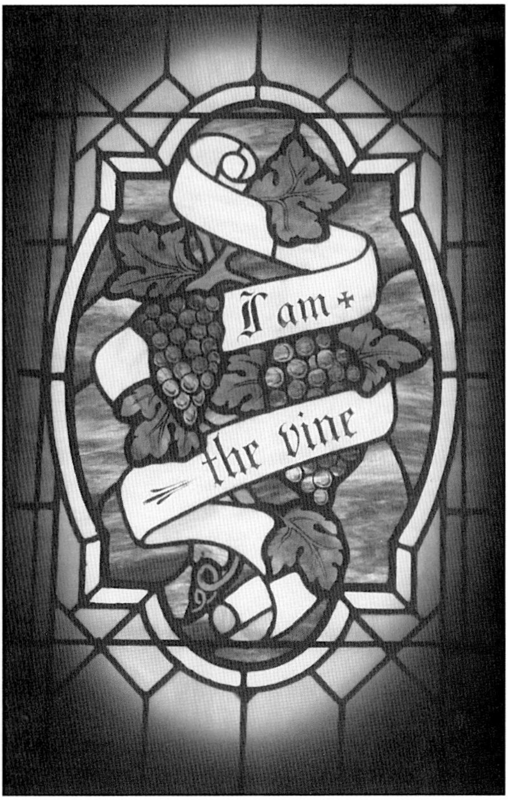

Vine Window. Denny Wright's photographs of the 1884 Methodist church's memorial windows enabled preservation of the windows in their previous colors, including this exquisite "I am the Vine" window, recalling Christ's message that he is the lifeblood of the church. Wright photographed the windows at the request of the town historian, a few years prior to the 1981 fire that destroyed the church.

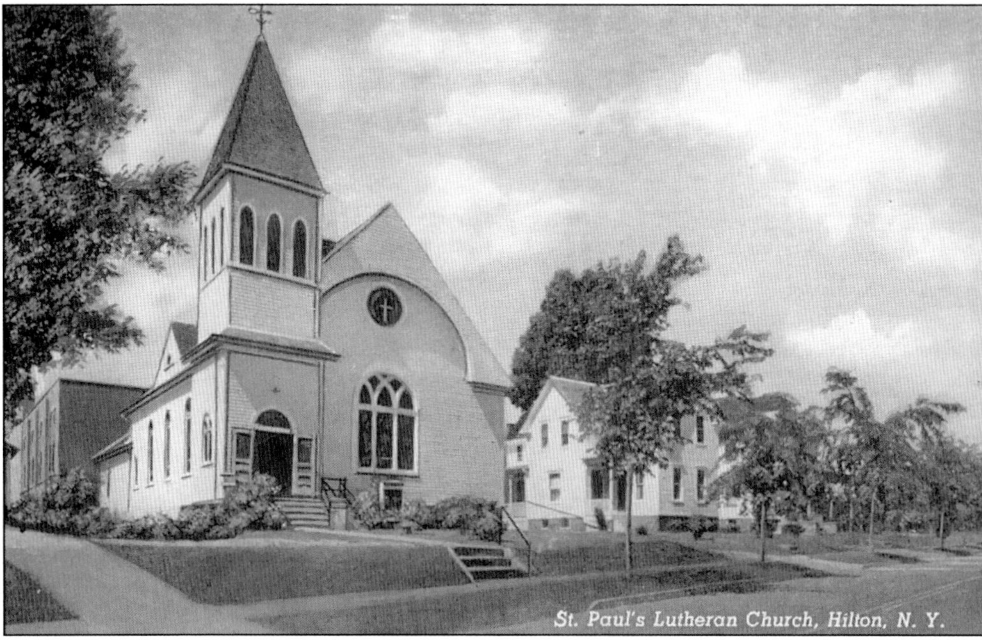

LUTHERAN CHURCH. St. Paul's Evangelical Lutheran Church was erected in 1899 to serve a German congregation. It had the community's loveliest stained-glass windows. Services were held in German for many years. Whenever a death occurred, the church bell tolled once for each year of the deceased's life on earth. Former members Donald Cairo and his wife, Marie Bauch Cairo, served in the African mission field after Reverend Cairo retired from other pastorates.

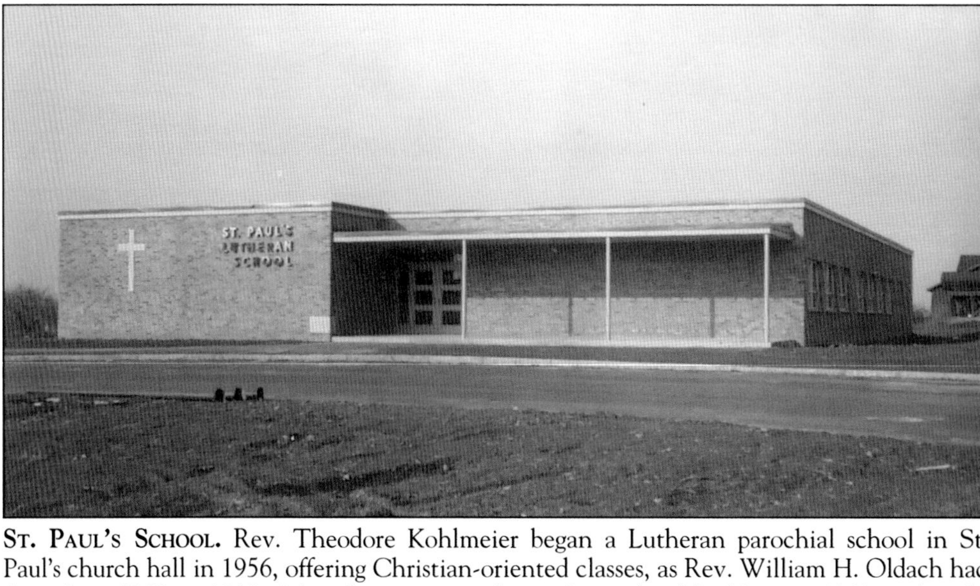

ST. PAUL'S SCHOOL. Rev. Theodore Kohlmeier began a Lutheran parochial school in St. Paul's church hall in 1956, offering Christian-oriented classes, as Rev. William H. Oldach had done from 1902 to 1918. After the erection of a modern school building in 1961, a church-owned residence was moved to Wilder Road and the beautiful sanctuary was demolished. Also demolished was the 1945 church hall, built under Rev Paul Boriack's leadership, where the school's first classes were held.

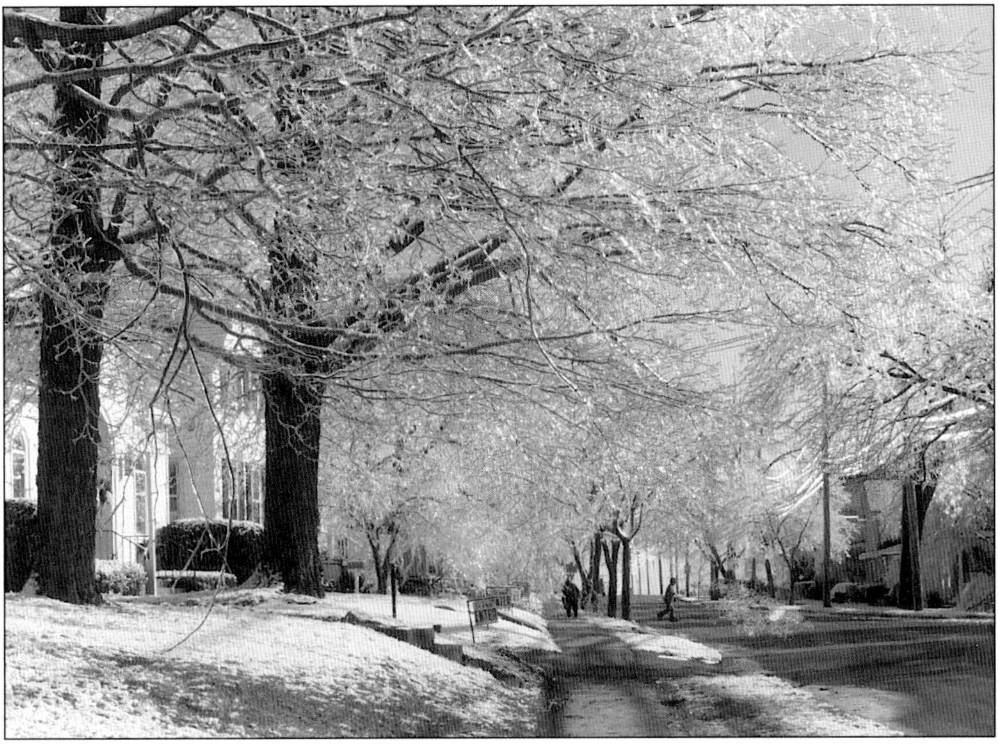

Ice Storm. Ann Kolb's photograph shows a picturesque scene along East Avenue near her home and St. Paul's Church during the 1981 ice storm. During Prohibition days, the Kolb home was the residence of Frank "Watermelon" Johnson, who is said to have smuggled bottles of liquor concealed inside watermelons from his nearby storage building. He had a wine cellar and recreation room in his basement and a private billiard room where only gentlemen were admitted: Hilton's version of a speakeasy.

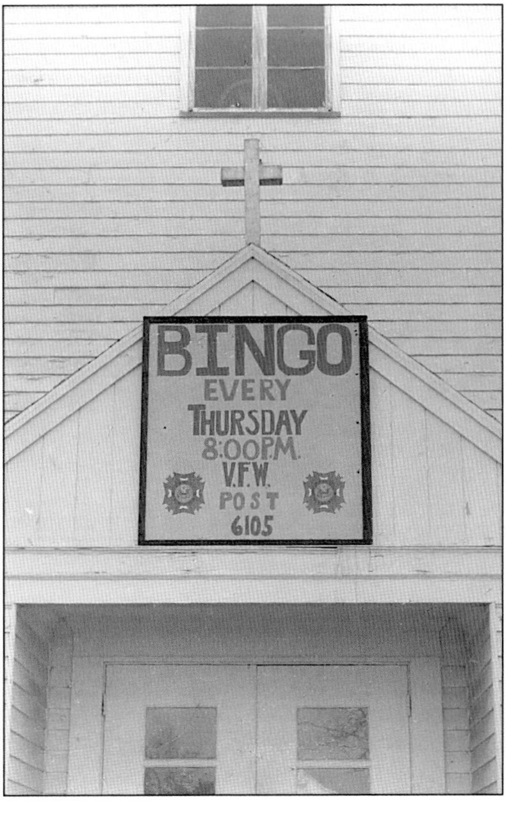

St. Leo's Church. Founded by French Canadians, old St. Leo's Church, built in 1883, has been utilized for community activities including bingo games, veterans' programs, flea markets, and dance classes. Rev. Fr. Nilus Hubble, C.P., a church member, was a marine combat chaplain for the navy during the Vietnam War. Devoutly faithful Bertha Kirchgessner attended Mass every day, greeting everyone with a smile and the happy comment, "Isn't it a lovely day?" regardless of the weather.

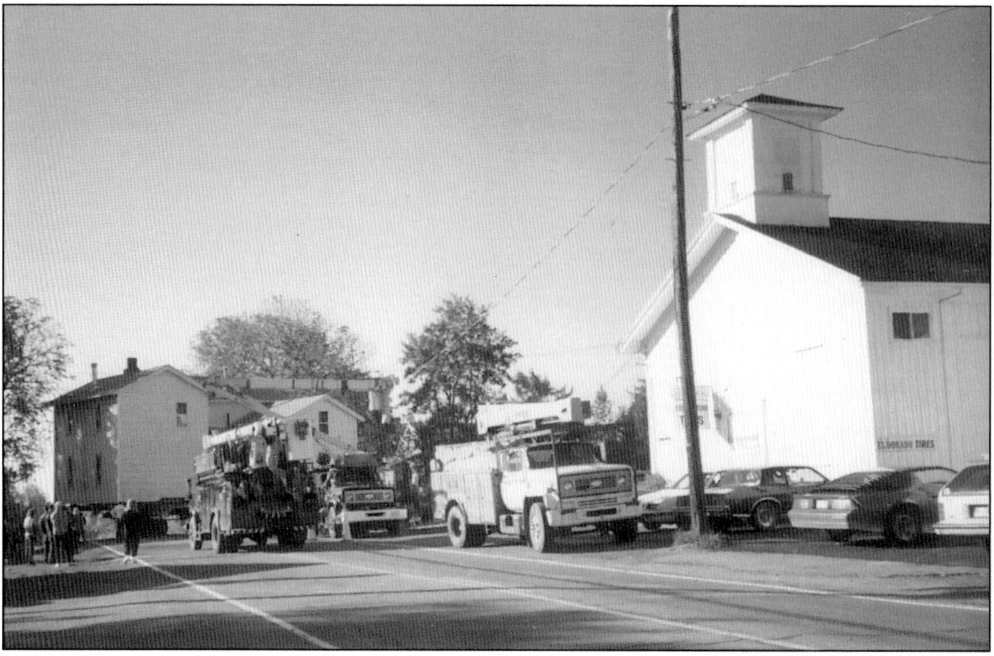

PARSONAGE ROLLS. Motorists were startled one day to see a house going down the road in front of them. Moving the parsonage of Parma Center Free Methodist Church insured its preservation as a residence, while making parking space for Dale & Wilma Zarpentine's tire shop, operating within the former church sanctuary. Some of the church windows were reinstalled in the new Free Methodist Church.

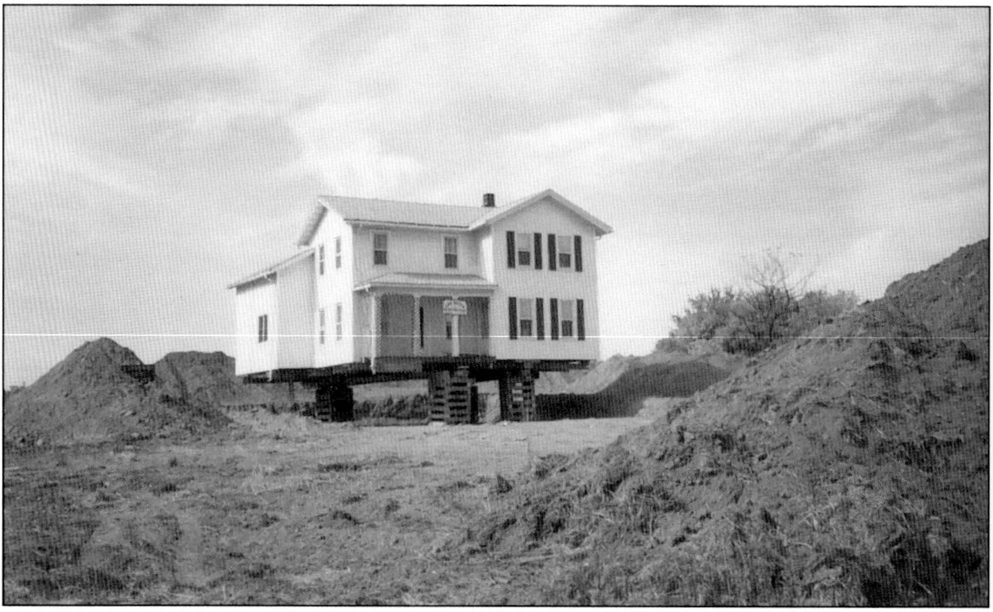

NEW LOCATION. The former Free Methodist parsonage is now located at 1253 Hilton-Parma Road.

Seven

Business and Industry

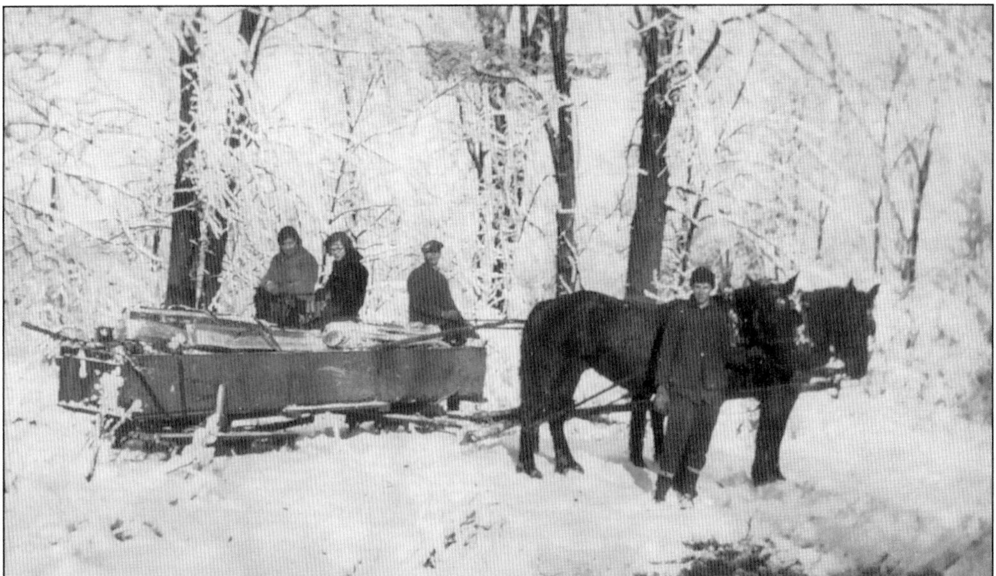

Winter Wonderland. Photographer Harry McCarty captured the enchantment of a winter morning near a snowy woods, probably on the McCarty Farm on Parma Center Road. Because a horse and bobsled had no trouble traversing the snow, tree trimming was an early spring activity, while trees were dormant. Tons of fruit were produced every harvest season and shipped out on the Hojack railroad line. In the village cannery, women patiently worked in the frigid temperatures required to preserve the apples, using heavily gloved hands to place nearly frozen apples on the trimming machines, or as peelers trimming off tiny bits of apple peel missed by the machines. The scent of applesauce perfumed the air as the fruit was processed and canned. Various brands bore labels printed at the *Hilton Record*, although the same applesauce was in every can, whatever the label.

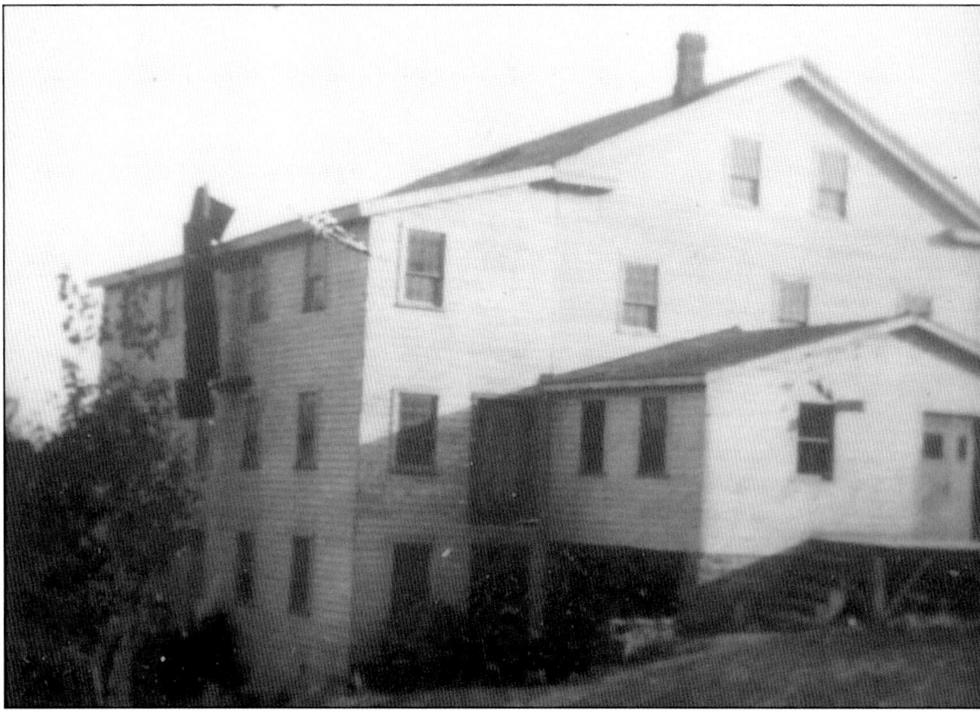

Fowler's Mill. Chauncey Fowler's gristmill on Salmon Creek beside Ridge Road was mentioned in road records in 1807. It was one of Parma's early gristmills along local streams busily grinding grain into flour and animal feed. Another mill was Whittier's on Hinkleyville Road, the successor to Rev. Jonathan Hinckley's mill—which, to the dismay of Adams Basin Presbyterians, enabled whiskey production. Genesee Valley wheat, because of its soft gluten, was not as good for baking purposes as that grown in Midwestern wheat fields.

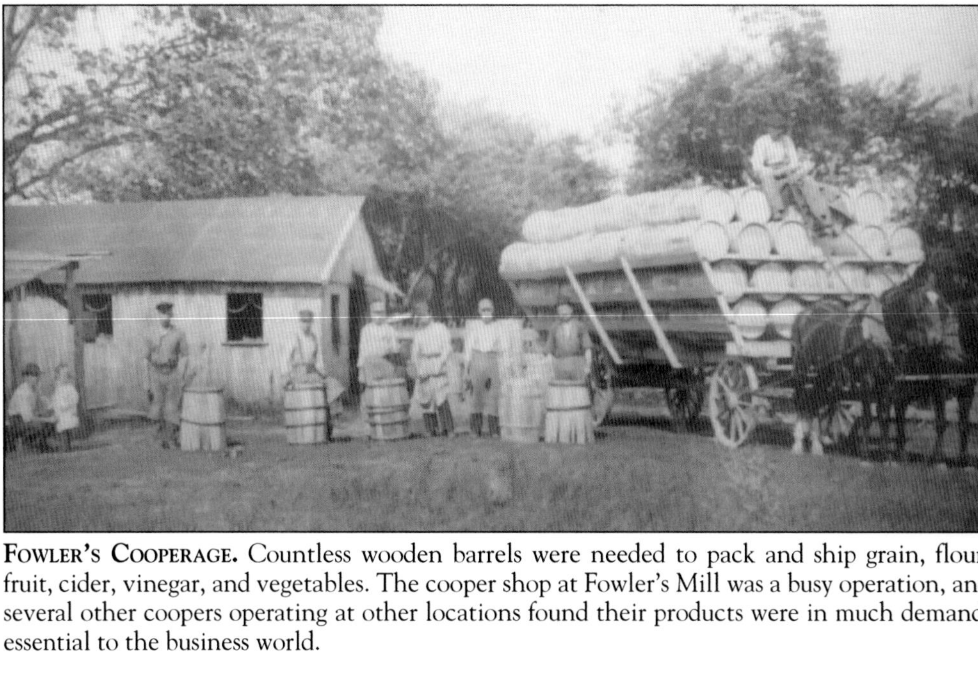

Fowler's Cooperage. Countless wooden barrels were needed to pack and ship grain, flour, fruit, cider, vinegar, and vegetables. The cooper shop at Fowler's Mill was a busy operation, and several other coopers operating at other locations found their products were in much demand, essential to the business world.

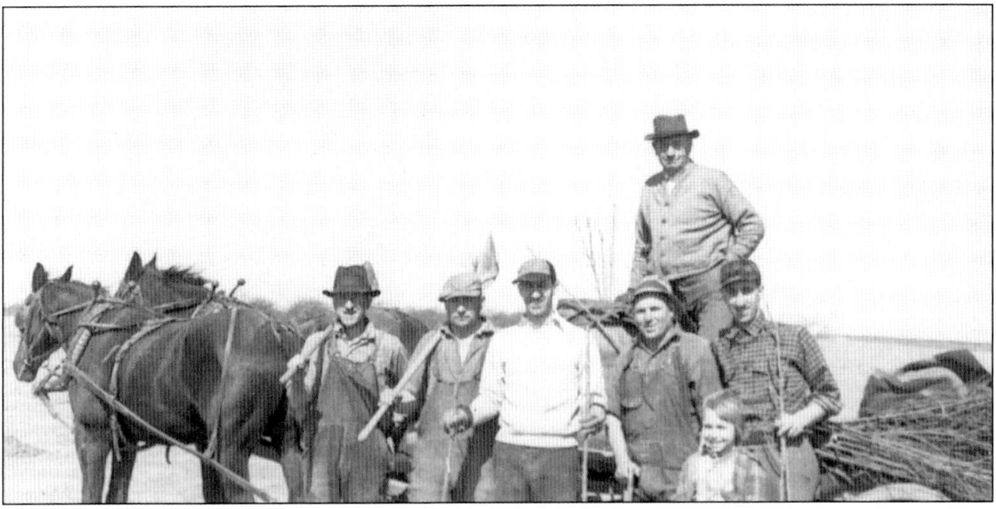

Farm Crew. A work crew planting peaches on the Hill Farm includes Otto Semmler and his daughter Doris, members of the Hill family, and hired man Zeke Heffner. By the 1950s, Parma had 291 farms, greater in both number and acreage than any other township in Monroe County. Parma was the top producer of apples and sweet cherries; the second highest producer of sour cherries, tomatoes, and cucumbers; and the third highest of potatoes, corn, turkeys, milk cows, pears, and grapes.

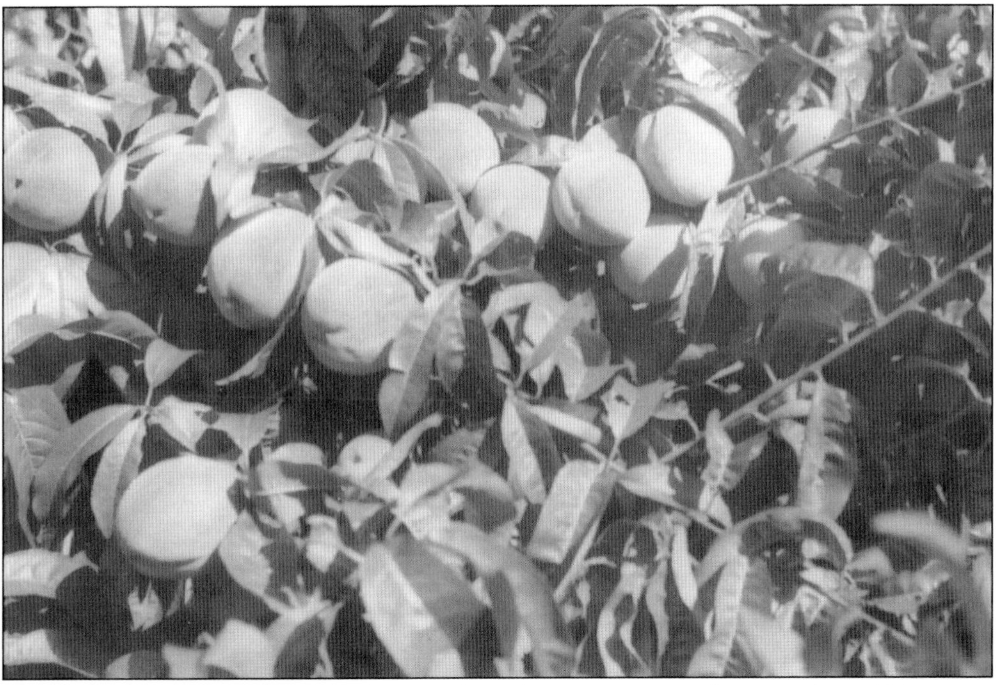

Peaches. This is a sample of the luscious fruit that once grew in Parma, where 134 growers reported that 1,938 acres were devoted to the production of apples, cherries, berries, peaches, pears, grapes, plums, and prunes in 1954. An adult baseball team was even named the Peaches in appreciation for the tons of excellent fruit once shipped out on the railroad to Canadian buyers or other markets. The State Bank of Hilton had an apple printed on the center of each check.

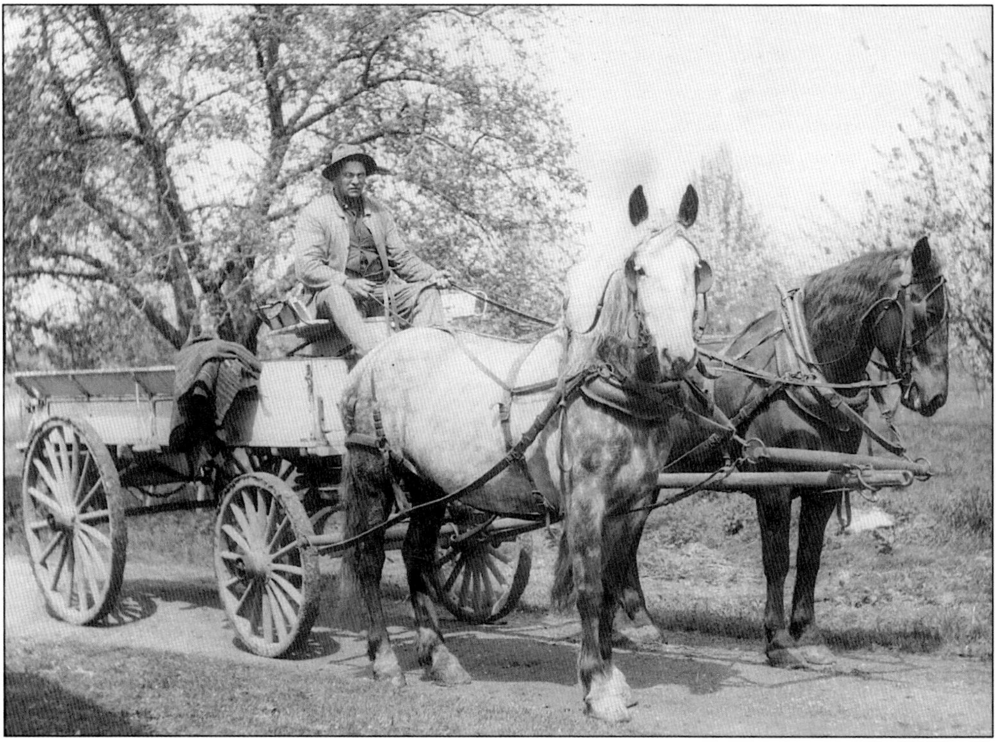

Migrant Labor. This Harry McCarty photograph shows an orchard worker, probably one of the countless African-American migrant workers who helped harvest crops here and all across the United States. Clothing and temporary housing for migrants was not attractive and sometimes barely adequate. Poor sanitation and angry fights over card games sometimes made migrant camps a dangerous place to live. Seasonal Italian workers were housed in tiny row houses beside Hilton's Peck & Pratt cannery.

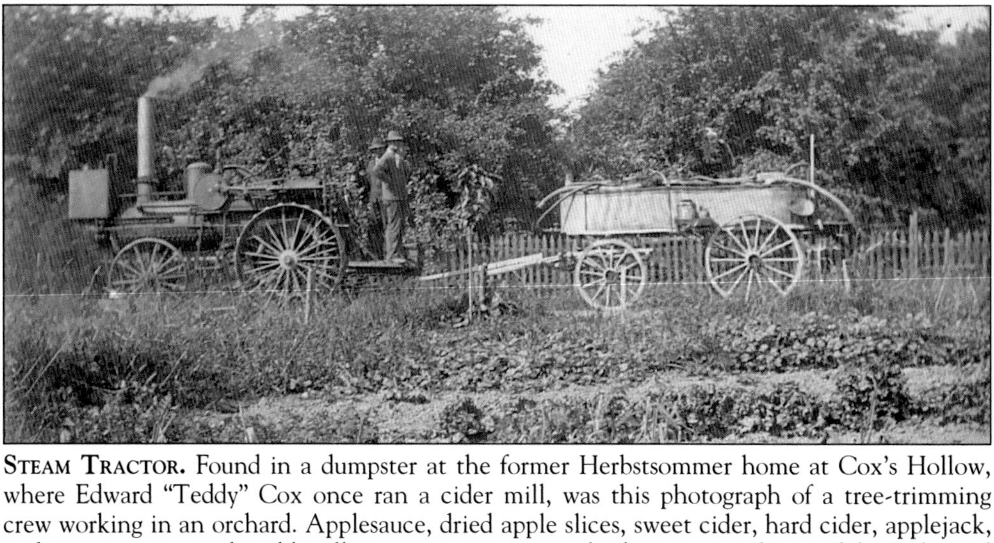

Steam Tractor. Found in a dumpster at the former Herbstsommer home at Cox's Hollow, where Edward "Teddy" Cox once ran a cider mill, was this photograph of a tree-trimming crew working in an orchard. Applesauce, dried apple slices, sweet cider, hard cider, applejack, and vinegar were produced locally, as steam tractors and other new machines of the Industrial Revolution improved production. Unfortunately, Bill Herbstsommer's son Kenneth never realized his longtime dream of living in Australia.

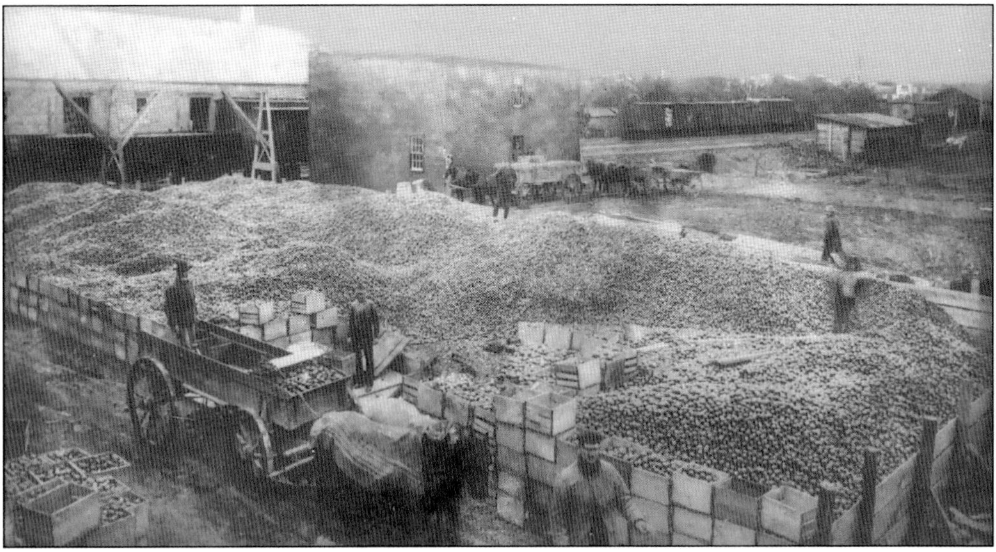

Fruit Piles. Thousands of apples are stockpiled behind the American Fruit Company at 24 Gorton Avenue in this *c.* 1906 photograph. At a number of local "dry houses," apple segments were dried by evaporating water from the fruit, first by hot air only and later with steam. Shipments were made across the nation and even to India. Joseph Heinrich donated this photograph to the town archives. The Heinrich Collision shop now occupies the site.

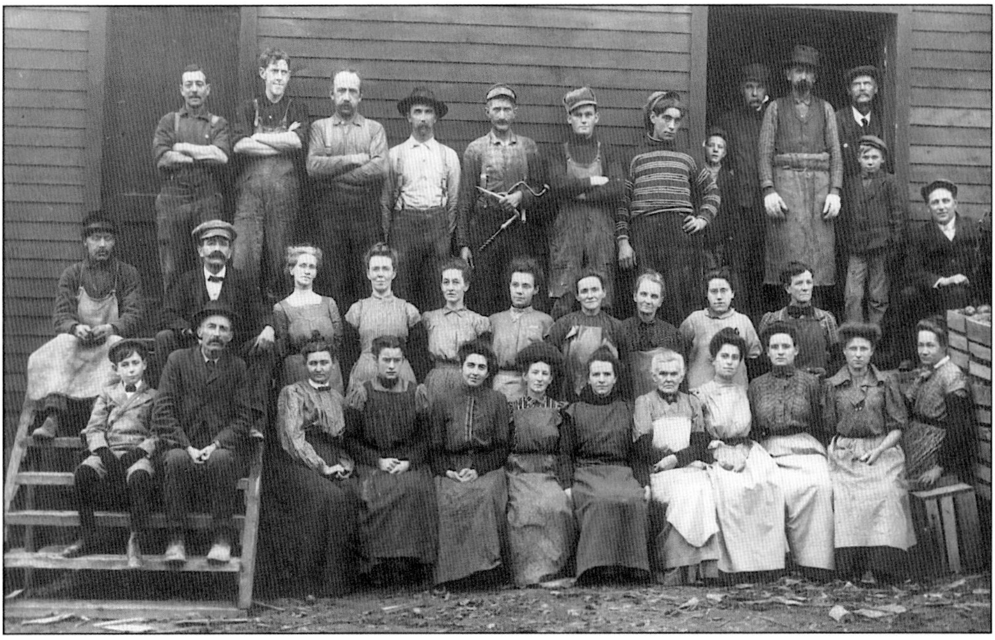

Fruit Workers. Mayor Larry Gursslin provided this picture of American Fruit Company workers. Among the workers is Gursslin's ancestor, Leon Doud (back row, second from the left). Supt. W.W. Winchell and his young son are seated on the stairs. Damaged by fire in 1957, the Gorton Avenue plant was typical of several local processing businesses offering seasonal employment to both men and women. Protective aprons were customarily worn while working.

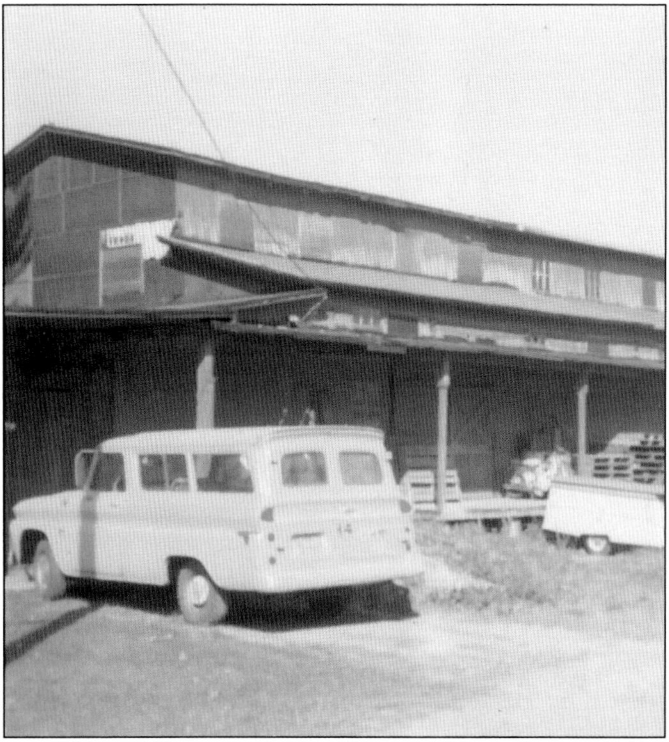

Apple Warehouse. The Collamers, the Bennetts, and the Tennys operated several local fruit-processing structures. This 1971 photograph shows a warehouse that stood until 1999 adjacent to the Collamer orchards. Nearby is the Hilton Packing and Storage building at Collamer Station, known as the Collamer storage, built in 1909 on Collamer Road, not in Hilton village. Under the direction of Arthur W. LaBaie, the plant produced apple cider vinegar, frozen cherries, and fancy mushrooms. Surplus foods, including many pounds of butter, were stored there.

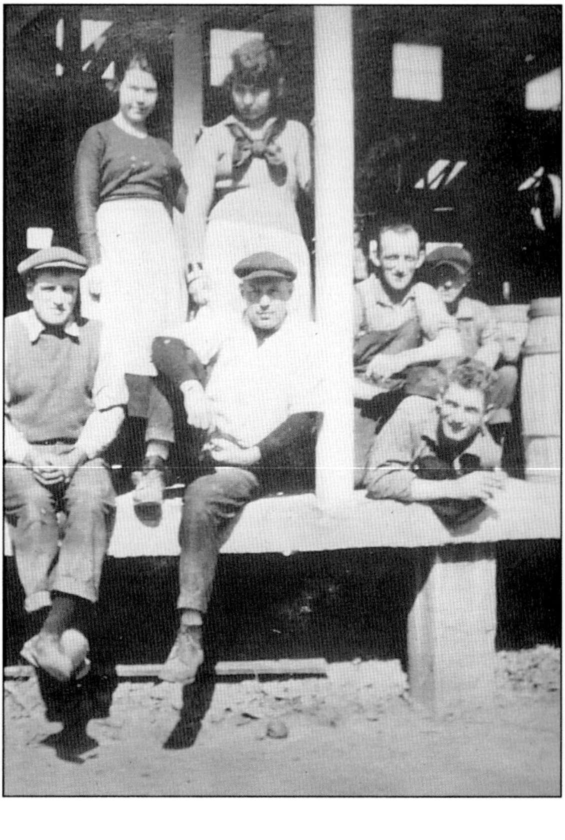

Work Break. Workers at Collamer's warehouse take a short break. Some of them were probably members of the Collamer family. The 1885 Singleton & Collamer warehouse in Hilton village just north of Hilton Baptist Church was the site of the first village election, on July 28, 1885. The Collamers later operated a storage for a time in the former two-room school building beside the railroad tracks, now Ciciohotti's Music Store.

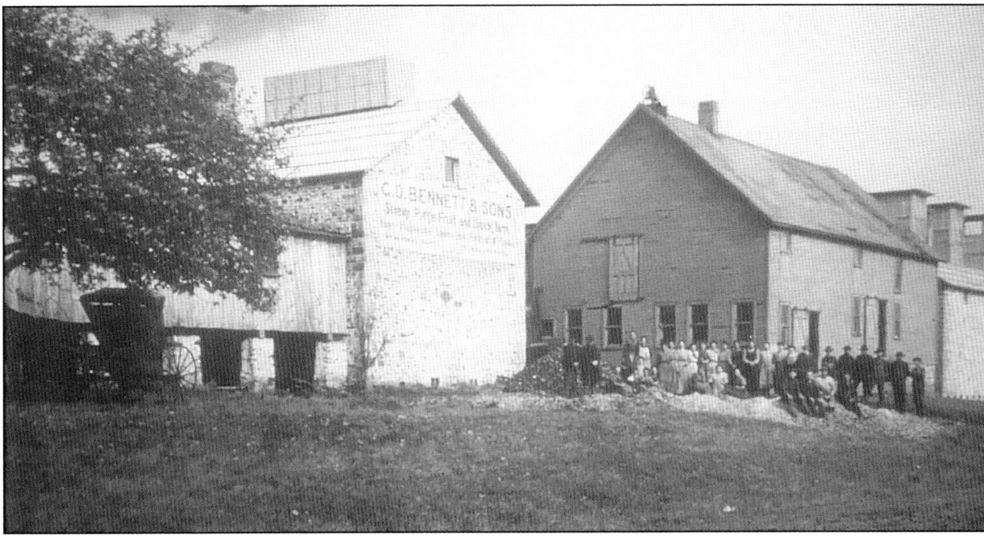

LARGEST EMPLOYER. The largest evaporating plant in the area, thus the largest employer, C.O. Bennett & Sons' firm was destroyed by a fire in 1914. Insufficient insurance coverage made its restoration from the $20,000 in damages unfeasible. Gradually, the fieldstone walls fell apart. A modern house is now on the site. A Free Methodist Church across the road is also long gone, as is the Curtis Mill south of Curtis Road, but Philander Curtis's cobblestone house nearby on Curtis Road is one of several Parma landmarks listed on the National Register of Historic Places.

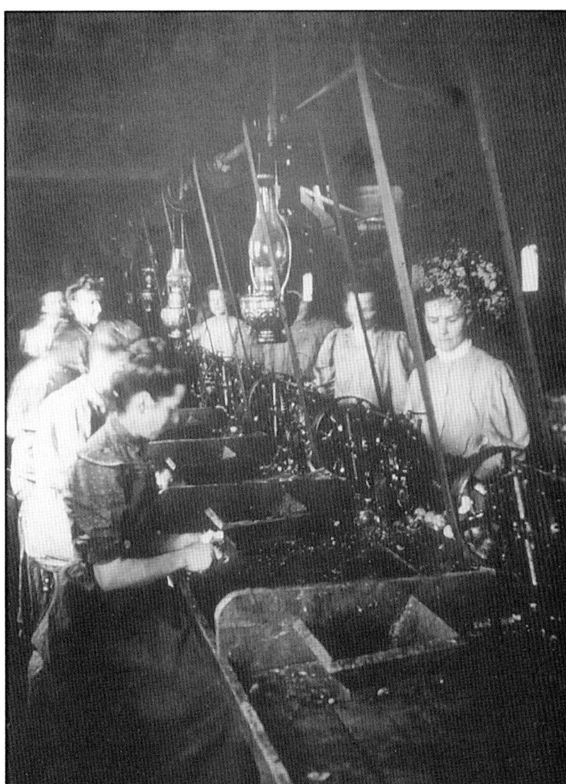

FRUIT LINE. Bennetts' Stoney Ridge Fruit and Stock Farm prided itself on offering fancy evaporated apples and fruit of all kinds, as well as livestock. The evaporator was on the northeast corner of Bennett and Curtis Roads, near a spring. One of the workers shown here on Bennetts' fruit line is Grace Cox Cross (front right). The woman on the front left may be Julia Cross Kentner. Note the hanging oil lamps. Women pared and trimmed the fruit; men performed heavier tasks, lifting fruit barrels and shoveling coal into the furnaces.

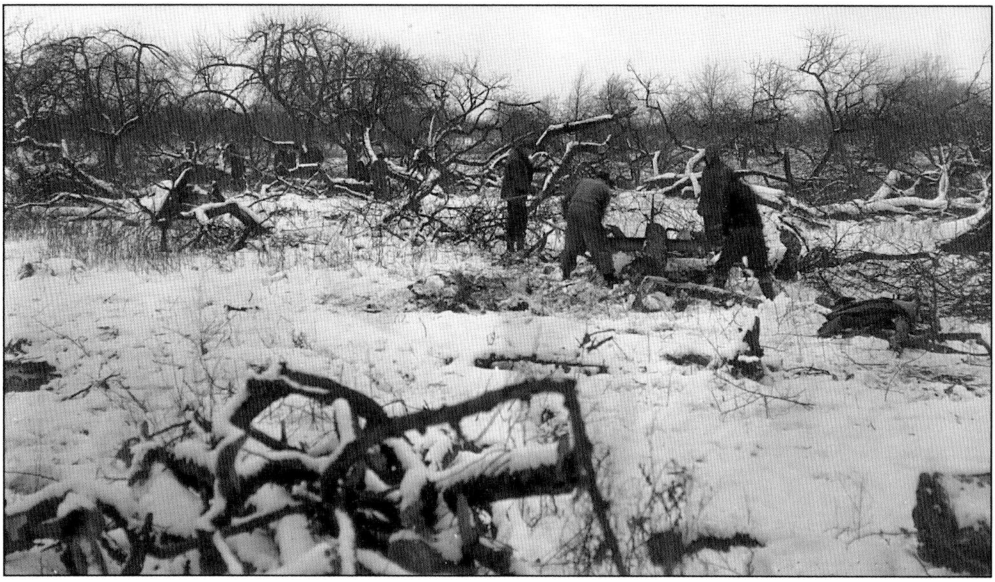

Frozen Fruit. The end of the fruit-packing industry drew near for the entire community when a disastrous freeze in 1934 destroyed nearly half of the fruit trees: 41,158 trees were frozen and 50,158 survived. Lake Ontario was frozen from shore to shore, one of the few times in its history that it became unnavigable. Not until the blizzard of 1966, the 1981 ice storm, and the 1999 snowstorm that brought 43.2 inches—the largest snowfall since 1900—did the weather become such a topic of concern.

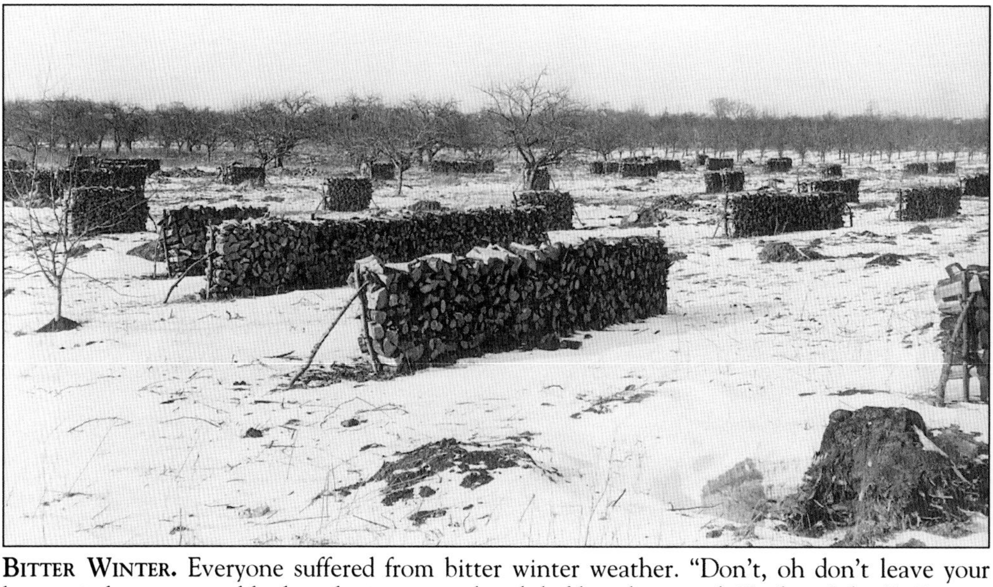

Bitter Winter. Everyone suffered from bitter winter weather. "Don't, oh don't leave your horses tied to a post unblanketed—it is a cruel and shiftless thing to do!" editor John E. Cooper wrote in the *Hilton Record* in 1918, when temperatures reached 20 below. Less humane was the public opinion that those unwilling to chop wood should have no heat. Welfare recipients were forced to cut and split frozen trees into firewood after the disastrous 1934 freeze.

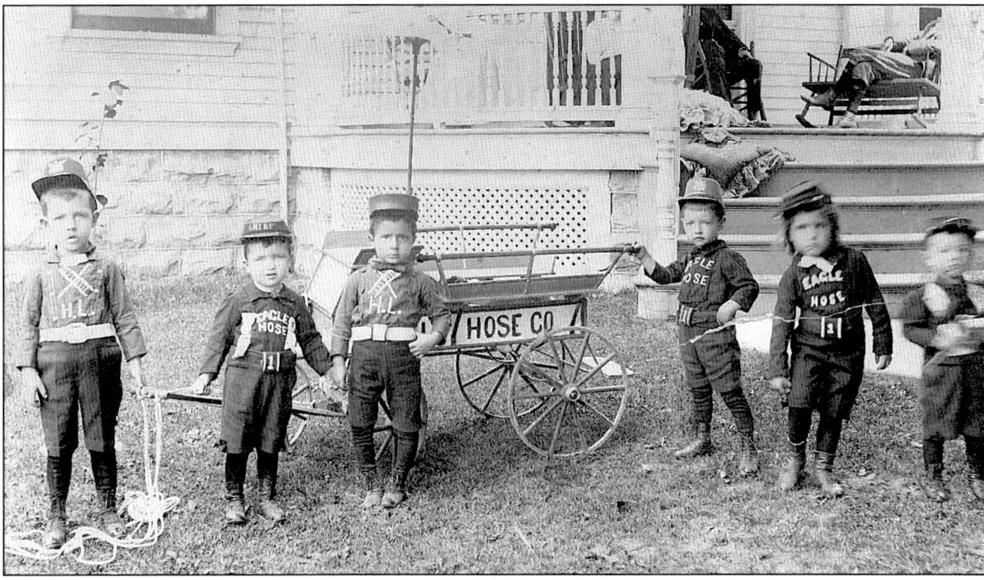

EAGLE HOSE COMPANY. Little is known about the Eagle Hose Company, pictured here in 1892. Could they put out a fire? Probably not, but neither could adult firemen, without water lines. The North Parma Fire Company of 1889 was succeeded by a new department with three separate companies, led in 1897 by Chief John E. Cooper. After interest again declined, the Hilton Hose Company was created in 1904. Chief George Lee reinvigorated the department in 1914. It was merged into one company in 1923 and was incorporated in 1928.

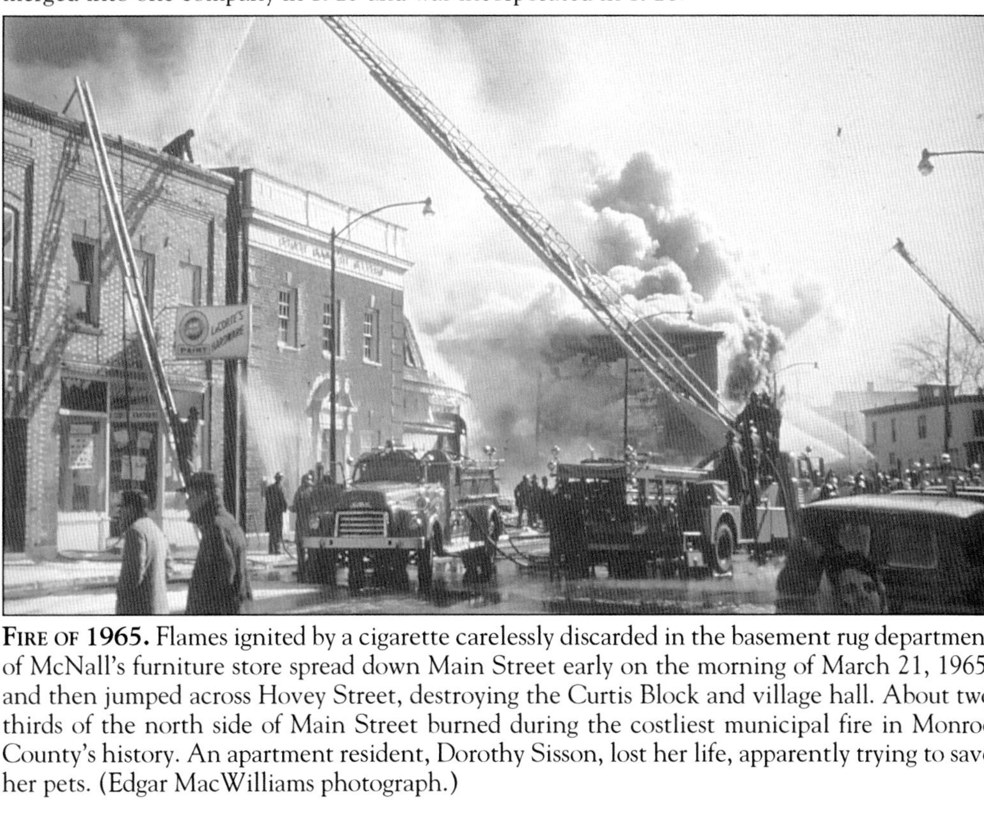

FIRE OF 1965. Flames ignited by a cigarette carelessly discarded in the basement rug department of McNall's furniture store spread down Main Street early on the morning of March 21, 1965, and then jumped across Hovey Street, destroying the Curtis Block and village hall. About two thirds of the north side of Main Street burned during the costliest municipal fire in Monroe County's history. An apartment resident, Dorothy Sisson, lost her life, apparently trying to save her pets. (Edgar MacWilliams photograph.)

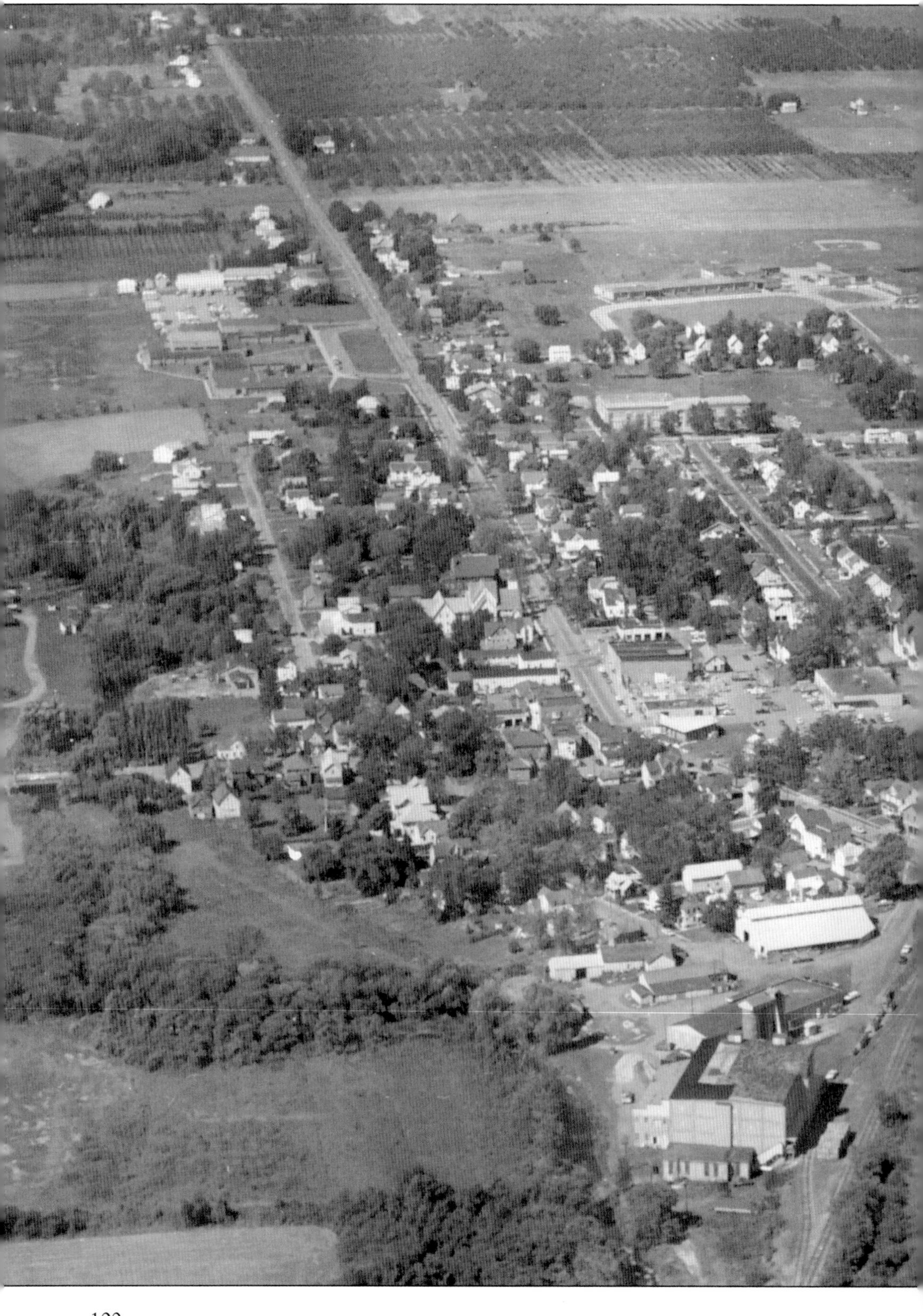

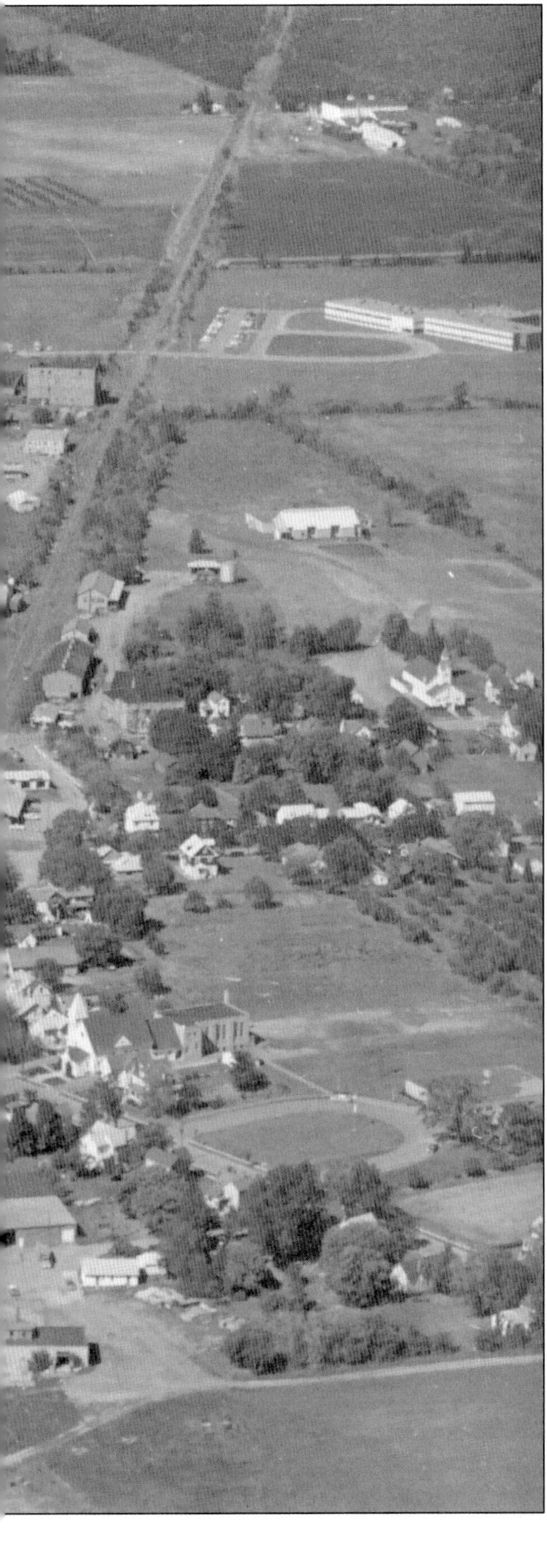

A 1965 Aerial View of Hilton. Industries hugging the railroad tracks are visible here, as is the gaping hole left in the heart of Main Street by the 1965 fire. The town's largest taxpayer was the Hilton Milling & Warehouse Company, in the foreground by the tracks. The company operated a sawmill, a stave and barrel factory, a coal yard, a flour and feed mill, and a fruit storage there. Unsuccessful as a fruit cooperative, Smithfield's cannery, east of the tracks, was torn down that August 1965. Its office building is now the Beautiful Angel gift shop; a warehouse became the Canning Street Square complex. Bud Hendershot's corn-drying building is now Carmestro's restaurant, where delectable foods are served.

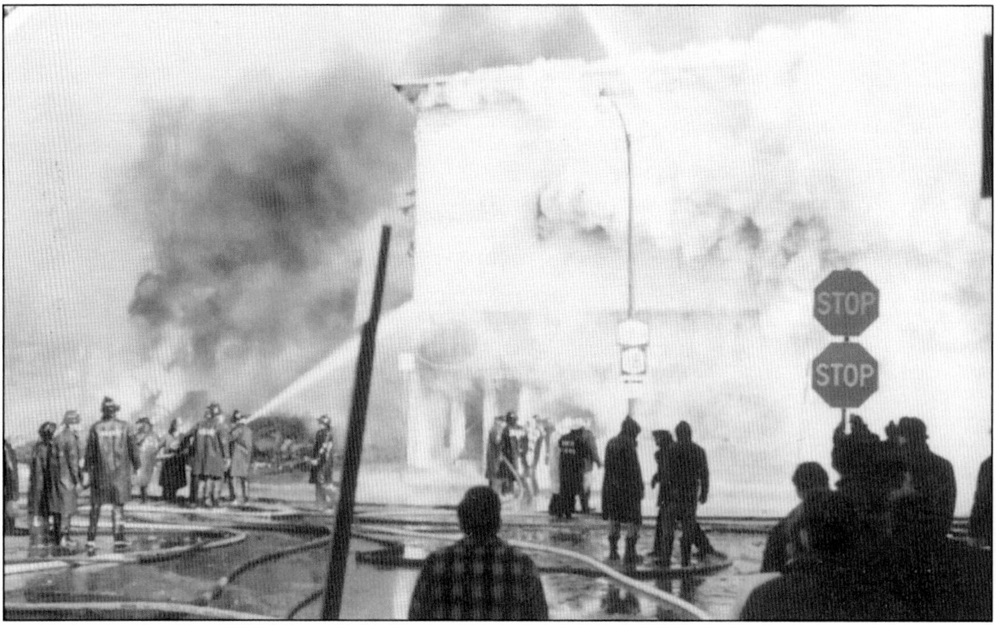

Main Street Fire. Several fire companies assisted in the effort to save the commercial area from the 1965 fire, but despite the loan of a snorkel truck, and despite gallons of water poured on roofs, the 1904 Curtis Block and the 1904 and 1907 Fraser Blocks were ruined, as was the 1912 village hall. The hall's brick-and-tile block construction stopped the fire. However, Fraser Block owner Violet Green, Curtis Block owner Clio Lodge, the State Bank of Hilton, the village of Hilton, and various merchants estimated losses of more than $1 million. (Donald Pisher photograph.)

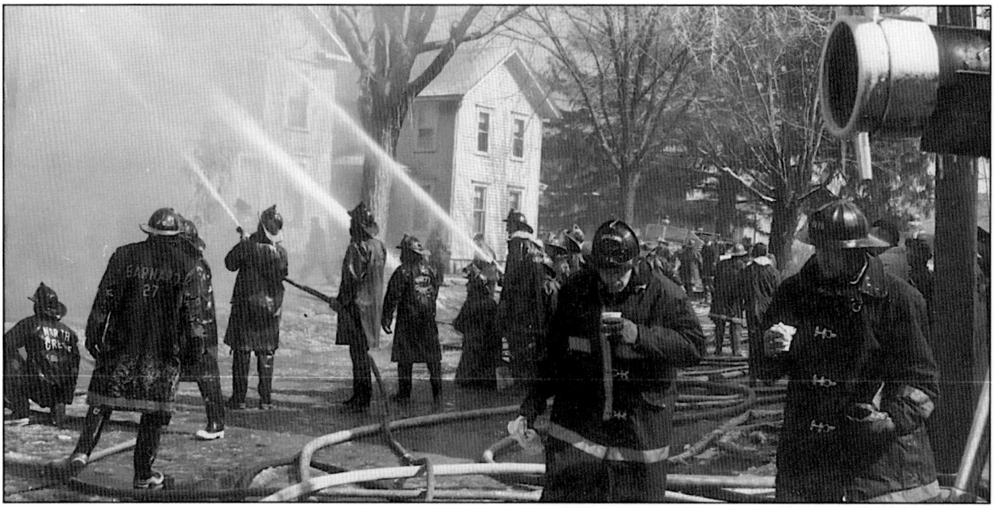

Firefighters. North Greece and Barnard firemen were among those rendering aid during the fire of 1965. Here, they are shown protecting the Elliott house, now the home of the Party Connection and The Hilton Dry Cleaners and Tuxedo shop. Businesses wiped out by the fire that never reopened included Clyde Robillard's jewelers, Archie and Grace Wilkins's Pleasure Shop soda fountain, and Vincent Barile's shoe store. Admired throughout the community, the ever-friendly Barile died on June 30, 1983; both he and his classy 1929 Model T Ford will long be remembered.

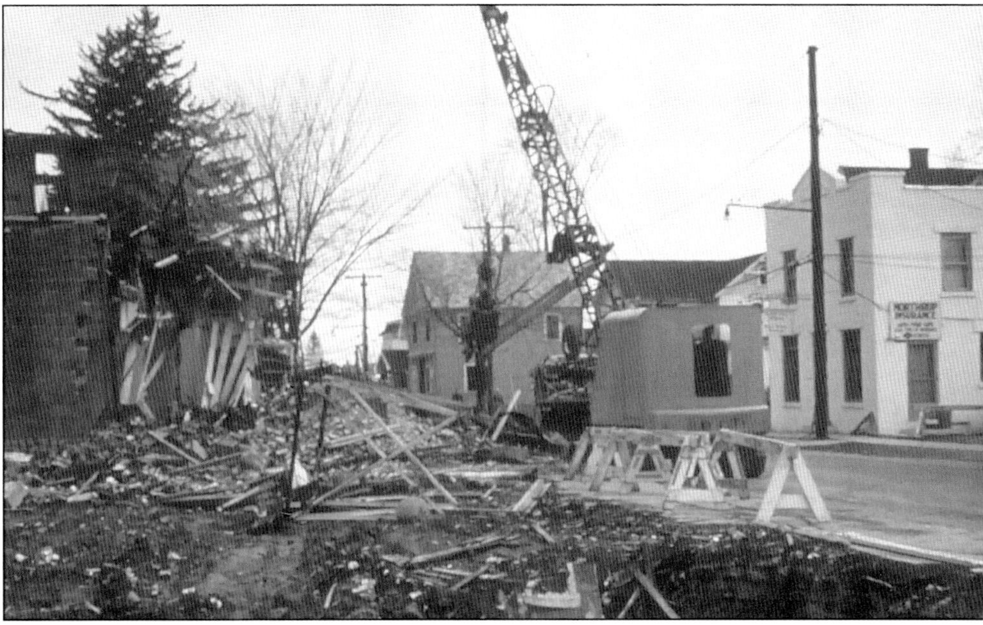

CLEANUP, 1965. A fire wall, although severely cracked, saved Main Street's brick buildings, but cleaning up the 1965 fire debris was a sad task. This photograph shows the 1912 Fisher Block at the right. John D. Klock and other civic leaders flew to Washington, seeking disaster aid. Congressman Conable obtained books for the public library. Klock's new building was leased for the Hilton Post Office. One by one, modern versions of the unadorned blockish architecture of past years were built in the burned out section. (MacWilliams photograph.)

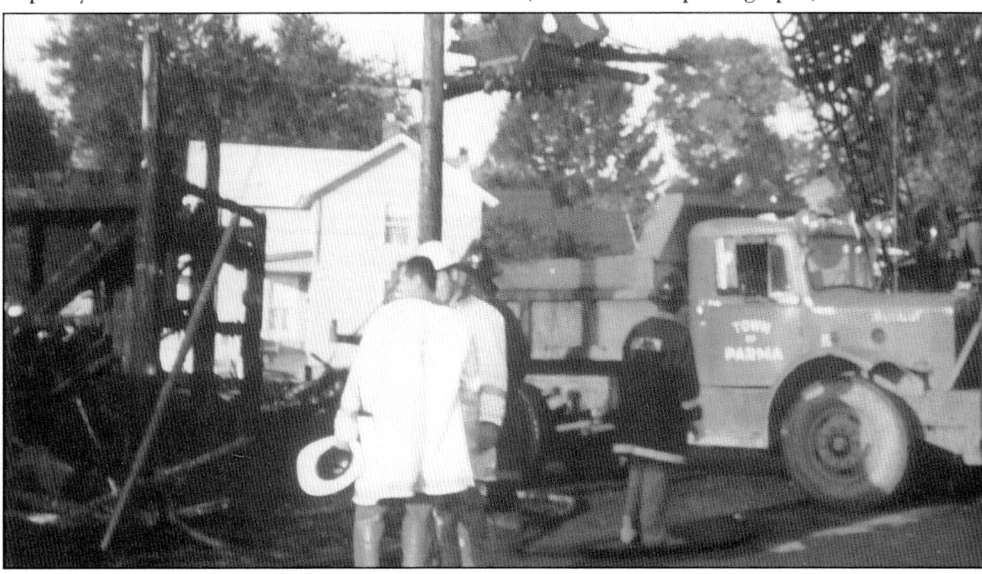

HILTON MILLING FIRE. Town of Parma trucks assisted with the cleanup operation after the Hilton Milling & Warehouse lumber shed burned in 1972. A man later confessed that he had set the fire, in which losses were estimated at $100,000. The business was owned by the Gioia brothers, Alfonso, Anthony J., Joseph A., and Horace P. The Gioia family enriched not only the local community but also the city of Rochester, where they ran a successful pasta plant on Canal Street.

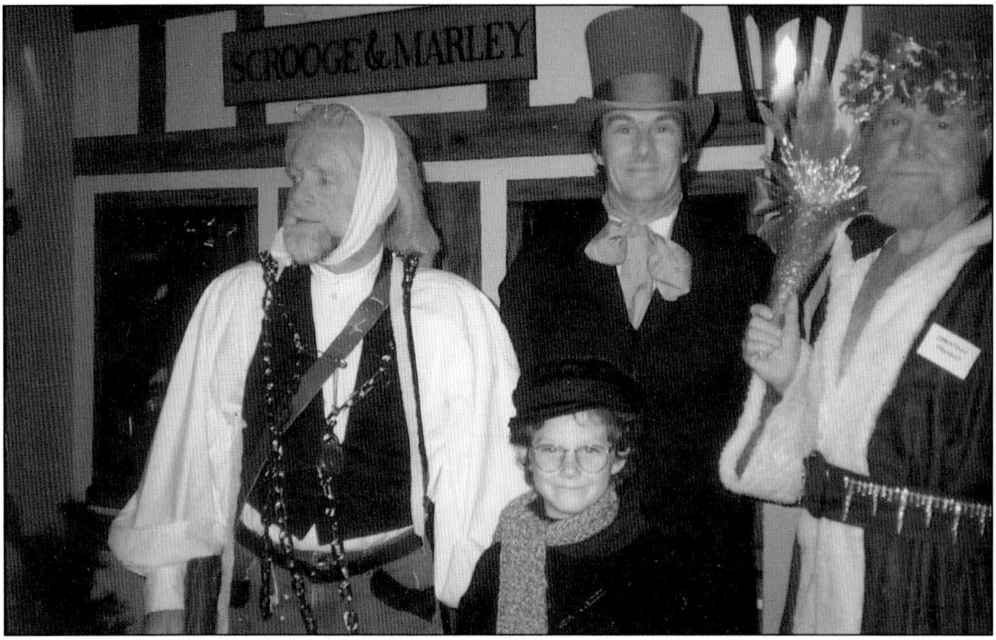

DICKENS FESTIVAL. The Smithfield Company's fruit warehouse became a furniture store after the 1965 fire wiped out McNall's Main Street store. Today, it is Marple's Canning Street Square complex, which houses The Greenery flower and gift shop (founded by the Hollenbecks in 1974), other small shops, and the Craft Antique Co-op (where special programs are held, such as the popular Dickens Festival in December). Pictured here, from left to right, are characters from Charles Dickens's favorite, *A Christmas Carol*—Jacob Marley, Tiny Tim, Bob Cratchit, and the Spirit of Christmas Present.

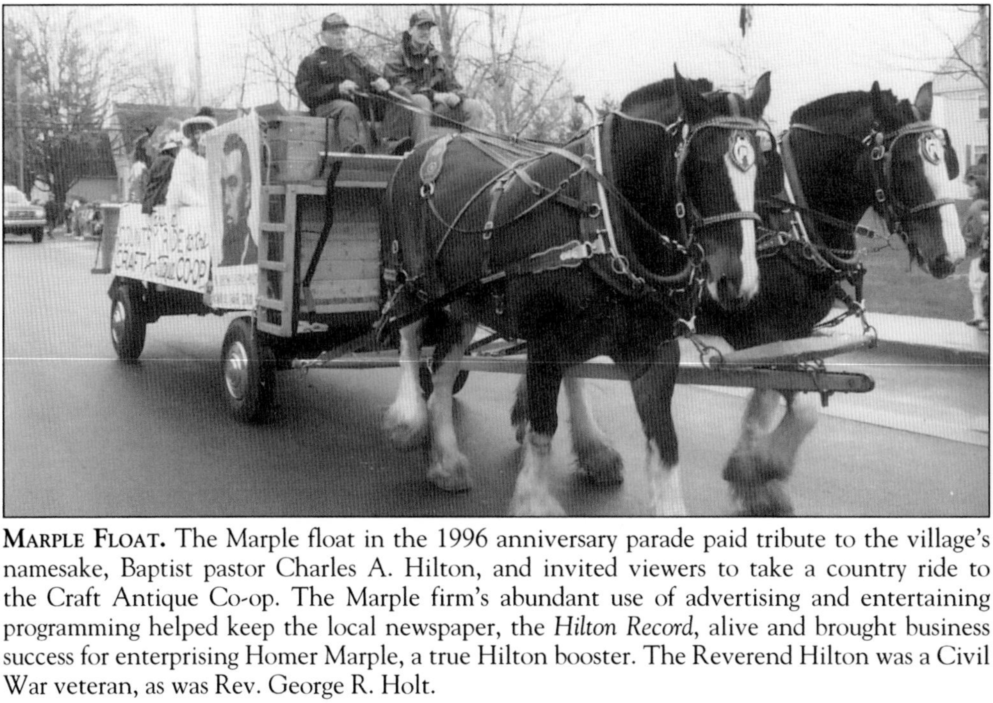

MARPLE FLOAT. The Marple float in the 1996 anniversary parade paid tribute to the village's namesake, Baptist pastor Charles A. Hilton, and invited viewers to take a country ride to the Craft Antique Co-op. The Marple firm's abundant use of advertising and entertaining programming helped keep the local newspaper, the *Hilton Record*, alive and brought business success for enterprising Homer Marple, a true Hilton booster. The Reverend Hilton was a Civil War veteran, as was Rev. George R. Holt.

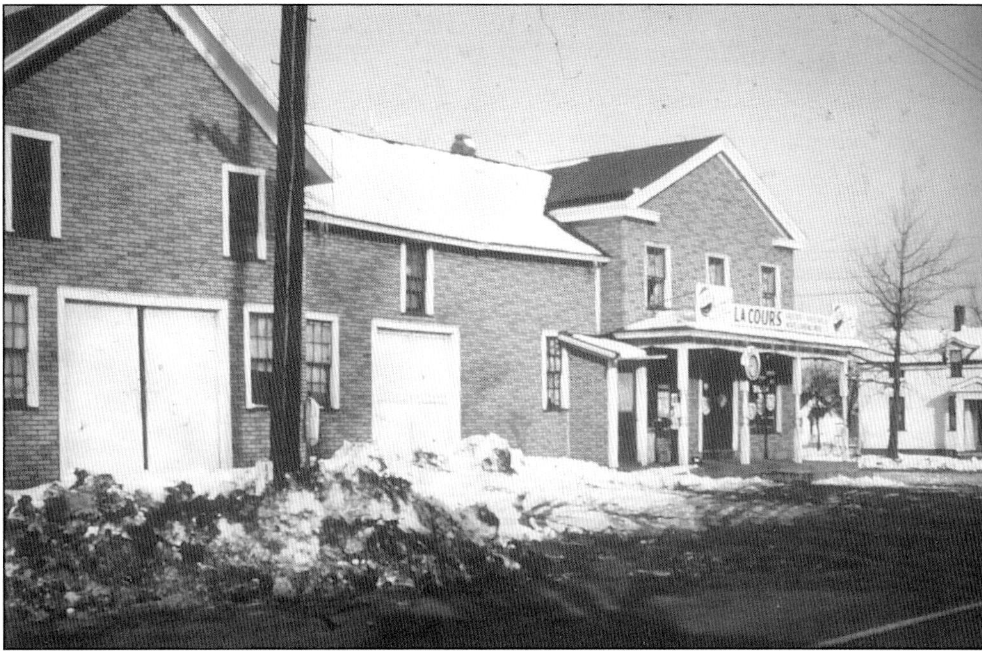

LA COUR'S STORE. The oldest business structure in Parma, dating back to 1827, was destroyed by fire in February 1994. The Parma Center general store was a station on the Underground Railroad, the birthplace of Parma Grange, a former post office and grocery, and the site of several other businesses. At the time of the fire, it housed Galaxie Auto Parts. Several storekeepers and the family of William Denniston, a state assemblyman, lived in the rear addition at various times over the years. In 1994, a phone call awoke the occupants, saving their lives.

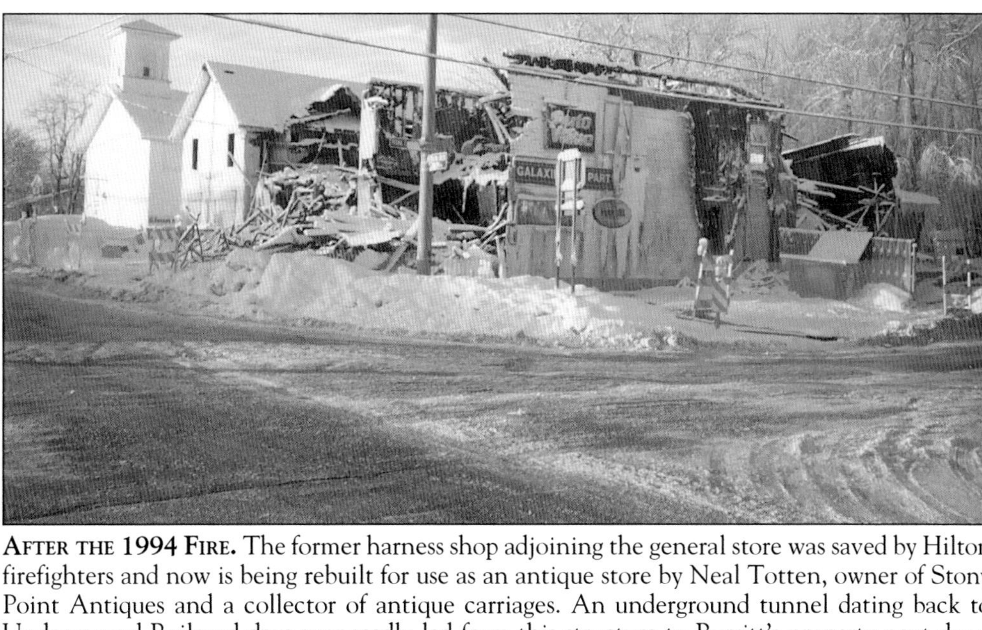

AFTER THE 1994 FIRE. The former harness shop adjoining the general store was saved by Hilton firefighters and now is being rebuilt for use as an antique store by Neal Totten, owner of Stony Point Antiques and a collector of antique carriages. An underground tunnel dating back to Underground Railroad days supposedly led from this structure to Burritt's property next door. (Brian Husted photograph.)

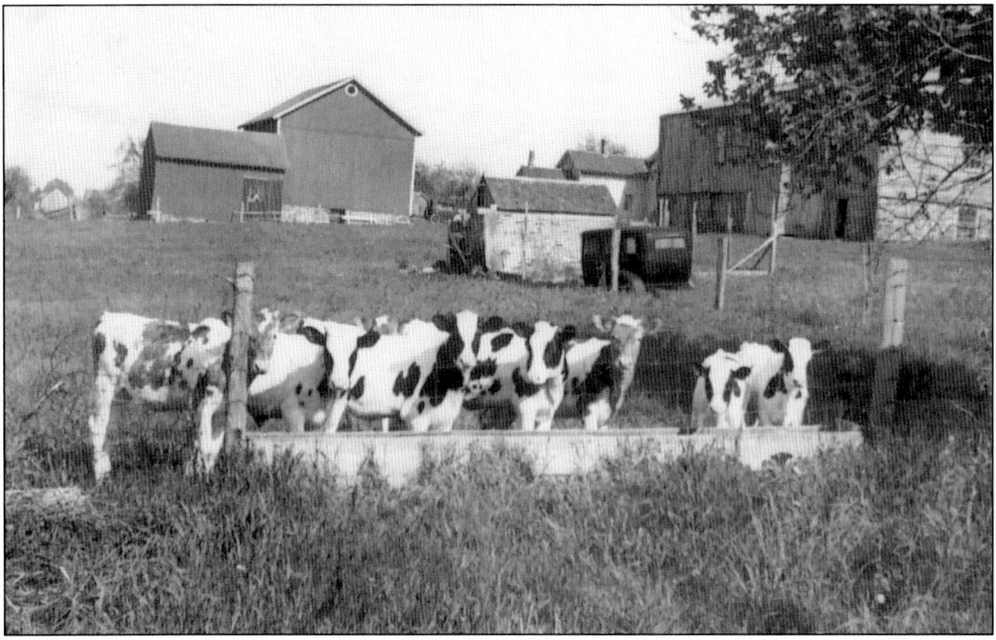

Calves on Gott Farm. The Hill family's calves gather at the feed trough on the Gott Farm off Ridge Road West, now the site of Pro-Carpets. The state's 1954 agricultural census listed 291 farms: 95 raising milk cows; 105 raising poultry, including 13,793 chickens; 11 raising turkeys; 114 raising corn; 123 raising wheat; 76 raising oats; and 134 raising fruit. Of the 23,083 acres of farmland, 11, 750 acres were producing crops. The end of agriculture as the town's main occupation was approaching.

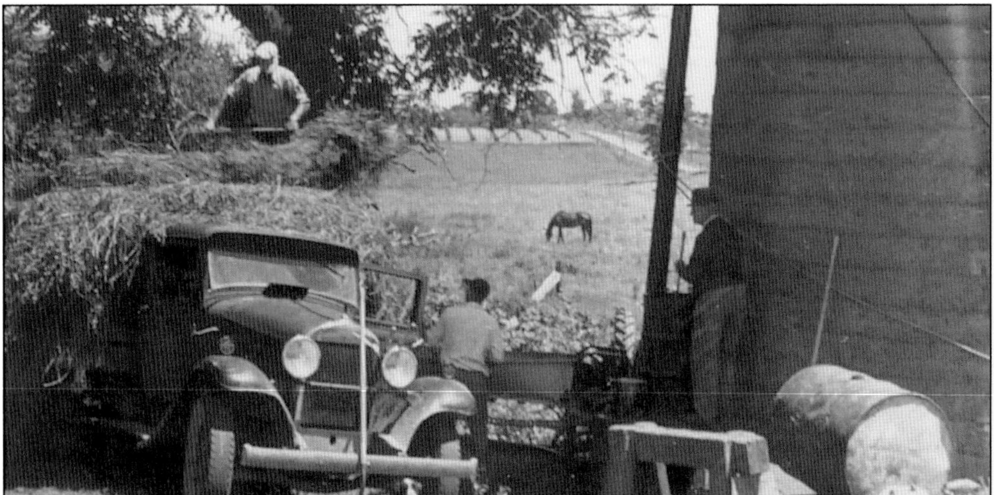

Filling the Hill Farm Silo. Hill's Moncony Farms, named after Monroe County, New York, became renown for registered holstein cattle. Fred Hill (right), a longtime superintendent of schools, was honored by the naming of a Brockport school in his memory. The Hill twins, Russell and Warren, are seen here filling the silo. Corn, wheat, tomatoes, potatoes, broccoli, carrots, cauliflower, cabbages, squash, beans, peas, cucumbers, and many varieties of fruit were produced on area farms. Twin Hills golf course, named after the Hill twins, now occupies part of a former Hill family farm.

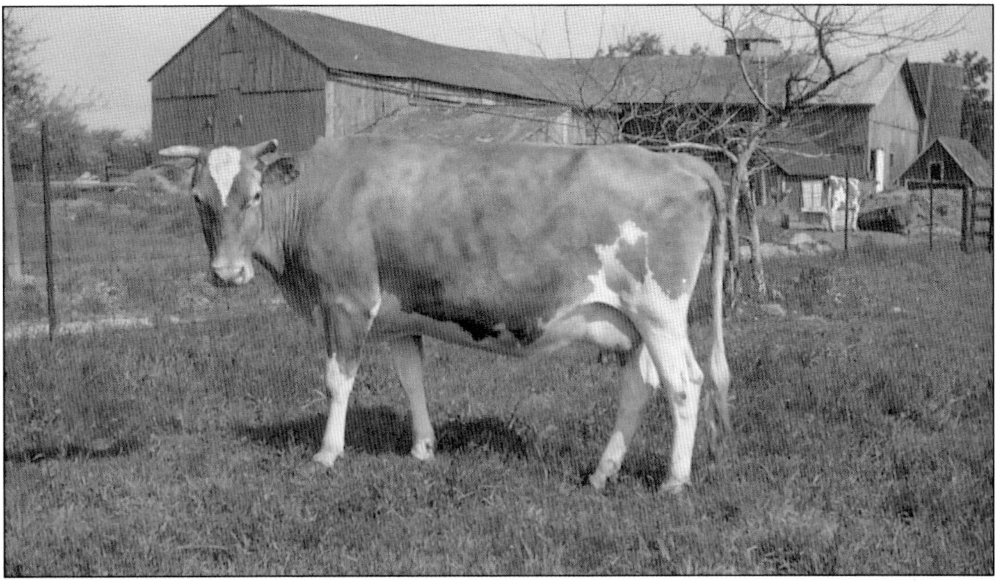

Mitchell's Dairy Barn. Dairy farms began going out of business in the 1950s, causing big cattle barns, such as this one on Ward Mitchell's Pleasant Vue Farm off Burritt Road, to become redundant. Many of the barns were beautifully constructed but, once unneeded, maintaining them became just too expensive. Soaring feed costs during World War II led to the demise of many poultry farms; dairy farms also experienced dwindling profits. Mitchell's Ruth No. 1 poses for this 1942 photograph. Note the heart-shaped marking on "Ruth's" hip.

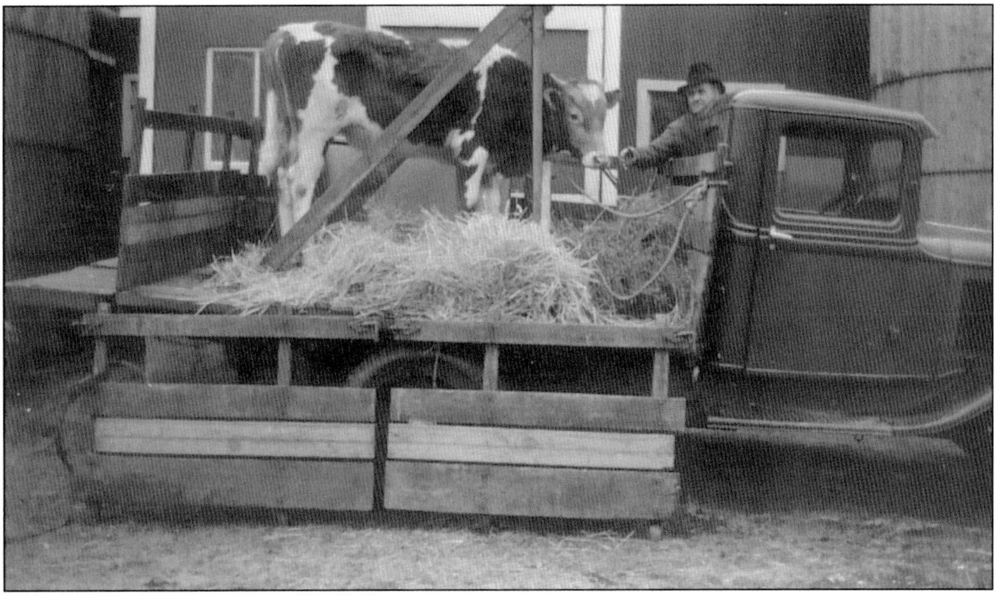

Moo-ve It!. Ward Mitchell had to struggle to unload this reluctant cow from his truck. Maybe he should have sung to it to calm it down, his forte being directing the choir at Hilton Methodist Church. Choir directing and cow directing is not quite the same thing (unless the cow enjoys "moosic"). Mitchell's daughter-in-law, Ruth Eberle Mitchell, was a music teacher and the Hilton Methodist Church organist from 1923 to 1958. His sister, Jennie Mitchell, Hilton High School's first graduate in 1899, was also a music teacher.

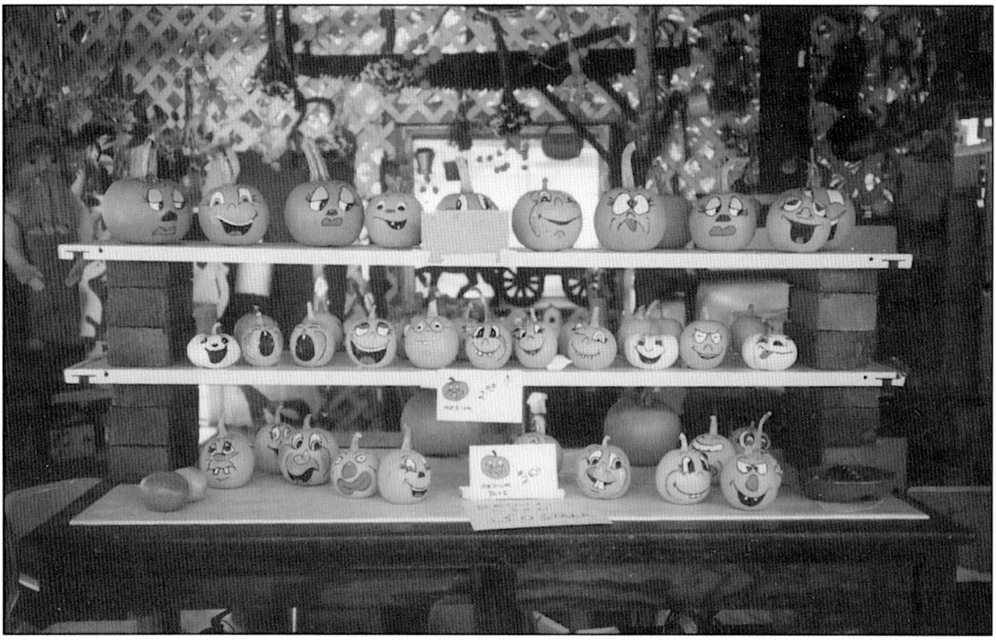

PAINTED PUMPKINS. Fall pumpkins greet customers at Wyant's Cobblestone Farm Market, one of the local producers of fruits and vegetables. Where Ray Wondergem once grew Irondequoit-type muskmelons, Sweeneys' greenhouses produce plants and hot house tomatoes. Local landscaping firms, florists, and garden stores sell plants, shrubs, and trees. Among them are Hawk's Nest Nursery, established in 1989 and specializing in perennials, and Justice Florists, once Shult's, the oldest floral firm, *c.* 1915. The main agricultural product is now field corn.

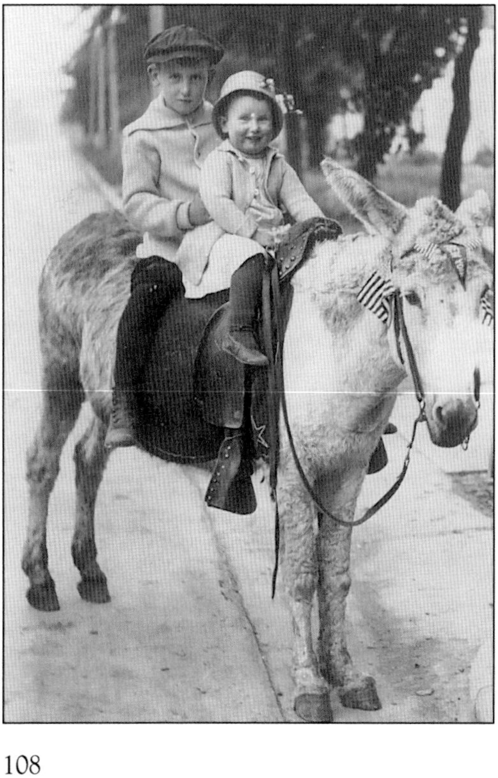

ADORABLE! This photograph from the Harry McCarty collection was donated to the Parma town historian's archives by Anne Pfarrer Hall. It was probably taken at a Fourth of July parade. Many of McCarty's photographs show animals, hunters, flowers, and fruit, revealing a deep appreciation of nature. McCarty apprenticed at Clarence Slaight's photography business in the village of Hilton.

Eight

HAPPY TIMES

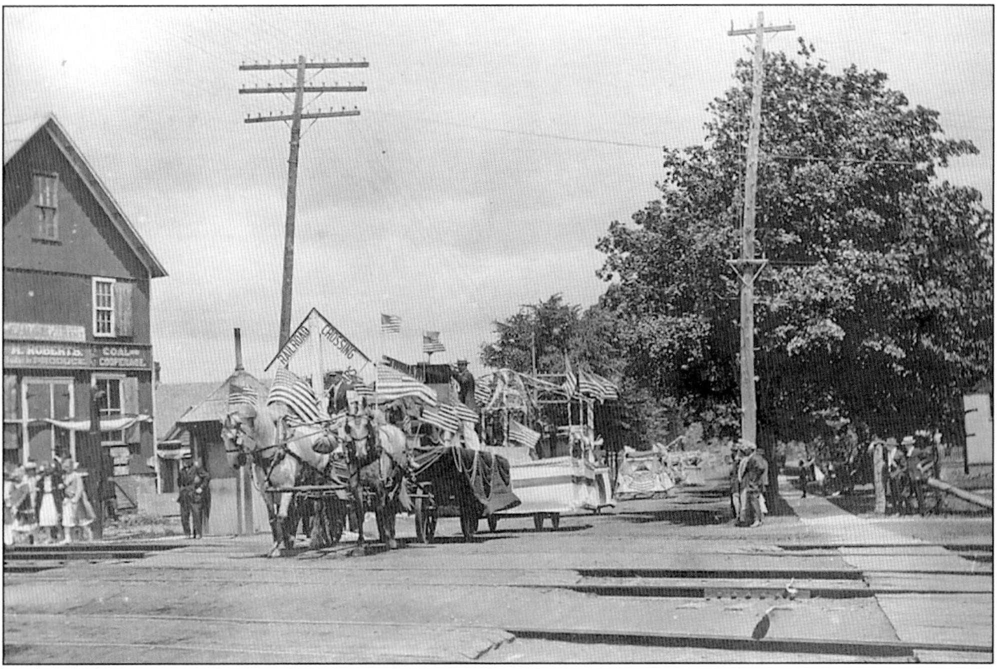

FOURTH OF JULY PARADE. Villagers filled their yards with flags on the Fourth of July. A great parade proceeded down Lake Avenue to the Lee farm on West Avenue, where folks picnicked and watched a ball game. Harry McCarty's photograph shows Edson Taber's ornate patriotic float approaching Myron Roberts' business, the 1889 Model Flour Mill, by the railroad tracks, later Ed Hiler's feed store. The GLF, now Hilton Agway, is the only feed store left in a town where mills once ground grain 24 hours a day. As the farms disappeared, so did the flour and feed business.

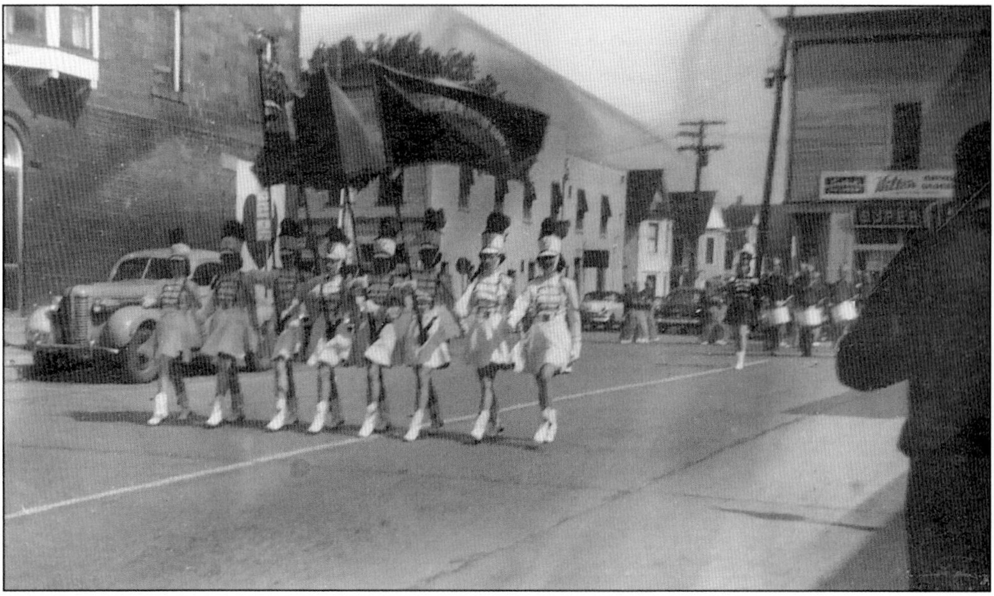

Color Guard. Motorized trucks enabled a fast response by Hilton Fire Department volunteers and more success in controlling fires. The department's ambulance corps, organized in 1936, has saved countless lives. Thus, parade appearances always draw appreciative applause. In 1947, the Hilton Fire Department made history when its new drum and bugle corps had the state's first all-female color guard—a small victory against male chauvinism, although some women said the skirts were too short.

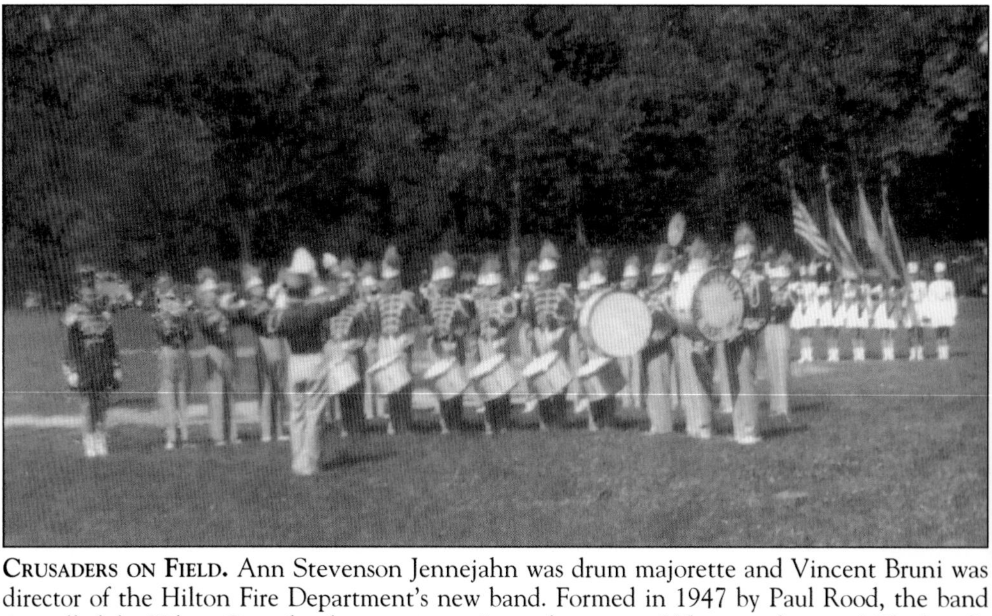

Crusaders on Field. Ann Stevenson Jennejahn was drum majorette and Vincent Bruni was director of the Hilton Fire Department's new band. Formed in 1947 by Paul Rood, the band was called the Hilton Crusaders because it was "crusading to put Hilton on the map." The band's soft gray-and-green uniforms, precision drills, and brilliant orchestrations by Eddie Mizma were a source of great community pride. The unit left Hilton in 1959 and became the Irondequoit Crusaders.

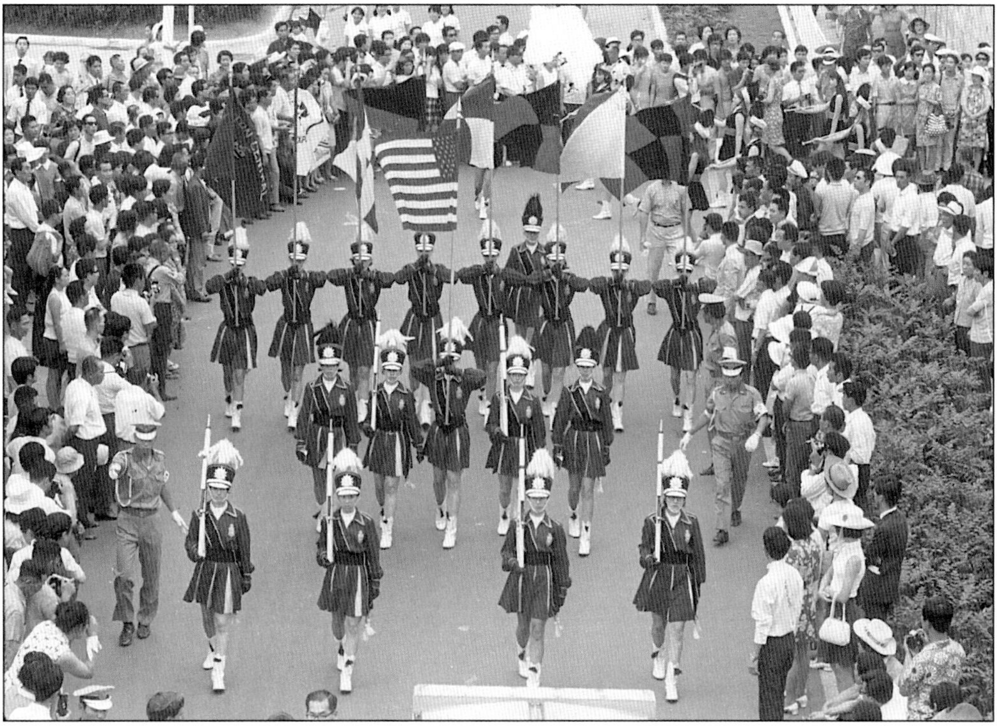

Crimson Cadets in Japan. Gordon Bascomb led the high school's Crimson Cadets at an appearance at Osaka, Japan, in 1970. The only American band at Expo '70, the Cadets were obviously well received. Charles Lucie was the music department supervisor and Thomas Younker the business manager. Under Lucie the Cadets also represented the United States at Expo '67, the Canadian World Exposition in Montreal. The Cadets also went on a 12-day tour of Europe in 1973.

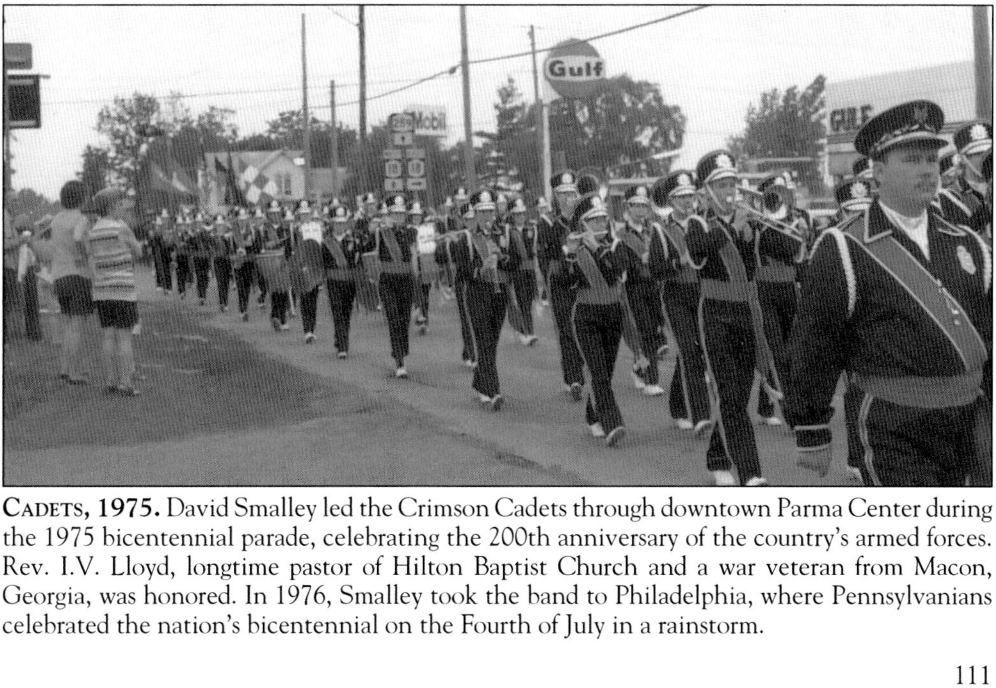

Cadets, 1975. David Smalley led the Crimson Cadets through downtown Parma Center during the 1975 bicentennial parade, celebrating the 200th anniversary of the country's armed forces. Rev. I.V. Lloyd, longtime pastor of Hilton Baptist Church and a war veteran from Macon, Georgia, was honored. In 1976, Smalley took the band to Philadelphia, where Pennsylvanians celebrated the nation's bicentennial on the Fourth of July in a rainstorm.

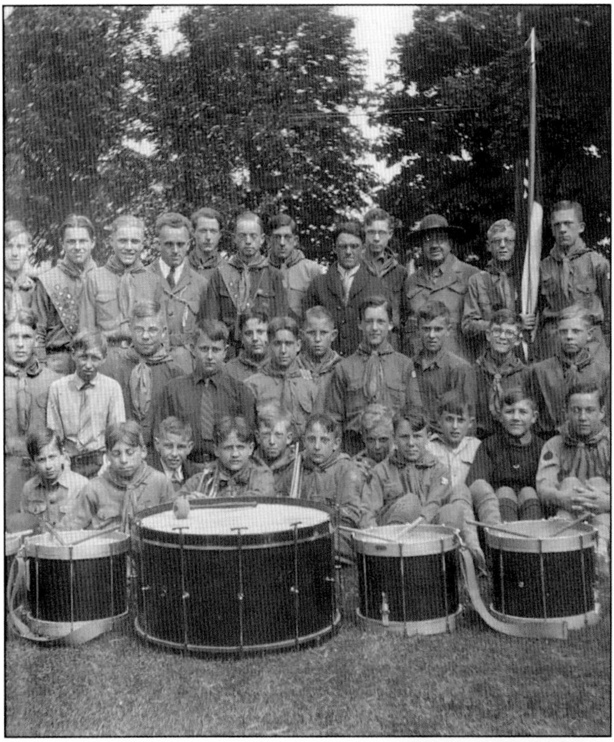

Boy Scout Troop. No parade would be complete without a contingent of Scouts. This early Troop 99 group picture includes the following, from left to right: (front row) Evan Smith, Tom Massam, Digs Quinlan, Whitney Nixon, Martin Wright, Lavergne "Shorty" Stothard, Warren Rowley, C. Harlan Cooper, Norman Kerrison, Eddie Moyer, and Garfield Cornish; (middle row) Jack Cooper, Floyd Conley, Ernest Kerrison, Cuba Cosman, George Laisney, Floyd Parker, Tillie Williams, Paul Rood, Earl Kerrison, Gordon Castle, and Royden Sawyer; (back row) Willard Odell, Chuck Kenyon, Herb Heinrich, Mort Wadsworth, Steve Burritt, Lee Wadsworth, Andy Albiker, Gordon Barringer, Ray Odell, leader Lewis Archer, Harry Dieckman, and Harold Sedler.

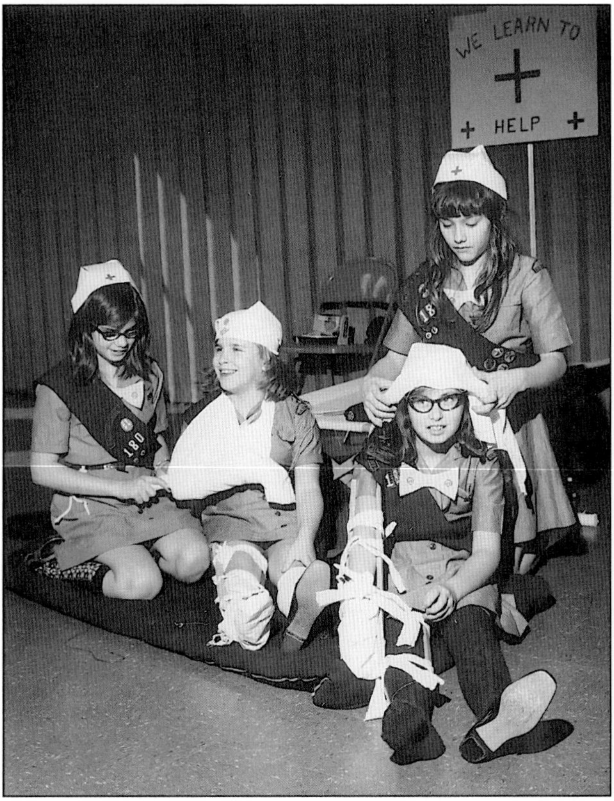

Girl Scouts. Joseph Choka's photograph of Girl Scouts during a first-aid lesson brings back memories of the many appearances of Scouts and Brownies during parades and public ceremonies. By their example, leaders such as Helen Burritt Latif, Marie Mikel, Ethel MacDermand, Barbara Hendershot Miles, Marion Newcomb Rowley, Betty VanDorn Keller, Muriel Collamer, Naomi Flood, and Beulah Albiker Hilfiker taught the girls some of life's best lessons.

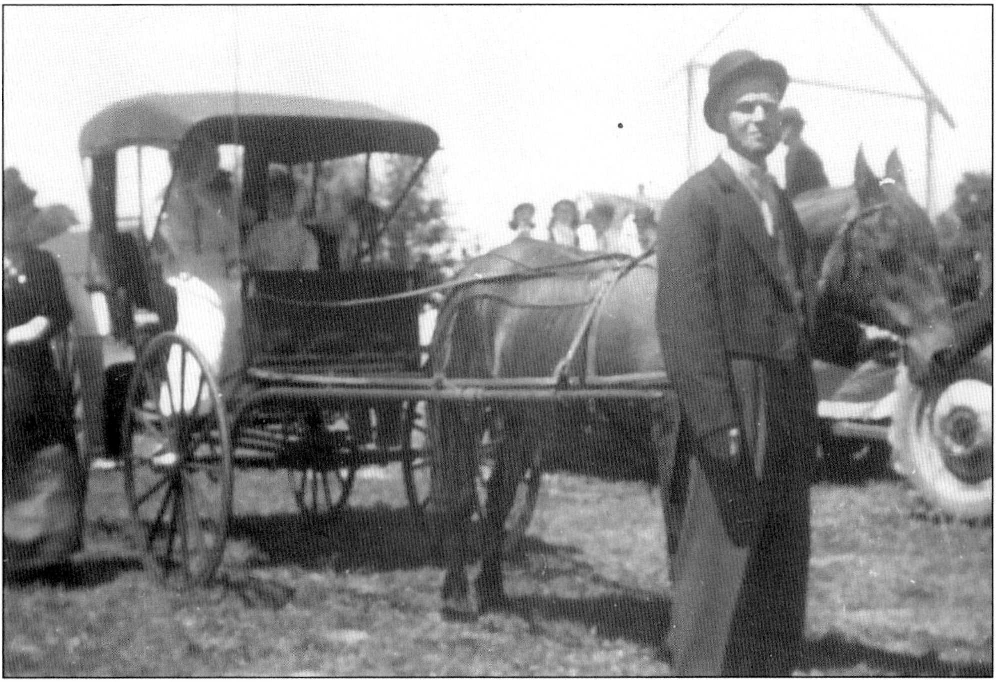

Ryan Family. Gerald Ryan and his family were a big hit at the town of Parma's 1959 sesquicentennial parade when they passed by in this antique carriage. Another favorite was a rig carrying Eddie Burritt and family.

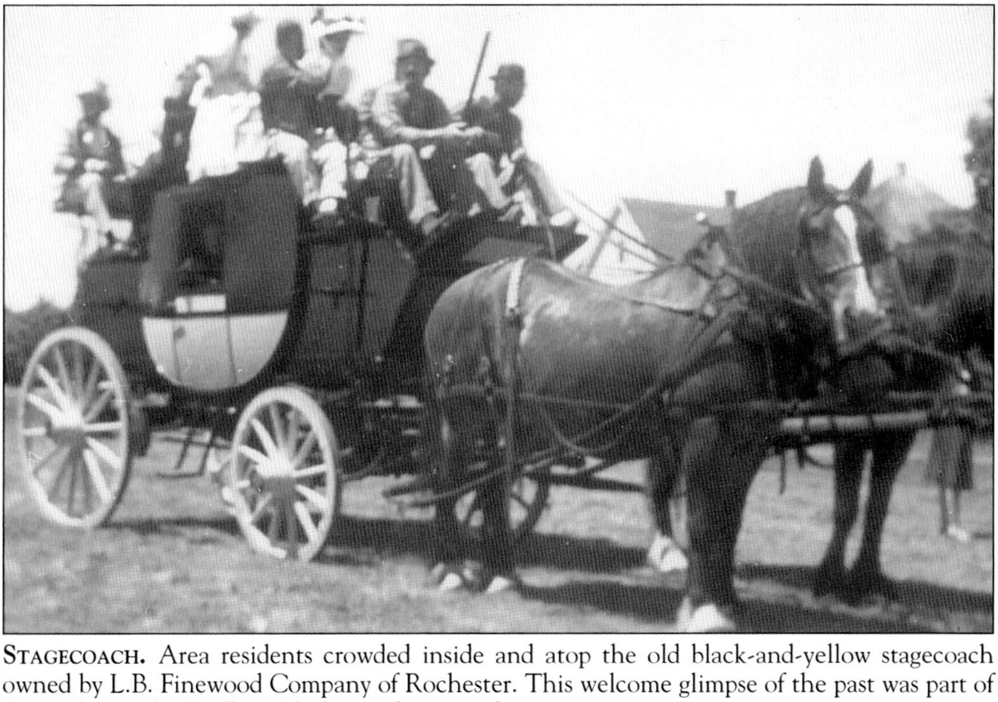

Stagecoach. Area residents crowded inside and atop the old black-and-yellow stagecoach owned by L.B. Finewood Company of Rochester. This welcome glimpse of the past was part of the 1959 parade. Wallace Kluth was the stage driver.

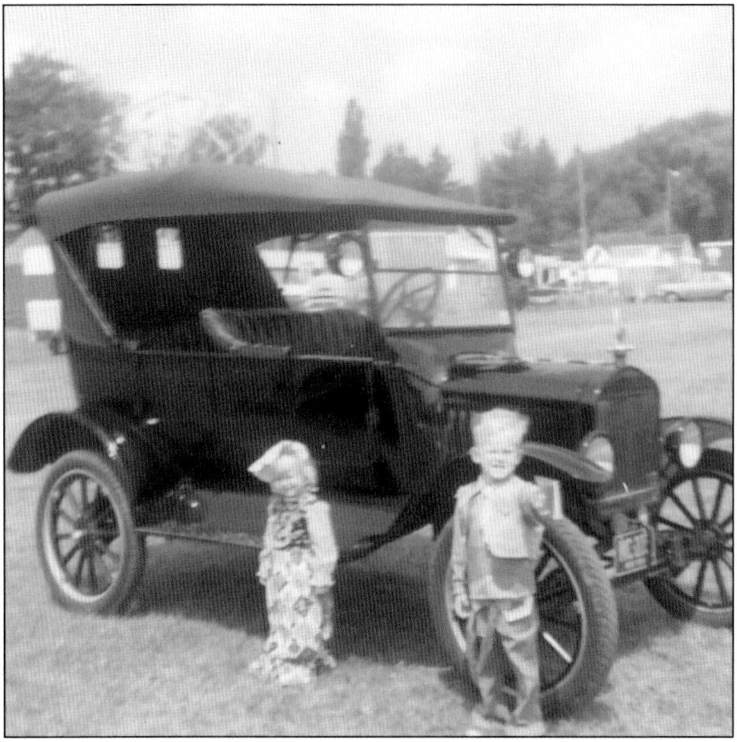

PIONEER DAYS. Rosemary and Brett Husted were among the many people admiring a lineup of old automobiles at the 1971 Pioneer Days observance at the Hilton Fair, honoring the 150th anniversary of the county of Monroe. Frank Cox attempted to turn the annual firemen's carnival into a fair with fireworks, shows, and special events, but it has remained small, still providing carnival-type entertainment.

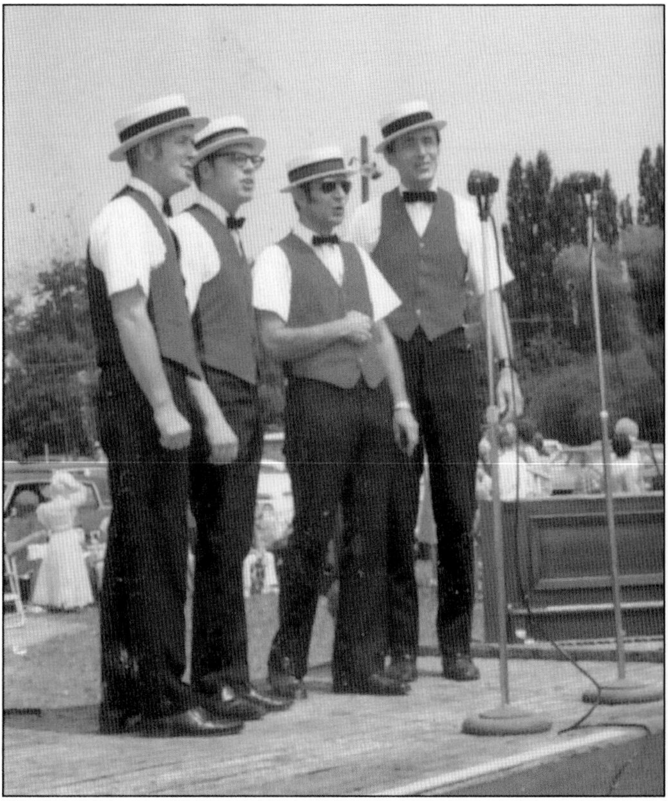

HILTONES. At the county sesquicentennial and other events, the Hiltones barbershop quartet added class and rollicking music whenever they appeared. Here, they serenade the 1971 crowd at Hilton Firemen's Field.

In the Crowd. Enjoying the Pioneer Days activities are, from left to right, Eileen Neal, Grace Goodell Witty, Mabel Black Goodwin, Velma Kelly Badgerow, Eleanor Stothard, and Blanche Roberts Newsome.

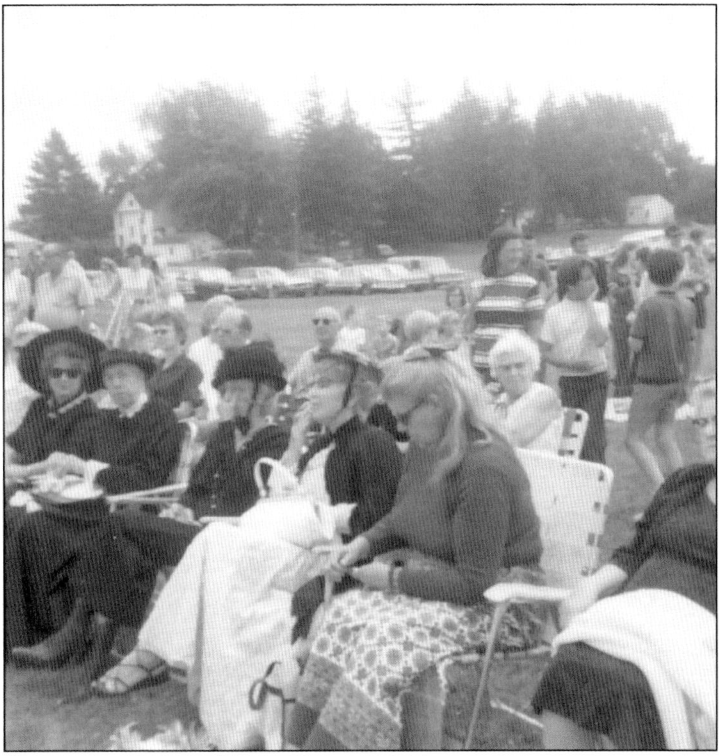

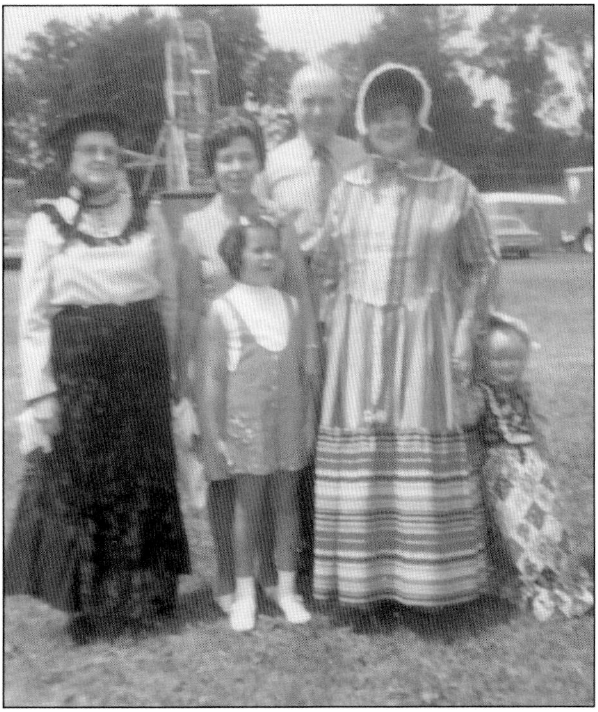

Descendants. Attending the 1971 county sesquicentennial were descendants of Revolutionary soldier William Cox of Elbridge. From left to right are Leith Cox Wright, village historian, emblem designer, and 1999 distinguished Hilton Central graduate; Phyllis Cox Reddick, Parma's first Apple Blossom Queen in 1935; Donna Reddick; Mr. Audrey Reddick; Shirley Cox Husted, town historian; and Rosemary Husted. A new village street, Leith Lane, now honors Mrs. Wright. Phyllis Reddick was buried in Fairfield Cemetery on September 30, 1999.

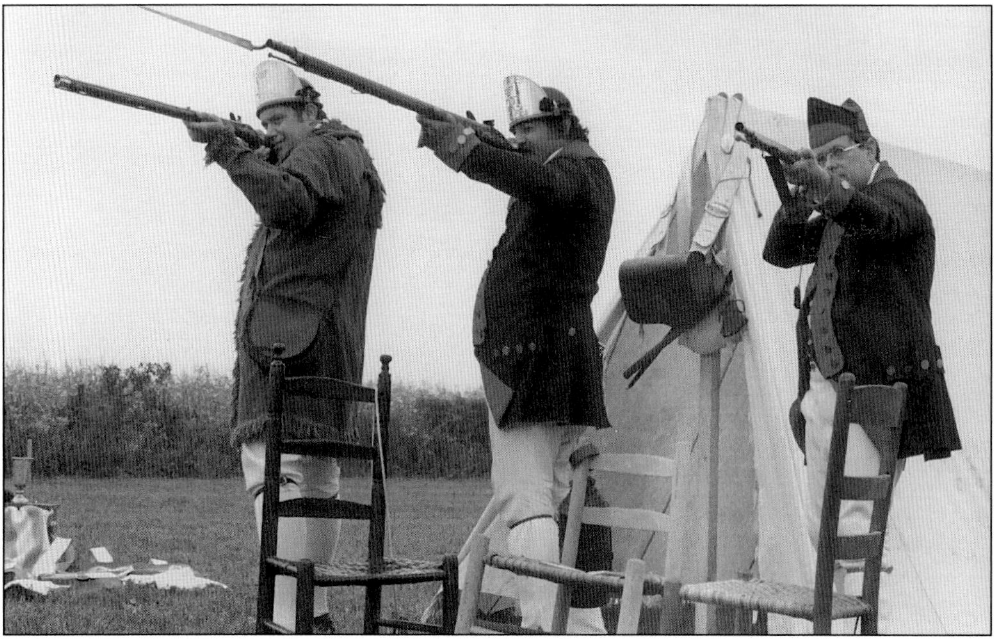

Reenactment. Donald Cox (far right) was a Roby's Continental Regiment honor guard, recreating Colonial army camp life at Parma's 1975 bicentennial. Mike Boyle's camera captured this firing demonstration at the Continental campsite. Other members of the Cox family included Teddy Cox, who operated a Ridge Road hotel, Streb's Arlington; Leon Cox, who built the Dutch Mill restaurant; and Eddie Cox, a noted race car driver who began the Welcome Ranch, now Sullivan's Charbroil.

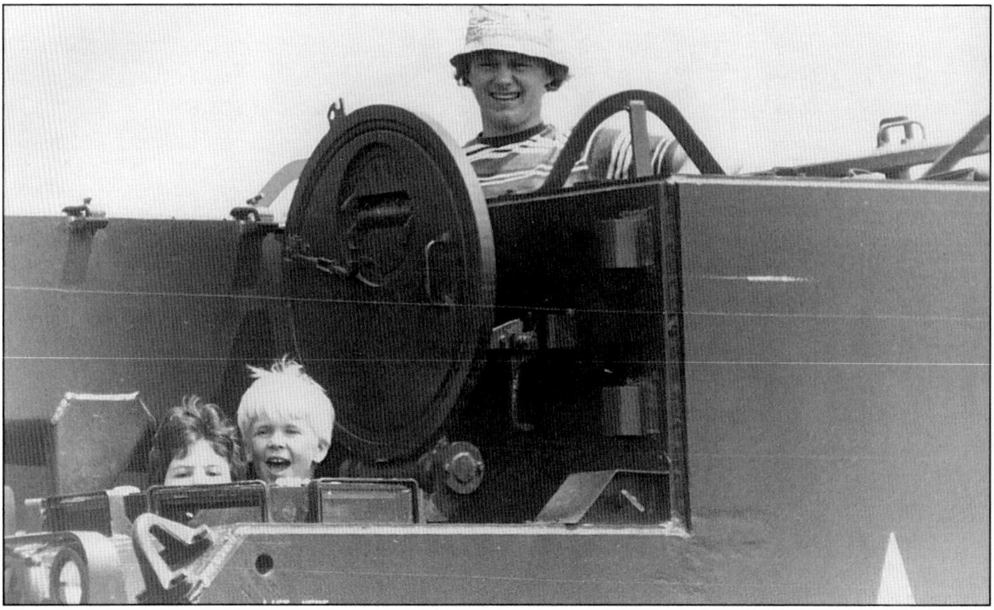

Army Tank. Riding around the town hall grounds in a real U.S. Army tank was a special treat for youngsters at the 1975 commemoration of the 200th anniversary of the armed forces. An army helicopter was also displayed. (Mike Boyle photograph.)

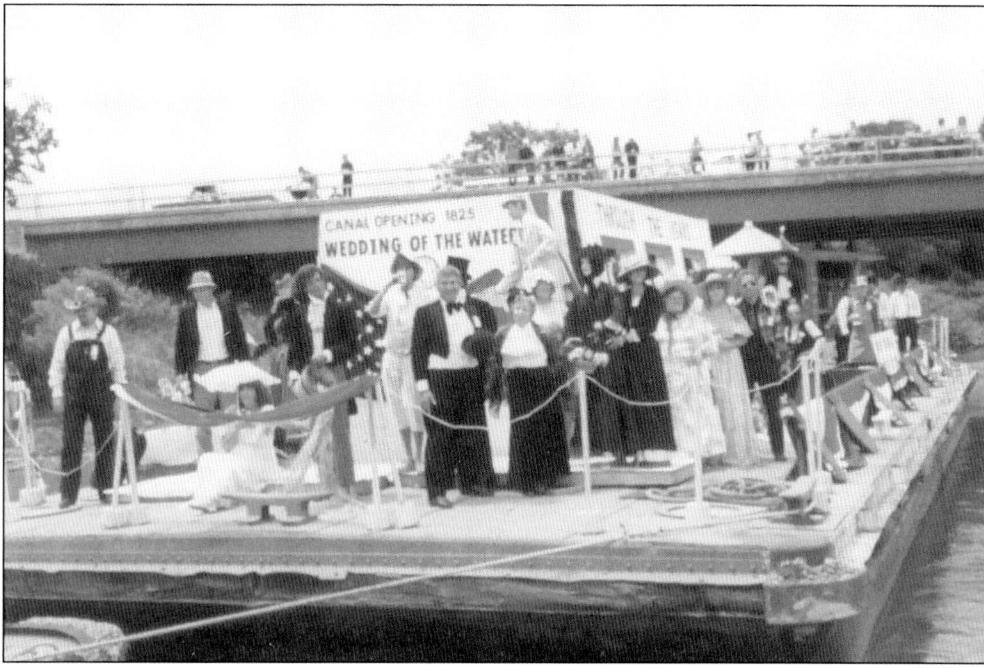

BARGE. Local people greatly enjoyed a bucolic afternoon cruise on the Erie Canal aboard the Parma-Hilton 1984 barge. The occasion was a water parade of boats from Spencerport to Genesee Valley Park. A long, long submarine sandwich served the crowd. Dave Smalley and Tom Younker led the singing—some of it a little bawdy, but an appropriate reminder of the lusty crews that sailed the Erie Canal.

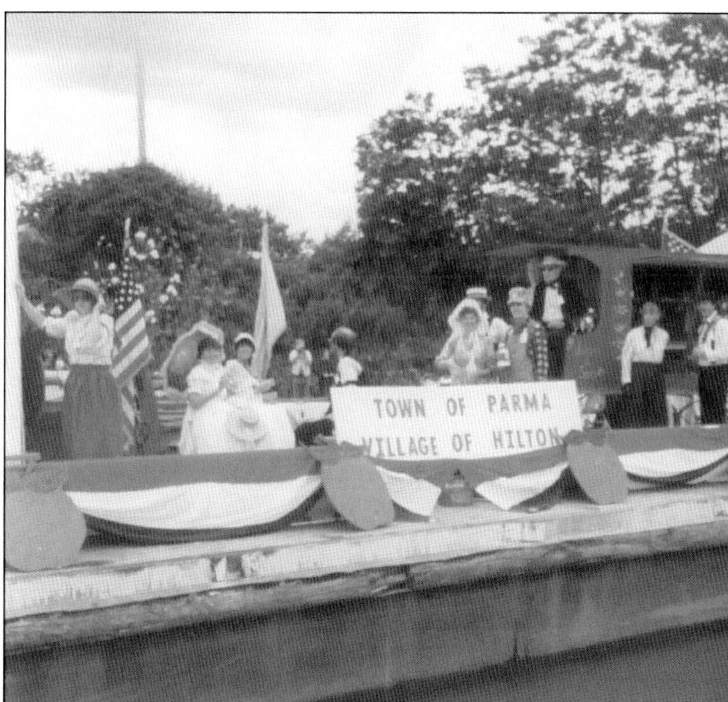

DANCING ON THE DECK. There was dancing aboard the Parma-Hilton 1984 barge, and when the boat arrived at Genesee Valley Park, the passengers serenaded the bystanders. The occasion celebrated was Rochester's 150th anniversary.

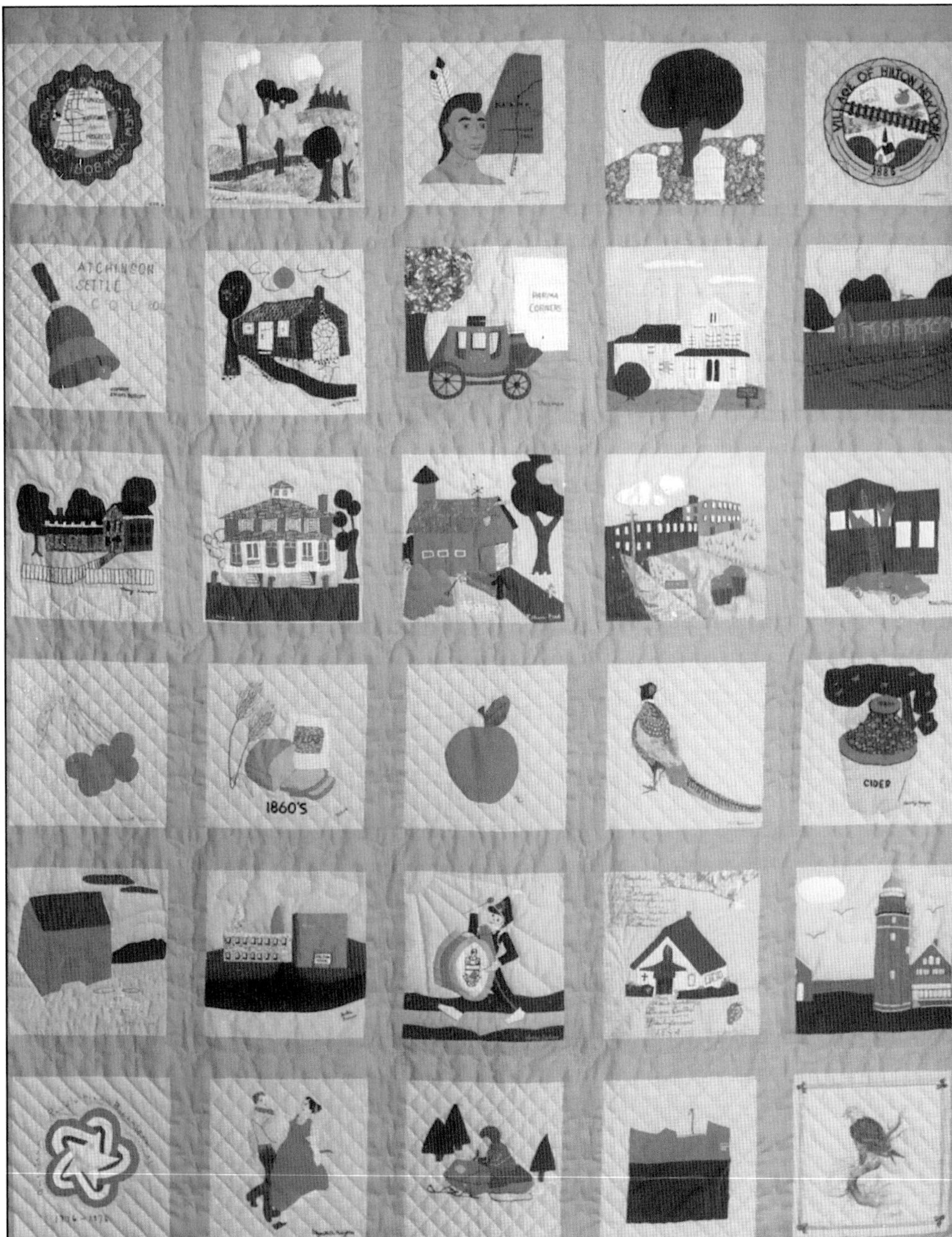

BICENTENNIAL QUILT. Parma's bicentennial quilt portraying the history of the township hangs in the Old Parma Meetinghouse Museum. Verna Chasman of Hill Road chaired the quilting project, which won a second-place award at the 1976 Monroe County Fair. The Chasman home was built for Bezaleel Atchinson Sr., a Revolutionary War veteran, whose descendants came to Parma in 1796. His grave is in the Atchinson cemetery nearby.

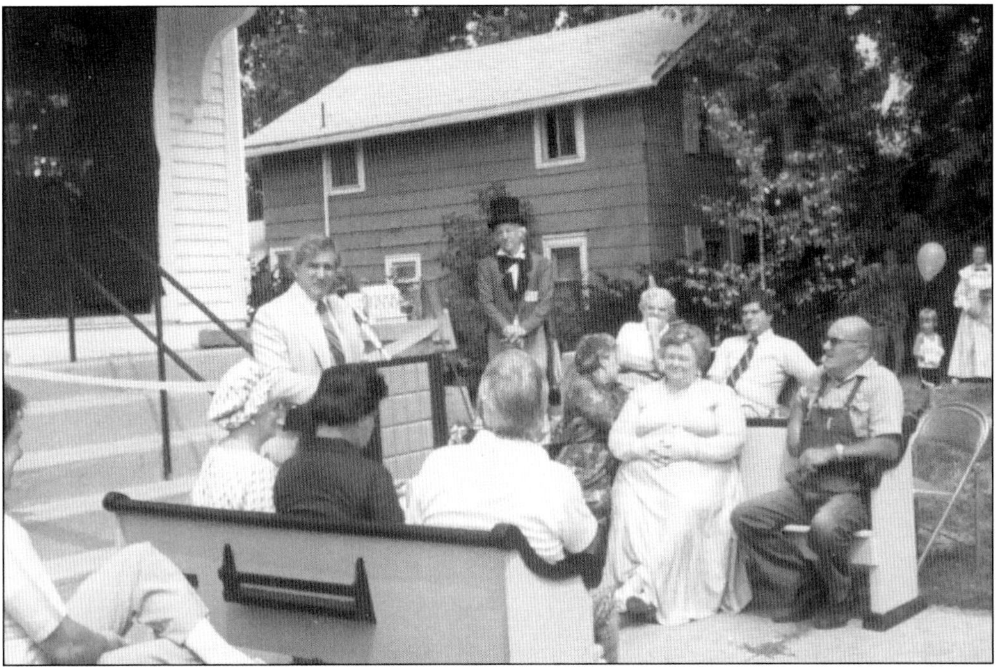

Museum Dedication. Among the many dignitaries attending the dedication ceremonies to open the Parma Meetinghouse Museum were Legislator Edwin Foster, Judge Kenneth Keir, town board members Donald Foster and Mary Gavigan, Supvr. Thomas Younker, "Nathaniel Rochester," town board member Maggie Van Dorn, Richard Husted, Shirley Husted, town board member Robert Ingham, and village historian Leith Wright.

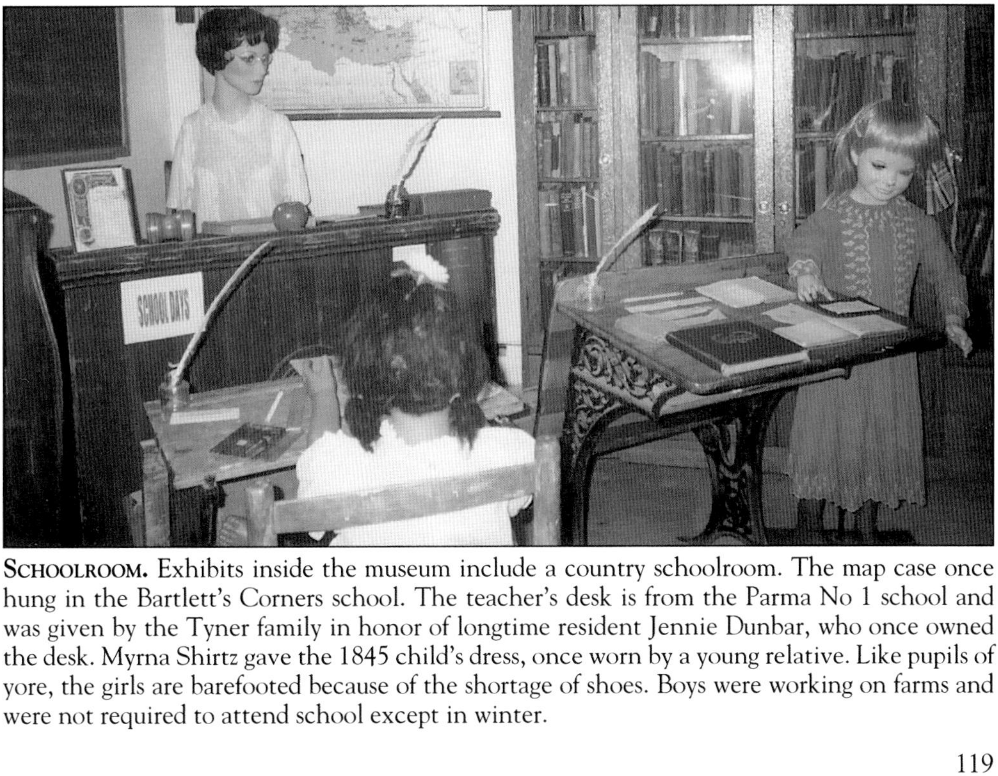

Schoolroom. Exhibits inside the museum include a country schoolroom. The map case once hung in the Bartlett's Corners school. The teacher's desk is from the Parma No 1 school and was given by the Tyner family in honor of longtime resident Jennie Dunbar, who once owned the desk. Myrna Shirtz gave the 1845 child's dress, once worn by a young relative. Like pupils of yore, the girls are barefooted because of the shortage of shoes. Boys were working on farms and were not required to attend school except in winter.

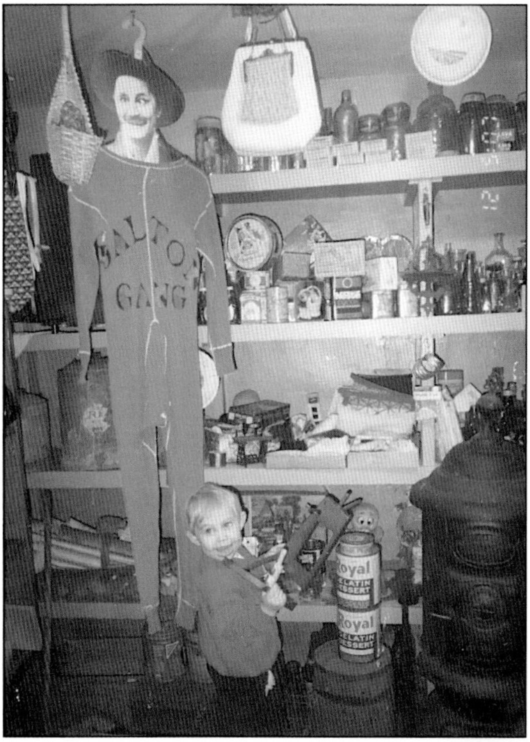

COUNTRY STORE. Jacob Husted looks like a mannequin himself, as he admires the museum country store's display of underwear, jokingly attributed to the notorious Dalton Gang of horse thieves. Three stores, the schoolroom, a 1920s kitchen, military items, a history library, antique hats and gowns, and a church wedding scene are among the museum's displays. Pictures, quilts, and artifacts bring back memories of past days; mannequins came from Sibley's, Edward's, LaBorie's, Penny's, and other stores.

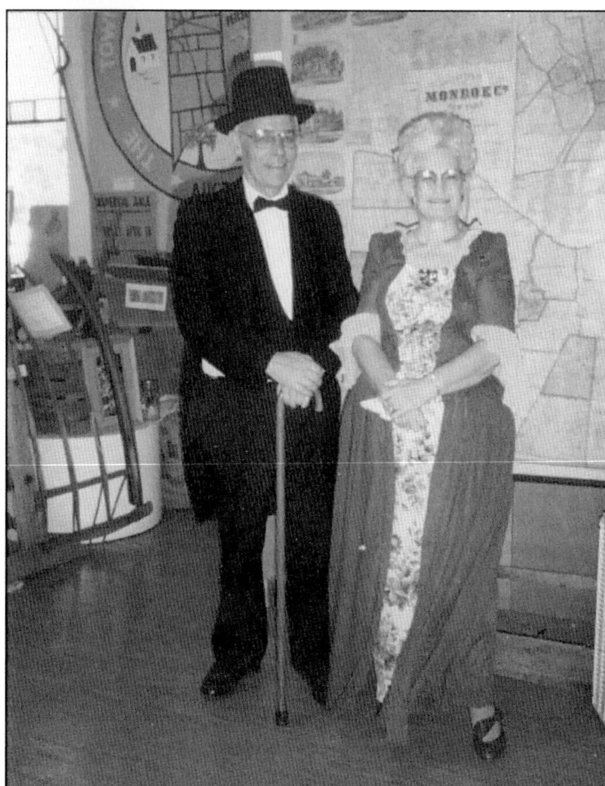

WARM WELCOME. Fashionably dressed R. Alfred Bergeron and Eileen Neal portrayed the spirit of the past as they welcomed guests to one of the museum's open houses. Bergeron is a member of the Friends of the Parma Meetinghouse organization, an unsalaried citizens' group (not a historical society) that supports museum programs and raises funds for new acquisitions. This year the group contributed two stained-glass windows that recreate the history of Parma, the Apple Capital.

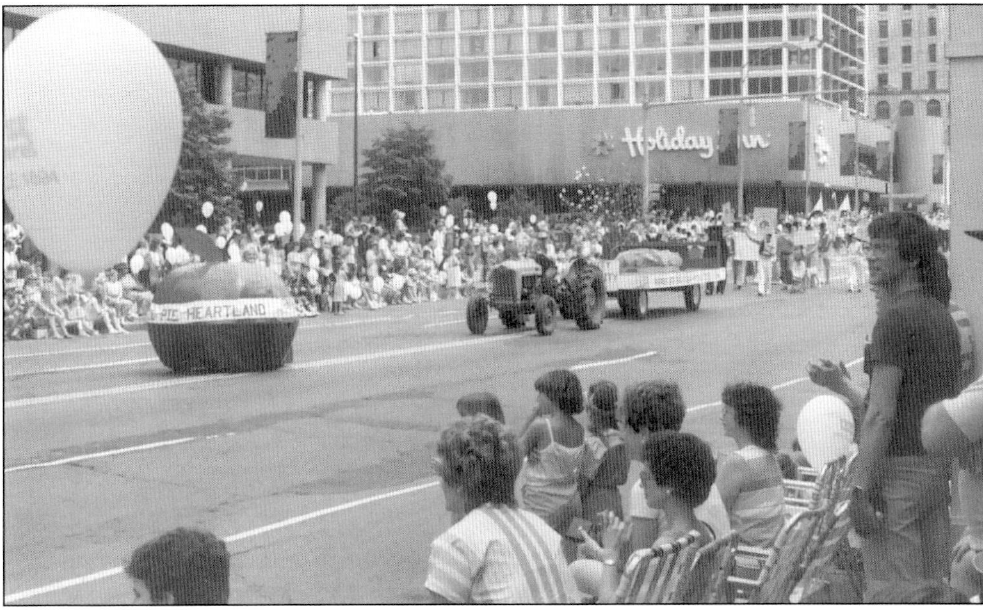

APPLE FLOAT, 1984. When the city of Rochester celebrated its 150th anniversary at a 1984 parade, Parma's float featured its long-gone apple industry. Mary Gavigan drove a motorized apple leading the float down Rochester's Main Street. Parma had settlers before Rochester did, and Parma pioneers helped hew the city's first roads through the wilderness. Josiah Fish, an early Rochester mill operator, later made his home on Ridge Road in Parma.

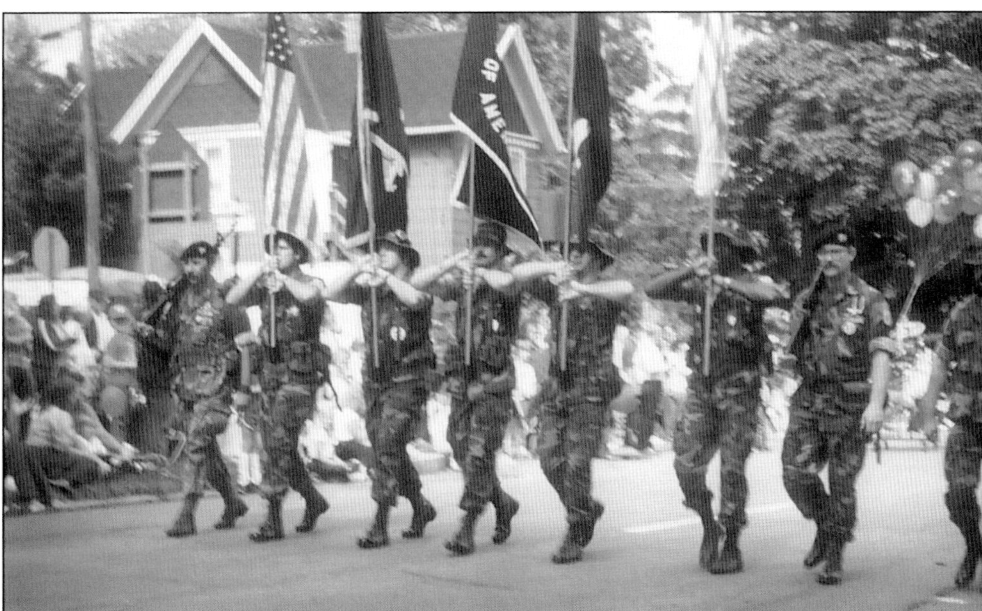

VIETNAM VETERANS. Vietnam veterans marched proudly in the 1985 Hilton Centennial Parade along West Avenue. Although the Vietnam War was unpopular, no one questioned the bravery, patriotism, and personal sacrifices of America's military. Then, as during other conflicts, the *Hilton Record* sent free newspapers to local men and women in the service across the world to help keep them in touch with events at home.

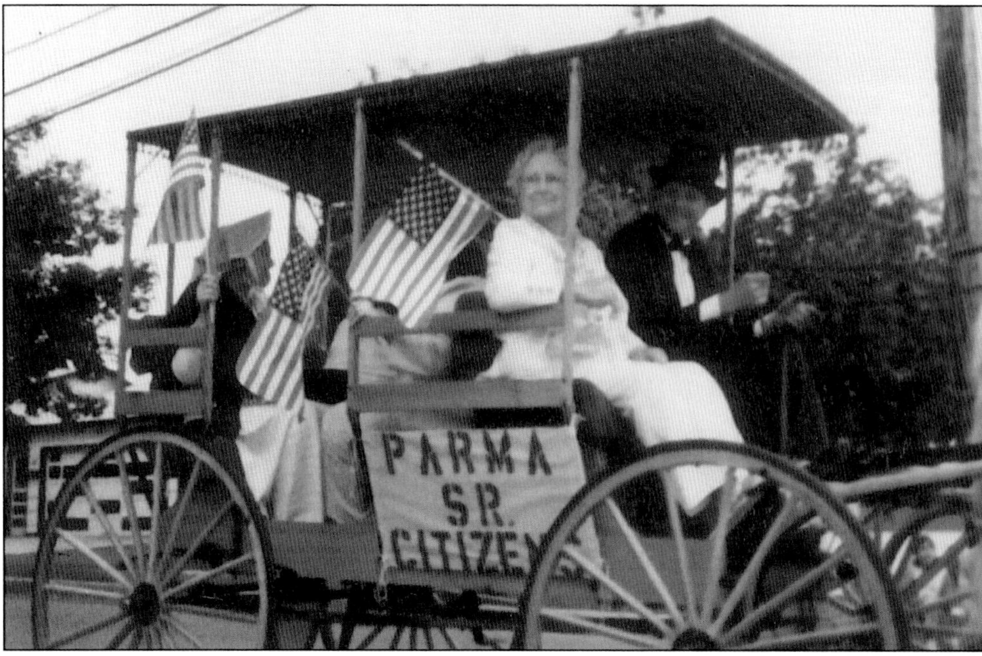

PASSENGER WAGON. Several senior citizens rode in the centennial parade in Lauren G. McCracken's very first passenger wagon. Mildred Chase McCracken (front left) could have reminisced about bygone days when her husband, Robert G. McCracken, drove his team to Hilton GLF for bags of feed or drove to town to deliver loads of peas to the Heinz plant. Bob invented a fast unloading device, envied by other farmers who had to unload their wagons shovel by shovel.

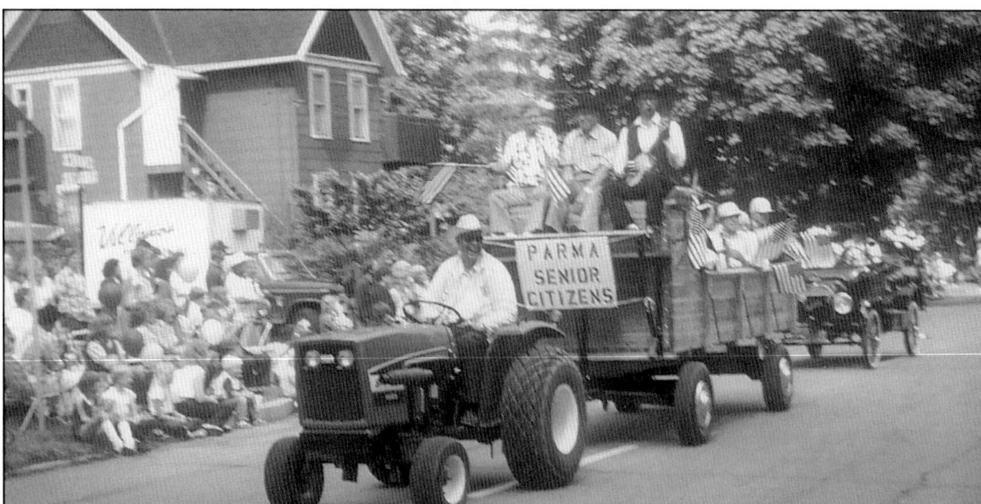

SENIOR FLOAT. The Senior Citizens float in the centennial parade was followed by antique vehicles, like some that the seniors may have ridden in years ago. Appreciation for Parma's seniors began with town-sponsored programs initiated at the urging of town clerk Arthur Kirchgessner and now conducted by Hilton-Parma Recreation. Alice Frisbee Stothard also encouraged programs for seniors at Hilton Baptist Church, where Wilbur Hermance is now very active in outreach activities.

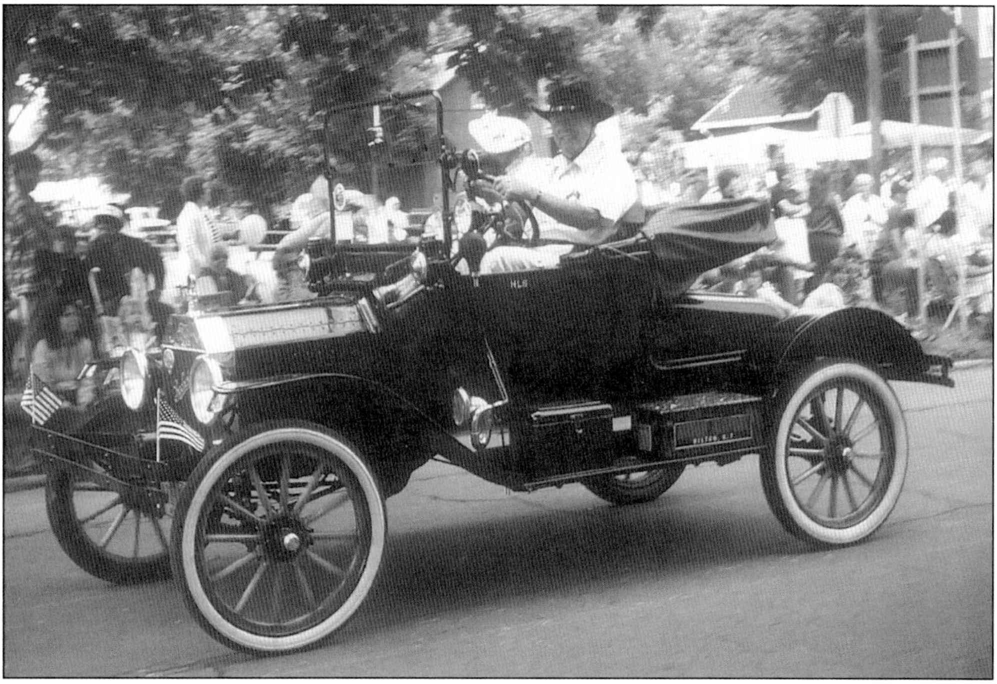

Early Automobile. Oh, for a car like this and gasoline at 15¢ a gallon! The coming of automobiles, telephones, telegraph lines, radios, and airplanes changed the world during the administration of Pres. Theodore Roosevelt. Mount Rushmore and the stuffed toys named teddy bears in his honor are reminders of the President's popularity and his efforts for environmental protection. Ironically, auto exhausts became a major polluter of the environment.

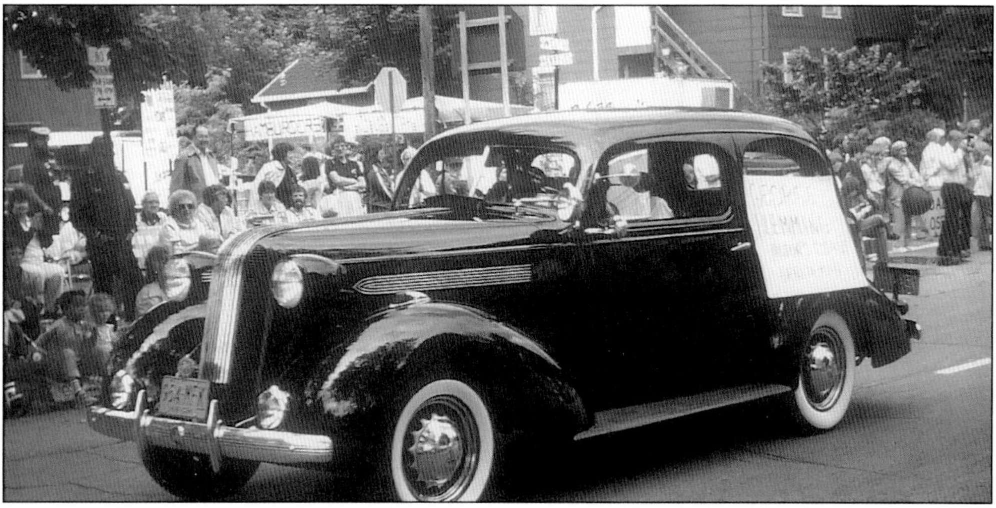

Classic Car. This classy vehicle drew a lot of attention in the centennial parade. Similar automobiles were on the roads whenever gas rationing allowed travel during the 1940s. After Pres. Franklin Delano Roosevelt proclaimed war against the Japanese because of their attack on Pearl Harbor on December 7, 1941, travel was frowned upon except for business purposes. Earlier, Roosevelt initiated a national Social Security plan, which today is a great aid to senior citizens and the chronically ill.

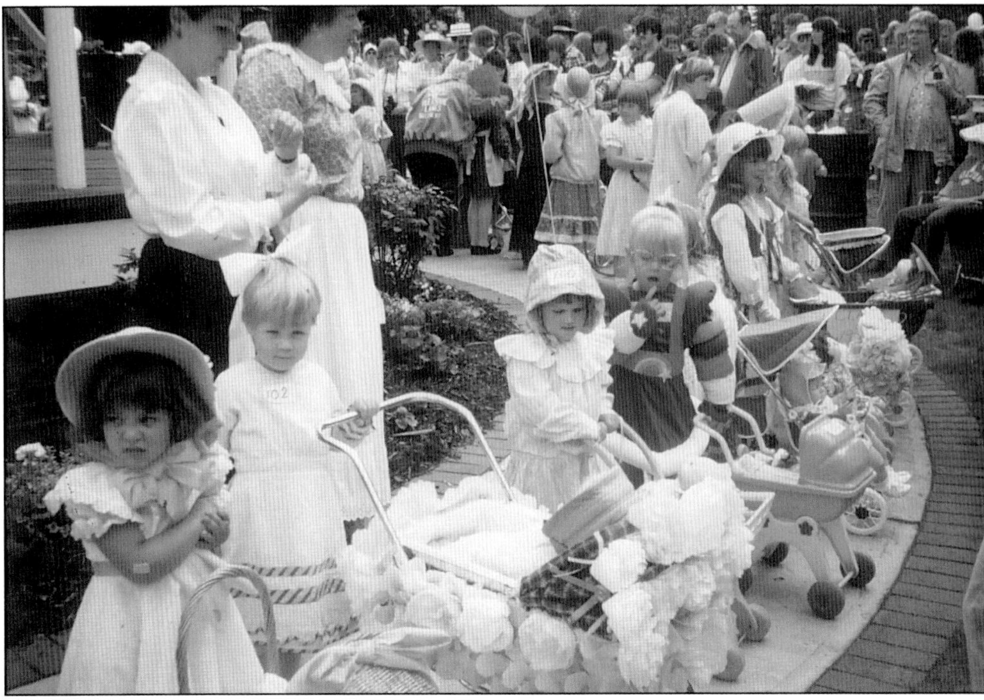

DOLL PARADE. The most adorable sight at the centennial observance was the doll parade. This photograph shows the young "mothers" waiting beside the gazebo for the parade to begin.

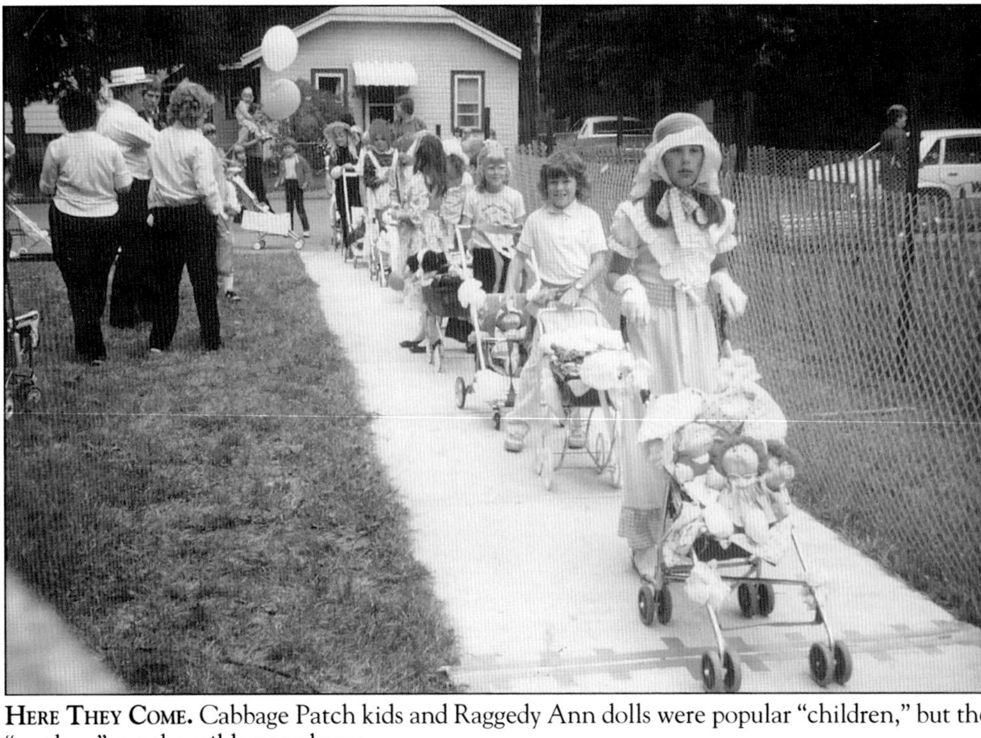

HERE THEY COME. Cabbage Patch kids and Raggedy Ann dolls were popular "children," but the "mothers" got the wildest applause.

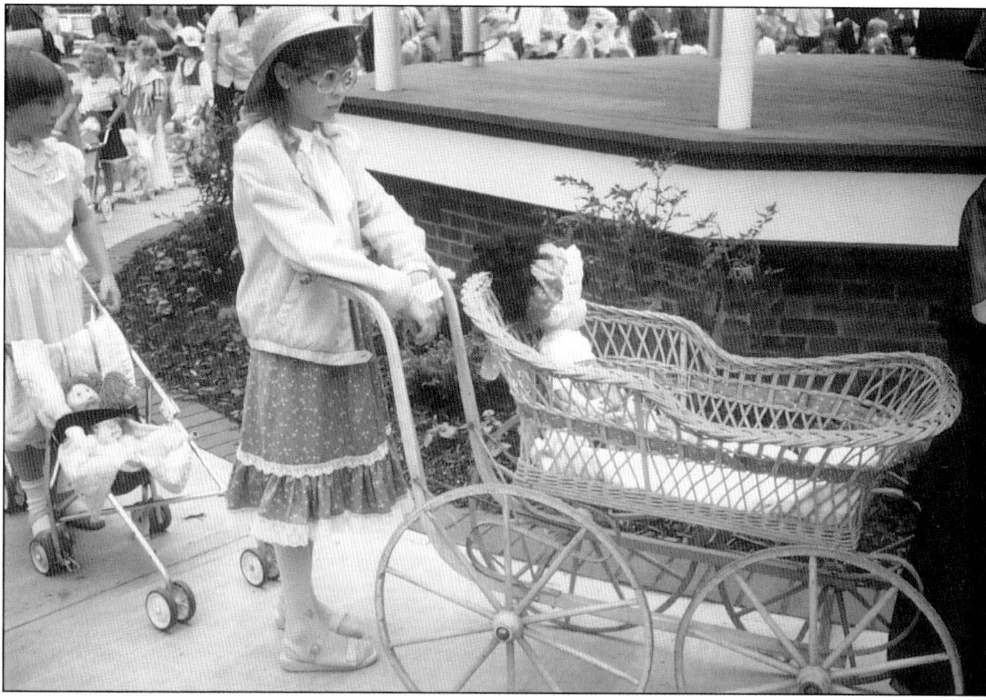

Wicker Carriage. This outstanding baby carriage was wicker made from willow tree branches, the material used by Native Americans for seating and reclining. Before the coming of plastic, an important contribution to modern life, a wicker baby carriage was a stylish possession—and it still is. With proper care, wicker furniture and carriages will outlast plastic items for several generations.

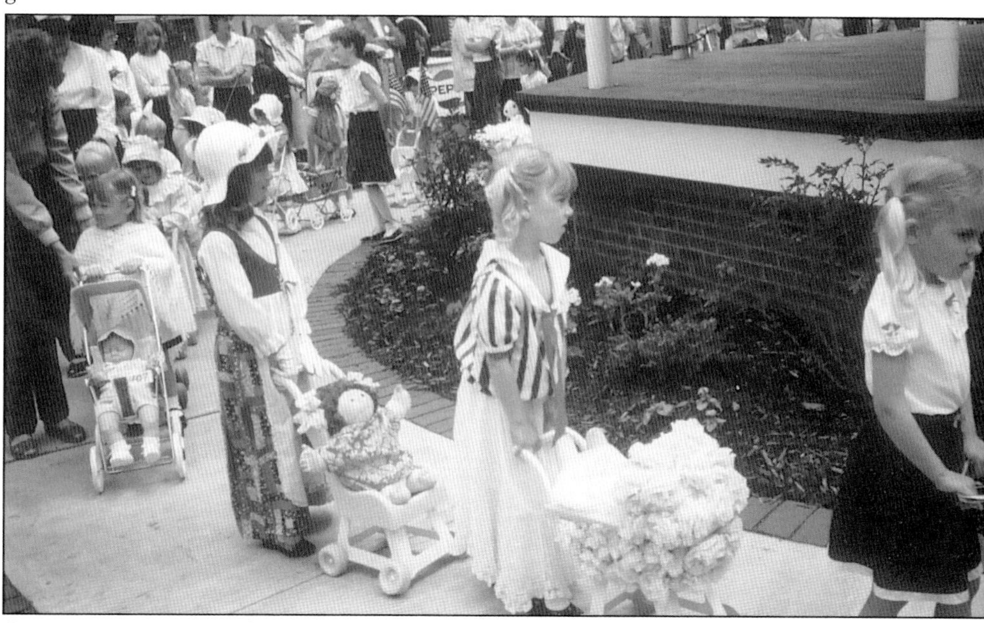

Collectors' Items. The little "mothers" of 1985 may be real mothers today, but they will always be remembered for their parade by the gazebo. Tomorrow, their "children" could become dolls that are in demand as collectors' items.

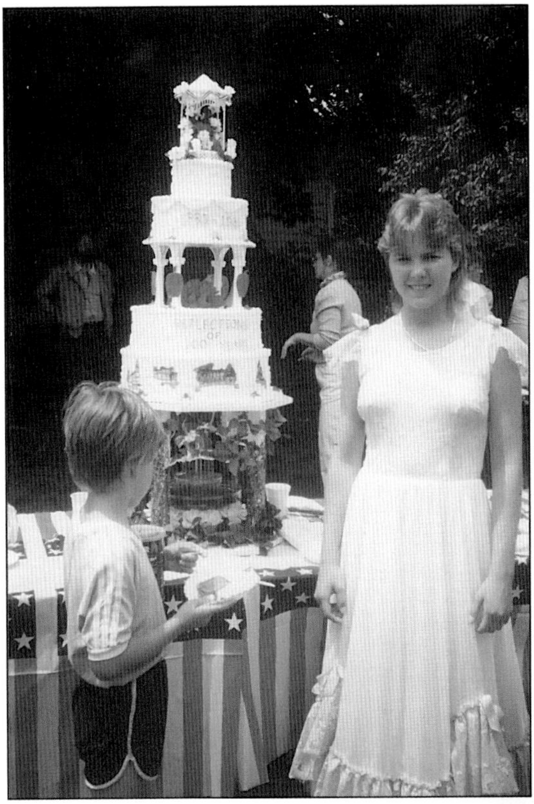

CENTENNIAL CAKE. Decorations on the 1985 centennial anniversary cake feature scenes from the village's history and a gazebo cake top. Miniature ceramic gazebos were sold at the event to raise funds. The gazebo is an appropriate reminder of community appreciation for music, as it is also appreciated in Parma, Italy, the birthplace of composer Giuseppe Verdi. Standing by the cake are Rosemary Husted in a period gown and a hungry boy with cake on his plate.

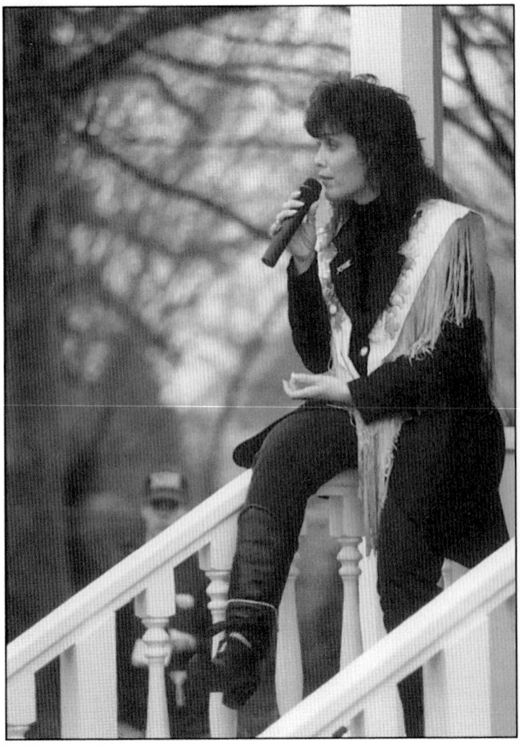

CENTENNIAL CONCERT. In 1996, the village of Hilton celebrated the 100th anniversary of its naming. As part of the festivities, Parma's popular country singer Josie Waverly gave a concert at the Centennial Gazebo. She was named a distinguished Hilton Central graduate in 1999. Olympic star Kathy Turner Bostley and committee chairman Walter Horylev distributed awards for 1996 sports activities.

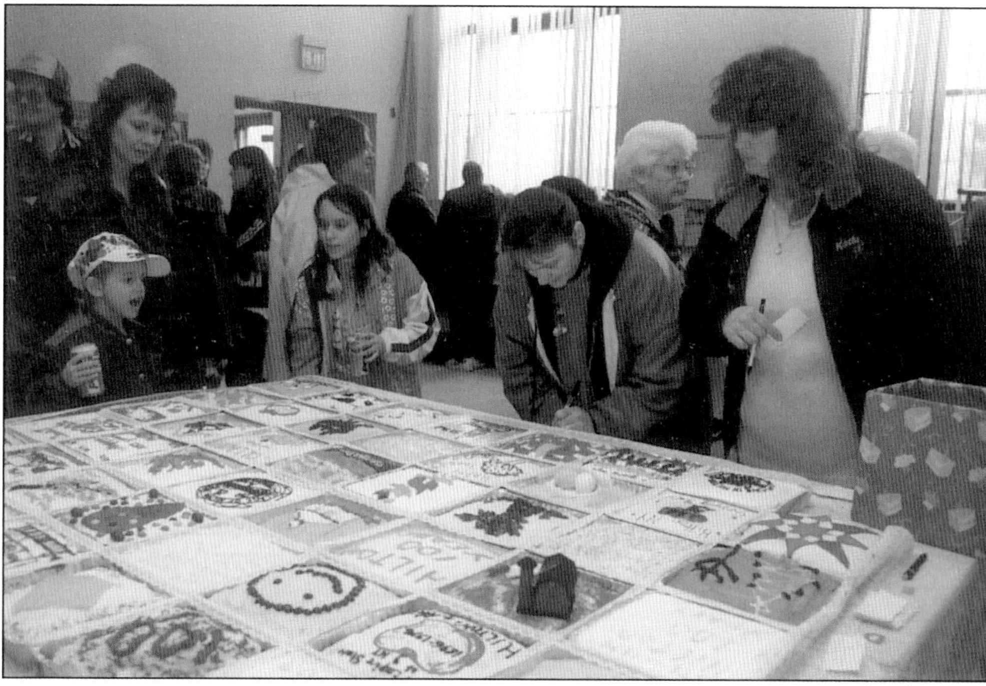

QUILTED CAKE. A cake featuring quilt blocks baked and decorated by local women was a special feature of the 1996 celebration. Senior citizens distributed free slices from the big birthday cake. Delores Belaire won first prize for her block, which featured the Gazebo, a landmark that symbolizes Hilton and home and happiness to many.

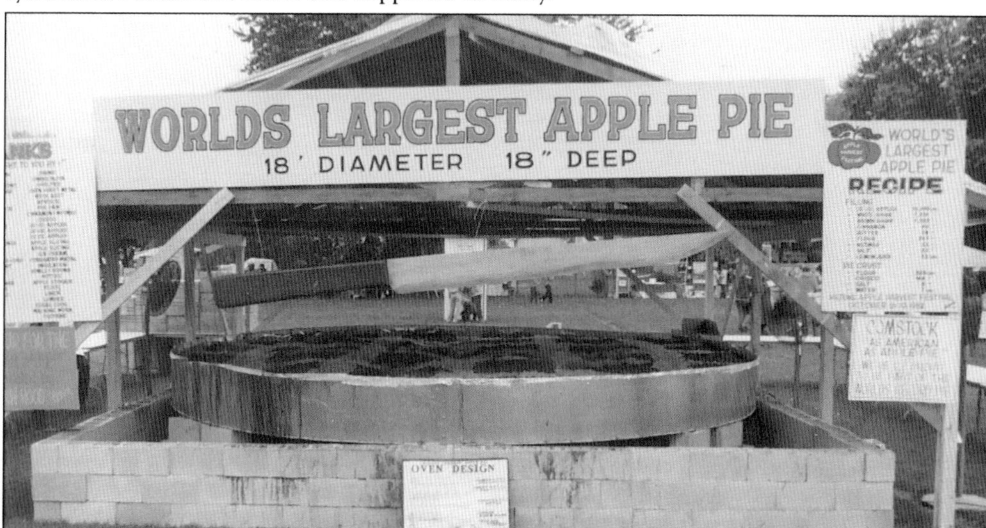

IMMENSE PIE. Intended to be the world's largest, this apple pie was made from 2,002 apples, 2,100 pounds of sugar, and 352 pounds of flour in 1982. As it turned out, this was not the world's biggest apple pie: British pie bakers took that record away from Hilton. Not to be outdone, the Applefest committee in 1983 sponsored the world's smallest pie, baked in a bottle cap. In 1975, Shirley Husted organized the first community festival held at the town hall. The festival was moved to Hilton in 1981. There, huge crowds gather every October to view outstanding crafts, antiques, old cars, quilts, and other exhibits.

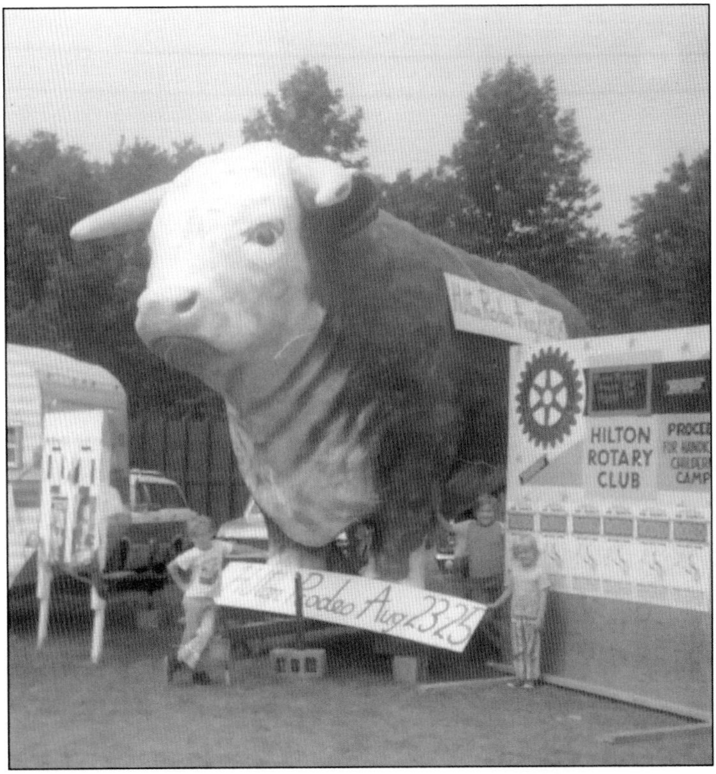

BIG BULL. When is a sign not a sign? When it's a bull—or vice versa. Seen here at the Rotary booth at the Hilton Fair is the huge fiberglass steer that once stood at 1619 Manitou Road. A source of controversy, the unwelcome bovine was forced to leave that location because it exceeded the size allowed by the sign ordinance. Given a new home outside a mid-state steak house, the cow had to mosey on again when that restaurant burned down. Reportedly, the cow continued its career at another restaurant.

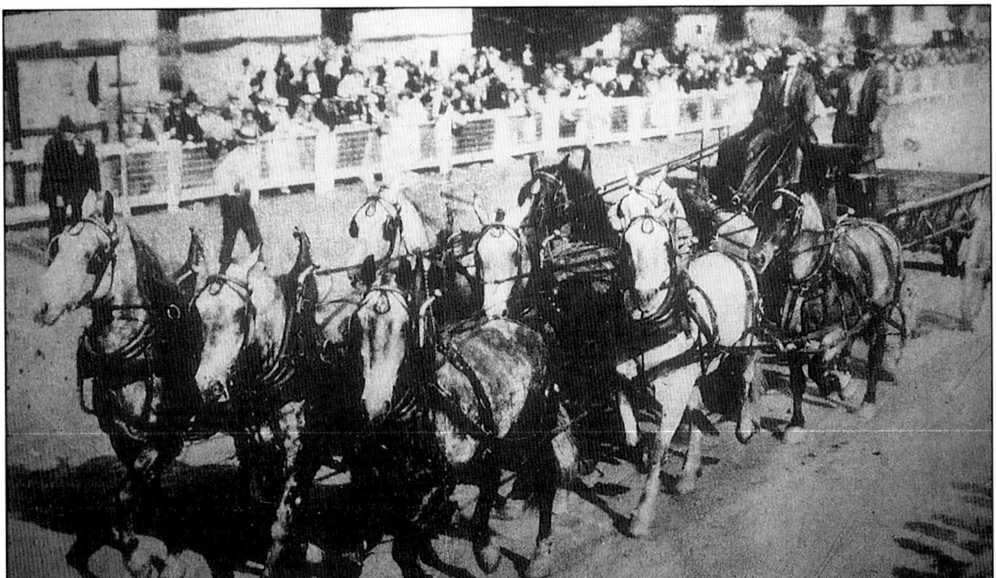

NINE-HORSE HITCH. Edwin B. Curtis was well known for his skill in training and handling draft horses, especially a nine-horse hitch, very difficult to control. In this photograph, Curtis holds the reins for his three beloved dapple grays, followed by four white beauties and two black steeds. Curtis operated a meat market and slaughterhouse at Hilton and built the impressive Curtis Block at East Avenue and Hovey Street, which later housed a grocery, dry goods store, ice-cream parlor, and F&AM Masonic lodge hall before it burned in 1965.